Some have argued the Black Church is dying or, even worse, dead. Others staunchly defend her and her indomitable spirit. In this well-written book, my brother and friend Thabiti Anyabwile cuts through the conjecture and anecdotes and offers a loving critique and hopeful encouragement for the church he loves and desires to see revived and faithful. *Reviving the Black Church* is both timely and refreshing. If you love the Black Church like I do, you will want to read this book and hope our beloved church's obituary has proved false.

—Tony Carter, Lead Pastor, East Point Church (East Point, GA)

Thabiti Anyabwile is one of my favorite authors (as well as one of my favorite people), so it is saying quite a bit for me to say that I think this is his best book yet. His powers of analysis have been clear in earlier works—his love and appreciation and hopes for African-American churches come to the fore in this book. Reviving is God's work we know, but the appearance of a book like this suggests that He is at work doing it even as we ask. Read this book and pray in hope.

—Mark Dever, Senior Pastor, Capitol Hill Baptist Church
(Washington, DC)

This is a must read for anyone who wants to know the truth of how we as a people gravitated toward emotional religion, instead of an expository relationship with our Savior. This book puts us back on track.

—Don Hayes, Pastor, Oakland Baptist Church (Alexandria, VA)

With her tradition of annual weeklong preaching services, the historic Black Church has always in some way been interested in being "revived." Thabiti's *Reviving the Black Church* points the way forward for her with biblically clear, precise, and extremely hopeful insights. I grew up in her, came to Christ in her, was married, licensed, and ordained to gospel ministry by her. If you love her as I do, then pick up several copies and pass them along to everyone you know, who is interested in the future of this sacred institution.

—Louis C. Love Jr., Pastor, New Life Fellowship Church
(Vernon Hills, IL) and Contributor, *The Front Porch*

Every now and then a book is written that is truly on time and speaks to a critical need in our lives. Every now and then a book is written that truly speaks what many of us in the body of Christ are thinking. Well, *Reviving the Black Church* is such a book. Thabiti Anyabwile has written a book that should be required reading for every pastor, every leader, and every member of a black church! For a lot of reasons, the Black Church is not as effective in our communities and our cities as she once was. Therefore our communities and cities are suffering the consequences of a church that seems to be sick and unhealthy. However this book gives us the prescription we need to revive the Black Church. As God asked the prophet Ezekiel once, can these bones live? Well Anyabwile through this book would say YES!! I highly recommend this life-giving book!

—Fred Luter Jr. Pastor, Franklin Avenue Baptist Church
(New Orleans, LA) and Former President, Southern Baptist Convention

Though many have grown discouraged, the Black Church is ripe for revival! Remaining faithful to our historical tradition and our biblical foundation, Thabiti Anyabwile is a prominent voice in the area of church health. *Reviving the Black Church* is a thoughtful, respectful, and challenging treatment of the viability of the African-American church. This book renews excitement and zeal for the great move of God taking place in our local faith communities.

—Dr. Bobby Manning, Pastor, First Baptist Church of District
Heights (MD) and author of *Saving Our Sons:
Effectively Engaging Young Men of Color*

Reviving the Black Church makes me as jealous as it does joyous: How I have longed to express these ideas for my people in such simple terms! Thabiti provides a blueprint for refashioning the Black Church to make a transformational impact in the African-American community and the world. Its loving, biblically-guided, yet biting, no-nonsense, manifesto calls the Black Church away from a syncretistic association with the culture to a redemptive relationship with the culture. Unflinching in his call to recover a New Testament church, Thabiti's proposal is sure to draw naysayers and enemies as he prioritizes identifying the people of God over seeking social significance. But such critics should give the work a full and judicious hearing, for the sake of the exaltation of our people, and for the salvation of people everywhere. Out of deep love for the Black Church, Thabiti has spoken up loudly and timely, with grace and truth.

—Eric C. Redmond, Assistant Professor of Bible, Moody Bible Institute, and author of *Where Are All the Brothers? Straight Answers to Men's Questions About the Church*

This is the book for which I've longed. Anyabwile takes seriously the scholarly and activist chastisements of the Black Church, while himself offering a hopeful, gospel-driven challenge to black congregations on spiritual life support. The prophetic word is sure: dry bones can live again if we hear the word of the Lord and receive afresh God's invigorating breath. *Reviving the Black Church* should be read critically and receptively by everyone who loves God's blemished yet beautiful Black Church. If nothing else, it will convict us to pray for revival! Let it begin in me.

—CJ Rhodes, Pastor, Mount Helm Baptist Church (Jackson, MS)

Churches can die, because Jesus said they can. He warns that the church in Sardis was on the verge of death. Europe, the birthplace of Protestantism, is strewn with once vibrant but now spiritually dead churches. Like Thabiti, I fear that the "Black Church" is not well and is in dire need of revival. The question that every pastor must answer is *how can I help?* But unfortunately, pastors, like most men when we're lost, don't like to stop and ask for help. I've had a lot of "how do we help the church?" questions, and I think Thabiti answered all of them and more. This is simply the most helpful handling of the Scriptures about reviving the church that I have ever read. So if you are burdened with a concern for the urban church, please, please, read *Reviving the Black Church* and apply it.

—Bobby Scott, Co-pastor, Community of Faith Bile Church (Los Angeles, CA)

As pastor of a predominantly African-American church established by free slaves more than 150 years ago, I cannot express how encouraged I was to read *Reviving the Black Church*. This book speaks to the heart of every person who has a passion to see black churches thrive in the truth of the gospel. But this is not just a book to be read, but a reference tool to be consulted for guidance on how any church, but particularly the African-American church, can experience true revival. Thabiti pours into this book his personal experience, pastoral concern, sound wisdom, biblical support and a knowledge of the history, tradition, and culture of the Black Church. I highly recommend this book for those considering the call to ministry, newly installed into the ministry, pastoral search committees as well as church members.

—Victor G. Sholar, Senior Pastor, Main Street Baptist Church
(Lexington, KY)

Thabiti Anyabwile speaks as one who loved the Black Church, left the Black Church, was saved in the Black Church, and still loves (and hopes for!) the Black Church. His experience and biblical fidelity should merit a reader's attention. This book sounds like that old hymn, "Revive Us, Again."

—Kevin L. Smith, Assistant Professor of Christian Preaching,
The Southern Baptist Theological Seminary

Reviving the Black Church is an excellent resource for any pastor or lay member. Chapter by chapter and line by line, the reader can hear the cry of Thabiti Anyabwile's heart to recover a biblical approach to pastoral ministry and authentic Christian living. Brother Anyabwile provides innovative responses to the challenges that face not only the Black Church, but also the church community at large.

—Nelson Sneed, Senior Pastor, Little Forest Baptist Church
(Stafford, VA)

Reviving the Black Church is the book I've been waiting for from Thabiti Anyabwile. With a pastor's heart and a theologian's mind, Pastor Anyabwile strides right up to the wolves prowling in some black churches and scatters them with the rod of God's Word. But unlike others who coldly critique the church, Pastor Anyabwile speaks the truth in love, realizing that even with her flaws, the church is Christ's bride and the womb that nurtures our faith. While focused on the Black Church, this book will inspire believers from all church backgrounds to esteem God's Word more highly and work for the health of the body more diligently. If you love Christ and His church, this book will thrill and inform you.

—Jemar Tisby, President of the Reformed African American
Network and Director of the African American Leadership
Initiative at RTS Jackson

REVIVING THE BLACK CHURCH

THABITI ANYABWILE

REVIVING THE BLACK CHURCH

A CALL TO RECLAIM A SACRED INSTITUTION

PUBLISHING GROUP

NASHVILLE, TENNESSEE

Published by B&H Publishing Group
Nashville, Tennessee

Dewey Decimal Classification: 262
Subject Heading: BLACK CHURCHES \ BLACKS \ CHURCH

1 2 3 4 5 6 7 • 19 18 17 16 15

Dedication

Rev. F. D. Betts (Files Chapel Baptist Church)
Rev. John A. Cherry II (From the Heart Church Ministries)
Rev. Dr. E. R. McNair (Spring Garden Baptist Church)
Rev. John W. Cade (Files Chapel Baptist Church)
Rev. Peter L. Rochelle (Church on the Rock)
Rev. Mark E. Dever (Capitol Hill Baptist Church)

Men and pastors the Lord has used to bless my life.

Acknowledgments

"First giving honor to my Lord and Savior Jesus Christ." If you've ever sat in an African-American church when visitors are welcomed, you've no doubt heard someone stand and begin their introduction with those words. Aren't they fitting words? I've never done anything worthwhile that didn't entirely depend upon the grace of God. If this book proves to be worthwhile, the credit and honor will be due to God our Father. First, I want to acknowledge and honor God, apart from whom we can do nothing.

After the Lord, the second person to whom I owe thanks is Kristie, my wife, best friend, fellow foodie, and partner in everything. You deserve my undying appreciation for not only putting up with me but also making me better than I would ever have been without you. You have made me happy since the moment I first saw you. You are the "good thing" I've found and "favor from the Lord" (Prov. 18:22). "I see you in my eyes."

Several brothers read the manuscript and provided incredibly helpful insight and constant encouragement. My brother and partner in crime at *The Front Porch*, Louis Love, helped me keep perspective and make my thoughts clearer. Mark Dever read every word, called, or Skyped after each chapter, and spurred me on in completing the book. Eric Redmond kept me in dialogue with points of view different from my own and seemed to drop me notes each time I got distracted from writing.

Over the years the entire team at 9Marks Ministries has left so many deposits of grace in my life that it's sometimes difficult to know when an idea was my own or really should be credited to them. To each of you, thank you for being faithful to our Lord and for investing so richly in me and in so many churches around the world.

Devin Maddox, my editor at B&H, has shepherded this project with constant enthusiasm and care. I'm grateful not only for our partnership in this project but also for our growing friendship. Thank you for caring about the church and serving her with your talents.

Many of the ideas in this book have been tested and refined in the lives of at least four churches: Church on the Rock (Raleigh, NC), Capitol Hill Baptist Church (Washington, DC), First Baptist Church of Grand Cayman (Cayman Islands), and Anacostia River Church (Washington, DC). Thank you for allowing me the privilege of serving you and learning from you.

I know I risk missing someone I love who played an incredible part in this journey. If so, please forgive me and give me a hard time every chance you get so that I might learn to be thoughtful. But go ahead and buy the book and multiple copies for friends!

Contents

Part III—Revive through Membership and Mission

Is the Black Church Dead? Or, Can These Bones Live?

The hand of the LORD was upon me, and he brought me out in the Spirit of the LORD and set me down in the middle of the valley; it was full of bones. And he led me around among them, and behold, there were very many on the surface of the valley, and behold, they were very dry. And he said to me, "Son of man, can these bones live?" And I answered, "O Lord GOD, you know."
—EZEKIEL 37:1–3

"And to the angel of the church in Sardis write: 'The words of him who has the seven spirits of God and the seven stars. I know your works. You have the reputation of being alive, but you are dead. Wake up, and strengthen what remains and is about to die, for I have not found your works complete in the sight of my God. Remember, then, what you received and heard. Keep it, and repent. If you will not wake up, I will come like a thief, and you will not know at what hour I will come against you. Yet you have still a few names in Sardis, people who have not soiled their garments, and they will walk with me in white, for they are worthy. The one who conquers will be clothed thus in white garments, and I will never blot his name out of the book of life. I will confess his name before my Father and before his angels. He who has an ear, let him hear what the Spirit says to the churches.'"
—REVELATION 3:1–6

The Obituary

On February 24, 2010, in the waning days of Black History Month, Princeton professor of religion and Chair of African-American studies, Eddie S. Glaude Jr., hurled a grenade into the sleepy camp of the Black Church. Glaude posed and answered a question that many whisper in private, but few dare raise in public. They will debate with passion one-on-one, but not in a widely-read forum such as the *Huffington Post*.

In a single post, Glaude felled both the long-standing African-American principle of not airing your dirty laundry in public (read, ethnically mixed public) and the African-American belief that the Black Church is the one necessary institution in the African-American community.[1] In the post, Professor Glaude offered three reasons he believes the Black Church is dead.

First, he points to the *conservatism* of some black congregations, a conservatism at odds with the traditional narrative describing the Black Church as a progressive force in African-American and American life. Glaude points out that the true narrative is more complex than traditionally believed, and apparently the continuance of conservative black churches means the death of the venerable though mythic "Black Church."

Second, the *differentiation and diversity* of today's African-American communities mean there is no "center" of black life at which the church can stand. As Glaude puts it, "The idea of a black church standing at the center of all that takes place in a community has long since passed away. Instead, different areas of black life have become more distinct and specialized—flourishing outside of the bounds and gaze of black churches."[2] Glaude identifies competition with nondenominational and evangelical megachurches as another factor leading to the death of the Black Church. He sees these alternative worship communities attracting more African-American worshippers than was possible historically.

Third, and most important for Glaude, the "routinization of black prophetic witness" means that too many people assume the prophetic past of the church will continue to be true for today's social and political context. They mistakenly think the church is inherently prophetic and active rather than necessarily redeployed in fresh and changing contexts by each successive generation. According to Glaude, "Prophetic energies are not an inherent part of black churches, but instances of men and women who grasp the fullness of meaning to be one with God. This can't be passed down, but must be embraced in the moment in which one finds one's feet. This ensures that prophetic energies can be expressed again and again."[3]

Glaude poetically describes a dead black church from his view: "Memory becomes its currency. Its soul withers from neglect. The result is all too often church services and liturgies that entertain, but lack a spirit that transforms, and preachers who deign for followers instead of fellow travelers in God."[4] Consequently, the church loses its power because it becomes "alienated from the moment in which it lives." For Glaude, the most telling evidence of rigor mortis is the church's inaction on a range of social causes, including unemployment, health care, child poverty, incarceration, home foreclosures, and helplessness. He laments the absence of a coordinated national program of cooperation between churches to remedy these issues. For him, such inaction smells like death. Glaude's article reads like an obituary for a once-great person who survived long beyond his or her usefulness and prime.

The Wake

But Glaude is not the only person asking the question, "Is the Black Church dead?" Prompted by Glaude's provocative *Huffington Post* comments, Columbia University's Institute for Research in African-American Studies and their Institute for Religion, Culture, and Public Life sponsored in October 2010 a panel discussion on the topic.[5] In 2012, Professor Anthony Bradley, in a conference to promote his recently released book, *Keep Your Head Up: America's New Black Christian Leaders, Social Consciousness, and the Cosby Conversation,* featured a panel discussion asking the same question.

But, this is not a new question for the African-American community. It's a question that lingers in the minds of everyone who loves the Black Church, like heavy-hearted mourners at a wake wondering to themselves, *How did he die so soon? I didn't even know he was sick.*

I've been in informal and formal gatherings around the country where this topic has haunted conversation and dialogue. In one two-week period, I found myself discussing the health, sickness, or death of the Black Church in Atlanta, Louisville, and Los Angeles. A palpable fear and trepidation invaded the room each time someone posed the question. Faces sallowed. Shoulders slouched. Eyes fell to the floor, surveying tiles and shoelaces to avoid the daunting implications. No one wants to say aloud, "My loved one is dying," even if the doctors have already summoned hospice-care workers. Even if doctors have already uttered the dreaded words, "There is nothing else we can do," we feel unable to pronounce a family member's imminent demise.

But we do have a surprising ease and fluency at sharing the news of death in someone else's family. I can't recount the number of times I've heard my mother and other older ladies in the community share the news of someone's failing fight with cancer, sudden death in their sleep, or pig-headed avoidance of proper health care on the way to the grave. These older women spoke freely, in detail, and with the entire range of human emotion about deaths in other families. But those same ladies would press their lips tight before speaking that way about their own spouses, parents, or children.

So it is that Pentecostals call quiet churches "dead." Liberationists proclaim politically inactive churches "dead." Conservatives label liberal churches "dead." It seems everyone thinks churches not like their own ought to be given a proper burial and the news broadcast for others to know.

But Did Anyone Identify the Body?

Responses to Glaude's comments were steady and varied. For instance, Byron Williams—syndicated columnist, author, and pastor of Resurrection Community Church in Oakland, California—readily agreed with Glaude that the Black Church *is* dead but for different reasons than those proposed by Glaude. According to Williams, Glaude "is right because the institution that he critiques in his essay *never existed*" (emphasis mine). Williams called the Black Church of Glaude's essay a "straw man" made "for easy dismantling." According to Williams, "The myth of the black church being the storehouse of the nation's moral compass was created largely during the Civil Rights Movement of the 1950s and 60s. But history indicates that it is more accurate to suggest that there have been individuals who were products of the historical black church that were on the cutting edge of justice and equality issues than to offer the institution as pushing the nation *en masse* to live up to the ideals to which it committed itself in 1776."[6]

Williams reminds us that of the five hundred black churches in Birmingham, less than twenty actively marched with King. Many of Birmingham's black pastors opposed King by using the same "outside agitator" language white segregationists once used to describe the Civil Rights leader. Williams ends his essay by suggesting that the real difficulty lies with the inability of the Black Church proponents to "embrace the high and the low moments of the institution . . . with equal authenticity." The *mythic* Black Church is dead, or perhaps needs to die.[7]

Of course, not everyone agreed with Professor Glaude's assessment. Joel C. Gregory, a white professor of preaching at Baylor University's George W. Truett Theological Seminary and coauthor of *What We Love about the Black Church*,[8] took issue with Glaude's pronouncement of the Black Church's death. Gregory, a self-described veteran of preaching in "more than two hundred African-American congregations, conferences, and conventions in more than twenty states each year," found himself at a loss for an explanation of Glaude's statements. Gregory offered six signs of vitality in the African-American church, including: thriving preaching, vitality in worship, continuing concern for social justice, active community service, high regard for education, and efforts at empowerment. Gregory contends that these signs of life can be found in African-American congregations in every historically black denomination and in varying regions across the country. He writes:

> Where is the obituary? I do not know any organization in America today that has the vitality of the black church. Lodges are dying, civic clubs are filled with octogenarians, volunteer organizations are languishing, and even the academy has to prove the worth of a degree. The government is divided, the schoolroom has become a war zone, mainline denominations are staggering, and evangelical megachurch juggernauts show signs of lagging. Above all this entropy stands one institution that is more vital than ever: the praising, preaching, and empowering black church.[9]

The back-and-forth between those pronouncing death and those highlighting life reveals the difficulty of defining "the Black Church." In fact, we must admit that speaking of "*the* Black Church" remains a quixotic quest. "The Black Church" really exists as multiple black church*es* across denominational, theological, and regional lines. To some extent, we can define the Black Church by referring to the historically black denominations—National Baptist, Progressive Baptist, African Methodist Episcopal (AME), African Methodist Episcopal Zion (AMEZ), Church of God in Christ (COGIC), and so on. But increasingly we must recognize that one part of "the Black Church" exists as predominantly black congregations belonging to majority white denominations like the Southern Baptist Convention or even African-American members of predominantly white churches. Still, other quarters of "the Black Church" belong to nondenominational affinity groups like the many congregations involved in Word of Faith and "prosperity gospel" networks sponsored by leaders like Creflo A. Dollar Jr. and T. D. Jakes.

Clearly "the Black Church" is not one thing. Black churches come in as many flavors as any other ethnic communion. Indeed, many African-Americans have experiences with many parts of the varied Black Church world.

I grew up attending a Missionary Baptist congregation. I came to faith in the Lord Jesus Christ while visiting an AMEZ church. My first "church home" was a congregation belonging to the National Baptist Convention. Later, my family and I joined a team of families to help plant a predominantly African-American nondenominational church. A few years later we became members of an ethnically diverse but predominantly white Southern Baptist church in Washington, DC, before going to pastor a multiethnic largely Afro-Caribbean congregation in the Cayman Islands.

Speaking of "the Black Church" calls for careful differentiation. We have to identify the body before we can finally conclude a death has occurred. But at least the family has been called and alerted to the possibility that a beloved relative could expire.

What Makes a Church "Alive"?

Amidst all the autopsies, coroner reports, and death announcements, two questions often go unasked: What makes a church "alive"? And, can a "dead" church live again? Everyone assumes they know what constitutes "life" and simply mourns the impending or recent "death." And, surprisingly for a people whose Lord rose from the grave three days after death, few consider the resurrection of the church a real possibility.

Professor Glaude's pronouncement of the Black Church's demise construed that death largely in terms of the church's loss of "prophetic energy," its public insistence upon justice for the marginalized, poor, and vulnerable. A living church expresses itself in social action according to Glaude. However, others think of dynamic worship as the main indicator of "life" in a congregation. Still some others contend supernatural "signs and wonders" signify the presence of spiritual life. The *symptoms* and *activities* of life don't constitute life itself. But even a decapitated chicken mimics life after its fated encounter with the ax.

Where does "life" come from? What is the source?

The Lord Jesus taught the earliest followers, the apostles, where genuine spiritual life comes from when He said, "I tell you the truth, whoever hears my word and believes him who sent me has eternal life and will not be condemned; he has crossed over from death to life" (John 5:24 NIV). Life comes from hearing the Lord's Word and believing it. Or, as the Lord puts it in John 6:63, "The Spirit gives life; the flesh counts for nothing. The words I have spoken to you are spirit and they are life" (NIV). Spiritual vitality results from the Spirit of God using the Word of God to quicken faith in Jesus Christ. That life, though abundant, does not consist in the abundance of possessions (Luke 12:15), nor is it a matter of the "flesh," of human nature exerting itself in various deeds of righteousness (John 1:13).

Life comes *from* God *to* the church *through* His Word and Spirit *by* faith *in* Jesus Christ.[10] There is no other source of life. So the Master proclaims, "I am the way, and the truth, and the life" (John 14:6). Or, as Jesus puts it to Martha in the moving scene following the death of Lazarus, "I am the resurrection and the life. Whoever believes in me, though he die, yet shall he live, and everyone who lives and believes in me shall never die" (John 11:25–26). Life is bound up in the Son of God (1 John 5:11–12), who quickens everyone who believes in Him. Even though a person dies in Christ, he shall yet live and never die!

Which brings us to our second crucial question: Can a "dead" church live again?

Do We Need a Eulogy or a Birth Announcement?

Like most African-Americans my age and older, I have been touched by the virtue and disturbed by the failures of the African-American church. I have had some of the richest times of celebration and praise in local black churches. And I've also experienced some of the most perplexing and discouraging situations in this same institution. It was an African-American preacher who vouched for me when I was facing criminal charges as a rising junior in high school, making all the difference in my future. And it was the membership of a black Baptist congregation that nearly poisoned my love for the church when, as a new Christian, I witnessed the "brawl" of my first church business meeting. The preaching of the church gave me biblical tropes and themes for building a sense of self in the world. But a low level of spiritual living among many African-American Christians tempted me to believe that everything in the Black Church was show-and-tell, a tragic comedy of self-delusion and religious hypocrisy.

I left the Black Church of my youth and converted to Islam during college. I became zealous for Islam and a staunch critic of the Black Church. I welcomed much of the criticisms of radicals, Afrocentrists, and groups like the Nation of Islam. I cut my teeth on the writing and speaking of men like Molefi Kete Asante, Na'im Akbar, Wade Noble, and Louis Farrakhan. The institution that helped nurture me I now deem a real enemy to the progress of African-Americans, an opiate and a tool of white supremacy. I had experienced enough of the church's weakness to reject her altogether. The immature and undiscerning rarely know how to handle the failures of its heroes, to evaluate with nuance and critical appreciation. That was true of me before the Lord saved me.

In July 1995, sitting in an African Methodist Episcopal Zion (AMEZ) church in the Washington, DC, area, a short, square, balding African-American preacher expounded the text of Exodus 32. With passion and insight, he detailed the idolatry of Israel and exposed the idolatry of my heart. As he pressed on, more and more I felt guilty for my sin, estranged from God, and deserving of God's holy judgment. Then, from the text of Exodus 32, he preached Jesus Christ, the Son of God who takes away the sin of the world and reconciles sinners to God. He proclaimed the cross of Jesus Christ, where my sins had been nailed and the Son of

God punished in my place. The preacher announced the resurrection of Christ, proving the Father accepted the Son's sacrifice. Then the pastor called every sinner to repent and put their trust—not in themselves—but in Jesus Christ alone for righteousness, forgiveness, and eternal life. It was as if he addressed me alone though I sat in a congregation of eight thousand. That morning, under the preaching of the gospel from God's Word, the Spirit gave me and my wife repentance and faith leading to eternal life. I was a dead man when I walked into that building. But I left a living man, revived by God's Word and Spirit.

Can a "Dead" Church Live Again?

I agree with Raphael G. Warnock, pastor of Ebenezer Baptist Church in Atlanta, Georgia, when he writes, "If the black church *is* dead, as Glaude asserts, concern over its prospects for resuscitation and role as an instrument of liberation is very much alive."[11] For all her problems, I believe the Black Church *can* live again. In fact, the reports of her death may be greatly exaggerated. There remain significant signs of illness and weakness: immorality among pastors and leaders, false "gospels" preached and taught, materialism, unclear direction and mission drift, an overemphasis on entertainment and the sensational, confusion about gender roles and the widespread absence of African-American men. The Black Church, like all churches, has her problems. But hope also abounds.

As Eddie Glaude Jr. rightly points out, "The death of *the* black church as we have known it occasions an opportunity to breathe new life into what it means to be black and Christian."[12] Surveying the weaknesses and limitations of the Black Church, we may recall the dramatic biblical scene when YHWH addressed the prophet Ezekiel. Ezekiel cast his eye over an utterly destroyed and abandoned Israel. The sight must have rivaled modern photos of holocausts and genocides. Bones lay lifeless on the valley floor, gleaming white from the burning and brandishing sun. A once-great people lie in utter ruin. Then comes the urgent question, "Son of man, can these bones live?"

Dumbfounded by the scene, the prophet Ezekiel replies, "O Lord GOD, you know." Ezekiel represents that swirl of despair and desire, of helplessness and hope that so many feel who dare ask, "Is the Black

Church dead?" Oh, Lord, You know if Your church can live again! But how?

The Lord answers, "Prophesy over these bones, and say to them, O dry bones, hear the word of the LORD. Thus says the Lord GOD to these bones: Behold, I will cause breath to enter you, and you shall live. And I will lay sinews upon you, and will cause flesh to come upon you, and cover you with skin, and put breath in you, and you shall live, and you shall know that I am the LORD" (Ezek. 37:4–6). And when Ezekiel prophesies to the dry bones, life returns (Ezek. 37:7–10)! They live again! As the word went out, life came in. God's people rose!

Ezekiel's vision provides us a picture of how life might be breathed again into the Black Church—through the faithful prophesying of God's Word. If God's Word gives life, it's no surprise that a return to preaching His Word in truth will bring new vigor and vitality to the Black Church. As if to anticipate the tempting hopelessness of future generations of Israelites and a languishing church of Jew and Gentile, the Lord explained to Ezekiel:

> "Son of man, these bones are the whole house of Israel. Behold, they say, 'Our bones are dried up, and our hope is lost; we are indeed cut off.' Therefore prophesy, and say to them, Thus says the Lord GOD: Behold, I will open your graves and raise you from your graves, O my people. And I will bring you into the land of Israel. And you shall know that I am the LORD, when I open your graves, and raise you from your graves, O my people. And I will put my Spirit within you, and you shall live, and I will place you in your own land. Then you shall know that I am the LORD; I have spoken, and I will do it, declares the LORD." (Ezek. 37:11–14)

The Lord opens the graves of a spiritually dry, hopeless, and dead people. He puts His Spirit in His people and causes them to live. That's what the Lord intends the preaching of the gospel to accomplish—revival. That's what this book is about.

Reviving and strengthening the Black Church will require great wisdom and courage. Not every prescription will help. A wide range of pundits hawk their wares and remedies for what ails the Black Church. They tell us the church needs this or that. I'm adding my voice to that fray—not because I think I have greater wisdom than all the other speakers. I'm adding my voice as another who owes his salvation to the faithful gospel witness of the Black Church, and as one who loves the church.

The recommendations in this book harken back to another time, borrowing the wisdom of earlier Christians. It harkens back to the Bible itself, for there we find the divine wisdom needed to see any ailing black churches live again, thriving with the Spirit of God in her soul.

What to Expect from This Book

I have organized the book into three parts. Part I examines the necessity of reviving the Black Church by God's Word as the source and guide of black church life and practice. Chapter 1 attempts a vision for what it means for churches to replace the Bible at the center of their life and worship. What will black churches look like if the Word of God animates and informs all they say and do?

Chapters 2 and 3 make a case for reforming African-American preaching. Without question, the pulpit is the fulcrum of change in the church. Little will happen if those who preach and teach God's Word fail to do so faithfully and accurately.

In chapter 2 I make the case for biblical exposition as the best way to reform preaching and unleash God's Word in the congregation.

Chapter 3 anticipates and responds to potential objections to biblical exposition.

Chapter 4 meditates specifically on the core of the Bible's message— the gospel of Jesus Christ. Without a recovery of the gospel in a local congregation, all chances of life are lost.

Chapter 5 explores the critical role music and singing play as aspects of the ministry of the Word. I argue for viewing music and singing as another form of teaching and preaching, and for the use of God's Word as a rule for what and how we sing.

Part II calls for a revival of biblical pastoral leadership in black churches. The Word of God must rest in the hands of faithful, godly men.

Chapter 6 offers an examination of biblical qualifications for church leaders, asking whether such qualities have guided the selection of men who shepherd God's people and inform our models of church leadership.

Chapter 7 calls for a realignment of biblical authority to the appropriate offices and qualified persons in black churches.

Chapter 8 highlights clergy scandal across denominations and calls for removal of ungodly leadership in the church.

Chapter 9 concludes the section with a look at pastoral training in the local church as a means of growing a generation of true churchmen.

Finally, Part III makes the case that the revival of the Black Church depends upon healthy efforts at membership and mission.

Chapter 10 promotes the rekindling of personal piety and discipleship.

Chapter 11 encourages the redrawing of lines between the church and the world through healthy church membership and discipline practices.

Chapter 12 focuses on reclaiming African-American Christian men and families.

Chapter 13 concludes the book with a call for the Black Church to reengage in gospel missions around the world.

We have long lived with cultural rules forbidding public critique of the Black Church. It's now time, however, that those who love the Black Church speak up with grace and truth. Some black churches have been hijacked by a number of ideas and parties. It's my humble prayer as one who loves the church and God's people that this volume might be useful to pastors and faithful lay members in reviving at least some quarters of the Black Church for the glory of God. It's my prayer that this book might make some impact on churches of every ethnicity and location.

PART I

Revive
by the Word

CHAPTER 1

Re-center the Bible

Your statutes are wonderful;
therefore I obey them.
The unfolding of your words gives light;
it gives understanding to the simple.
I open my mouth and pant,
longing for your commands.
Turn to me and have mercy on me,
as you always do to those who love your name.
Direct my footsteps according to your word;
let no sin rule over me.
Redeem me from the oppression of men,
that I may obey your precepts.
Make your face shine upon your servant
and teach me your decrees.
Streams of tears flow from my eyes,
for your law is not obeyed.
—PSALM 119:129–136 (NIV)

Introduction

Everything about that Bible was white. The hardback binding with *faux* leather cover was white. The heavy pages with gold trim were white.

The praying Jesus—arms folded on a rock, flowing robe and hair, face turned toward heaven in gentle golden beams—was white. The Bible salesman that convinced my mama this Bible was worth several installments of her hard-earned paycheck because it would be "a family heirloom" was—you guessed it—white. Even the lace doily on which it rested appeared to me like a soft network of white clouds bedding a heavenly treasure.

The large white Bible rested on the living room coffee table for a brief period of time. Pretty soon it went where all the valuable treasures of our house went for permanent storage—my mother's room. Today, it remains on my mother's dresser, floating on that now-dingy doily, holding between its covers the records of significant family events—births, marriages, deaths, and a few newspaper clippings.

I don't think I ever saw a family member read that Bible or any other Bible while I was growing up. But we never questioned its content or allowed anyone to misuse it. When I was growing up, there were two oaths that could end any dispute or silence doubts about a boy's integrity—"I swear on my mama's grave" or "I swear on the Bible." Our mothers' lives and our families' Bibles were too sacred to play around with. I didn't know it at the time, but my family responded to the Bible the way many—if not most—African-Americans have always responded to it. We reverenced it without reading it.

Encounters with the Bible during Slavery

Before it was commonplace for African-Americans to learn to read, African-American Christians reverenced the Bible, the mysterious "talking book" they saw whites read and preach. Freed African slave James Albert Ukawsaw Gronniosaw (ca. 1705–1775) recounts his first encounter with the Bible:

> [My master] used to read prayers in public to the ship's crew every Sabbath day; and when I first saw him read, I was never so surprised in my life, as when I saw the book talk to my master, for I thought it did, as I observed him to look upon it, and move his lips. I wished it would do so with me. As soon as my master was done reading, I followed him to the place where he put the book, being mightily delighted with it, and when nobody saw

me, I opened it, and put my ear down close upon it, in great hopes that it would say something to me; but I was very sorry, and greatly disappointed, when I found that it would not speak.[1]

Another slave, John Jea, recounts a very similar impression of the Bible as a "talking book." Jea writes, "I took the book, and held it up to my ears, to try whether the book would talk to me or not, but it proved to be all in vain, for I could not hear it speak one word."[2] Despite these early frustrations, Jea persevered in his longing to know the Book. He writes, "Such was my desire of being instructed in the way of salvation, that *I wept at all times I possibly could, to hear the word of God, and seek instruction for my soul;* while my master still continued to flog me, hoping to deter me from going; but all to no purpose, for I was determined, by the grace of God, to seek the Lord with all my heart, and with all my mind, and with all my strength, in spirit and in truth, *as you read in the Holy Bible.*"[3]

These were the early encounters of an illiterate people with the Holy Scriptures. Their illiteracy was forced upon them through the cruel oppressions of slavery, and self-interested slave owners often used the Bible to justify enslaving Africans. But that did not prevent them from being drawn to this almost magical book. To be sure, not every African was drawn to the Bible or sought its content. But pretty soon, it became the great ambition of some enslaved Africans to know the contents of this book and preach it for themselves.

Dwight Allan Callahan, in his delightful survey of African-Americans and the Bible, points out: "If the genres of poetry and autobiographical narrative are the beginnings of African-American literature, even African-American literature does not properly begin with writing. It begins with religion, the Evangelical religion of slaves who heard the text of the Bible speak to them and made of its letters a sacred quest. The Bible was the chief goal of literacy for African Americans, for whom religion was both opportunity and mandate to acquire letters."[4]

From the earliest times, some African-Americans revered the stubborn book that pressed its lips together and swallowed its secrets. The Bible had a place in their affections, imaginations, and aspirations—a central place, if not a speaking place. My mother's desire to spend money hard-earned in North Carolina's furniture mills and our boyhood reverence for the Bible stemmed all the way back to some slaves' "chief goal" of reading the Bible for themselves, to have and hear the talking book.

We Believe the Bible: Early Doctrine of the Word of God

As African-Americans acquired the ability to read, they turned their attention to the Bible's content. They looked to master the Bible's content as a means to both spiritual and social understanding and empowerment. Their explorations of the Bible yielded a self-consciously high and evangelical doctrine of Scripture.

One of the earliest to articulate a more doctrinal understanding of the Scripture was the slave and father of African-American literature, Jupiter Hammon (1711–1806?). In 1760, Hammon became the first African-American to publish a work of literature. He expressed his belief in the Bible and exhorted his audience to read it in his famous *Address to the Negroes in the State of New York:*

> [T]he Bible is the word of God and tells you what you must do to please God; it tells you how you may escape misery and be happy forever. If you see most people neglect the Bible, and many that can read never look into it, let it not harden you and make you think lightly of it and that it is a book of no worth. All those who are really good love the Bible and meditate on it day and night. In the Bible, God has told us everything it is necessary we should know in order to be happy here and hereafter. The Bible is the mind and will of God to men.[5]

Daniel Alexander Payne (1811–1893) served as Bishop in the first African-American Christian denomination in the United States, the African Methodist Episcopal (AME) Church. Payne was instrumental in establishing and reforming the ministerial requirements for the entire denomination. A tireless educator, Payne's view of Scripture's importance, authority, and centrality were much like Jupiter Hammon's. In his most famous address, *Welcome to the Ransomed,* given on the occasion of the District of Columbia's emancipation of slaves, Payne pressed his hearers to "rest not until you have learned to read the Bible."[6] Payne argued that "an individual man or woman must never follow conviction in regard to moral, religious, civil and political questions *until they are first tested by the unerring word of God.*" The Bible was to be the exclusive source and norm for personal conviction and conscience. Payne continued:

> If a conviction infringes upon the written word of God, or in any manner conflicts with that word, the conviction is not to be followed. It is our duty to abandon it. Moreover, I will add that light on a doubtful conviction is not to be sought for in the conscience, but in the Bible. The conscience, like the conviction, may be blind, erroneous, misled, or perverted; therefore it is not always a safe guide. The only safe guide for a man or woman, young or old, rich or poor, learned or unlearned, priest or people is the Bible, the whole Bible, nothing but the Bible.[7]

In summary, the earliest African-American Christians held an evangelical view of the Bible. They believed the Scriptures to be inspired by God, to have authority over the people and the life of faith, and to be sufficient for discerning how one should live—even in the midst of wickedness and oppression perpetrated against them by white professing Christians.

But enslaved people were not uncritical or gullible in their appropriation of the biblical text. John Jea, already quoted as an example of early black reverence for the Scripture, also illustrates the ability of some slaves to distinguish between the reliability of the Bible's content itself and the unreliable teaching of the Bible in the hands of some white masters. Jea recalls:

> After our master had been treating us in this cruel manner [severe floggings, sometimes unto death], we were obliged to thank him for the punishment he had been inflicting on us, quoting that Scripture which saith, "Bless the rod, and him that hath appointed it." But, though he was a professor of religion, he forgot that passage which saith "God is love, and whoso dwelleth in love dwelleth in God, and God in him." And, again, we are commanded to love our enemies; but it appeared evident that his wretched heart was hardened.[8]

Jea's account and others like it teach us that African-American Christians trusted the Bible while they suspected the self-serving motives and Scripture-twisting actions of white preachers and slave owners. It's fascinating to consider that a highly oral people revered the Scriptures they could not read even while they rejected the oracles of co-opted preachers they could hear. One could say that African-American Christianity began with an unread Bible placed on the center of the church's ecclesial coffee table.

Diverse Ways of Reading the Bible

Few professing African-American Christians would argue against the notion that the Bible should be at the center of the African-American Christian life and experience. The typical African-American Christian takes this for granted. But there's a significant danger in taking for granted what early enslaved Christians actively sought—through such presumption the Bible may, in fact, lose its place at the center of African-American Christian life and practice.

I have argued elsewhere[9] that a significant change of emphasis happened with the rise of a more radical abolitionist movement in the 1830s and following. Prior to 1830, African-American calls for slavery's abolition and the emancipation of Africans depended upon rich biblical texts and themes. The early abolitionist movement self-consciously centered itself on the Bible's teaching. Subsequently, however, appeals for emancipation and abolition were increasingly based on social and political arguments. It was not that the Bible ceased to be used and quoted; rather, the Bible became one among a range of arguments and sources. In short, it began to lose the center as African-Americans scrambled to first gain their freedom and then to redefine life in Reconstruction, Jim Crow segregation, and the Civil Rights movements. Preachers preached the Bible less and less, opting for political and social commentary instead. The people took to the streets in protest, centering their lives more and more on social action. Not surprisingly, biblical illiteracy continued for much of the emancipated history of African-Americans. Eventually, at least three interpretative approaches to the Bible emerged.

Evangelical Hermeneutic

First, the evangelical Biblicism of earlier African-Americans like John Jea, Jupiter Hammon, and Bishop Daniel Alexander Payne continued in black church life and practice. In this stream, the Bible continued to be revered, believed, and preached. Evangelical interpretation assumes the Bible to be inspired by God (literally, breathed out by God), to mean what it says, and to be without error. The Bible is to be obeyed as an act of faith and piety.

Evangelical approaches tend to emphasize a literal interpretation of the Bible. Sometimes evangelical interpretations have been "wooden," forcing meanings without reference to the genre of Scripture being read (history, poetry, gospel, etc.) or the context of the passage. Interpretations can also be moralistic, fostering self-righteousness and losing sight of the grace of God necessary for salvation. But at its best, an evangelical interpretive approach seeks the meaning of the text according to its literary genre and its social, historical, theological, canonical, and grammatical context.

Among evangelical interpreters, the Bible provides the knowledge necessary for salvation. As the doctrinal statement of the African Methodist Episcopal (AME) Church puts it: "The Holy Scripture containeth all things necessary to salvation; so that whatever is not read therein, nor may be proved thereby, is not to be required of any man, that it should be believed as an article of faith, or be thought requisite or necessary to salvation."[10] The Bible's main theme is spiritual salvation, culminating in the Person and work of Jesus Christ, the Son of God. One must interpret the Bible in light of this overarching work of God. Good moral lessons and examples abound, but the primary matter remains spiritual life.

Liberation Hermeneutic

Another approach to the Bible begins with the assumption that liberation of the oppressed is the primary theme and emphasis of the Bible. The main proponents of this approach belong to the academic school called Black Theology, cemented by Professor James Cone with his publications *Black Theology and Black Power* and *A Black Theology of Liberation*. Cone rejected the Bible as the rule and normative source for black Christianity and called black people to use various sources for doing theology, including black history, culture, experience, and tradition. Cone argued, "To know God is to know God's work of liberation on behalf of the oppressed. God's revelation means liberation, an emancipation from death-dealing political, economic, and social structures of society. This is the essence of biblical revelation."[11]

Perhaps Cone stated his position most clearly in the preface to his later work, *God of the Oppressed*:

I still regard the Bible as an important source of my theological reflections, but not the starting point. The black experience and the Bible together in dialectical tension serve as my point of departure today and yesterday. The order is significant. *I am black first—and everything else comes after that.* This means that I read the Bible through the lens of a black tradition of struggle and not as the objective Word of God. The Bible therefore is one witness to God's empowering presence in human affairs, along with other important testimonies.[12]

Those who followed Cone and some who preceded him argue for "a hermeneutic of suspicion." They contend that African-Americans should approach the Bible with a kind of skepticism, a suspicion, helping to push against the oppressive uses and content of the Bible while simultaneously identifying the subversive, liberating messages of the Scripture. Theologian Howard Thurman (1899–1991) often receives credit for advancing a hermeneutic of suspicion among African-American theologians and biblical scholars. Thurman tells the story of his grandmother, an ex-slave, who resisted what she saw as oppressive implications of the biblical text.

"During the days of slavery," she said, "the master's minister would occasionally hold services for the slaves. . . . Always the white minister used as his text something from Paul. 'Slaves be obedient to them that are your masters . . . as unto Christ.' Then he would go on to show how . . . if we were good and happy slaves, God would bless us. I promised my Maker that if I ever learned to read and if freedom ever came, I would not read that part of the Bible."[13]

According to some writers in the field of Black Theology, the willingness of Thurman's grandmother to reject Pauline writings as inconsistent with her experience and her need for liberation represents a particular way of reading the biblical text that de-centers the text and creates flexibility, even playfulness when approaching the Bible.

What would prompt such thinkers to remove the Bible from its central and authoritative place in black Christianity? Michael Joseph Brown, professor of New Testament and Christian Origins at Emory University, has written an excellent critique of African-American biblical scholarship. Tracing the development of African-American biblical scholarship through several key authors, Brown, himself an adherent to Black Theology, concludes that "a great deal of African American biblical hermeneutics is a reaction or response to the perceived advancement of evangelical Christianity and fundamentalism in the African American community." In Brown's view, the evangelical view of the Bible furthers the oppression of the African-American community. He maintains that "efforts must be made to provide alternatives that liberate members of the community from a misguided biblical hegemony."[14] Perhaps this helps to explain Brown's lament over the fact that "African American biblical hermeneutics is a largely academic enterprise" that "has not found a place among the larger African American populace yet."[15]

Some proponents of Black Theology explicitly argue for the setting aside of the Bible as the rule for faith and practice in the Black Church. Ronald N. Liburd makes the point plainly. He contends, "A fundamental flaw in black biblical hermeneutics is the authority invested in the Bible as the Word of God in order to posit a theology of liberation." In other words, biblical authority must give way to a liberation agenda. Moreover, Liburd tells us, "An African American biblical hermeneutic in the sense of calling the Bible the Word of God is counterproductive, in that it has to allow for the oppressors' legitimate use of certain biblical texts to maintain their position of dominance."[16]

We should not miss what is being proposed here. Once African-Americans trusted the Bible and suspected the preacher, now some African-American biblical scholars argue that the scholar should be trusted and the Bible suspected! The effect of such a reversal would be to move the Bible to the periphery of black church life.

Prosperity Hermeneutic

A third approach to the Bible can be found in the interpretative methods of proponents of the "prosperity gospel." On the one hand, prosperity preachers subscribe to a Biblicism not too dissimilar from that held by most black evangelicals. They believe the Bible to be God's Word inspired by the Holy Spirit. But on the other hand, prosperity preachers approach the Bible in search of a liberation message, much like the liberationist. The difference, however, is that proponents of prosperity theology define liberation not in terms of social and political freedoms but in terms of personal wealth, health, and possessions.

We might tune in to see a smiling televangelist like Joel Osteen, pastor of Lakewood Church in Houston, Texas, standing with Bible held high and leading the vast congregation in reciting a mantra of sorts. "This is my Bible: I am what it says I am; I have what it says I have; I can do what it says I can do. Today, I will be taught the Word of God. I'll boldly confess. My mind is alert; my heart is receptive; I will never be the same. I am about to receive the incorruptible, indestructible, ever-living Seed of the Word of God. I'll never be the same—never, never, never! I'll never be the same, in Jesus' Name."

The mimicking congregation confesses that they are about to be "taught the Word of God," a rather evangelical confession. They expect through the teaching to become, have, and do what the Bible teaches. Such an expectation sounds entirely reasonable. Everyone who takes the Bible seriously might make such a proclamation of faith. It's not until we consider Osteen's actual teaching that we recognize the difference a prosperity hermeneutic makes. The bulk of the teaching centers on success, self-improvement, health, and wealth. Osteen mutes the message of eternal life that evangelicals contend is the main story line of the Bible. The call for group liberation vanishes as individual and personal prosperity takes center stage.

While Osteen is white, prosperity preachers and televangelists have a long history in the African-American community. Proponents include men like "Daddy Grace," Frederick K. C. Price, Creflo Dollar, T. D. Jakes, Eddie Long, and Leroy Thompson.

The prosperity hermeneutic relies on finding in the biblical text the promises of blessings and prosperity God makes to His people. Prosperity preachers use Old Testament covenantal promises from passages like Deuteronomy 28:1–14 as promises to be "claimed" by individual New Testament Christians. YHWH made these promises to Israel for their obedience in the Promised Land. However, a prosperity hermeneutic removes such texts from their contexts, ignoring the developments and progressions of the Bible's main story line. Adherents to a prosperity hermeneutic see in Jesus' death and resurrection not only the means of eternal salvation but also the means of earthly physical, social, emotional, and financial well-being.

Each school of interpretation—evangelical, liberationist, and prosperity—has contributed to the de-centering of the Bible. Evangelicals have allowed it to be de-centered through neglect, failing to read it and apply it to life and faith. Liberationists have rebelled against it, actually calling for its removal from the dominant place in theology and religion. And prosperity preachers have removed it from the center by misusing and misquoting it, using a Biblicism that sounds evangelical while focusing on worldly materialism and success.

The truly alarming reality is that most of these erosions to the Bible's centrality have been happening while the congregation's Bibles have been wide open! The loss of biblical centrality cannot be averted with a biblically illiterate pew. If the Bible loses its place of authority, the Black Church loses its life-giving power.

What's at the Center of Black Church Life Now?

If the Bible has lost its central place in black church life, what then has taken its place? The answer to that question varies.

In some places the pastor's authority replaces the Bible's. Local churches may be governed not by the Word of God but by the opinions and preferences of senior leadership. Many lead well and offer the best guidance they can. But despite a pastor's best intentions, man's ideas and opinions provide little replacement for God's wisdom. Such pastors can become dictatorial. Moreover, such men often come under extreme pressure and stress as they attempt to provide the things that only God can provide by His Word.

In other churches entertainment replaces the Bible. One gets the sense that the climax of the black church service—the sermon—can often become a show. Congregations can be built around one man's speaking prowess. That prowess may be felt without ever honestly and accurately dealing with the biblical text. A "good preacher" knows how to "move the crowd." He masters rhythm and cadence. He reads the congregation and he knows how to turn a phrase. Add to that an exceptional choir and you have a recipe for thoroughly entertaining worship. But we may be left to ask, "What happened to the Bible?"

When entertainment takes center stage, very likely authority gets vested in individual experience. What comes to matter most is how individuals and the church *feel* about this or that issue. Celebration and catharsis, pleasure and pain-avoidance become the aims of the Christian life. While emotion remains one gift God has given for expressing life and faith, making emotion central to the life of faith can actually weaken the church and reliance on God's Word.

Other churches might center themselves on social action. The key note sounded in such congregations might be the necessity of protest, "speaking truth to power," and one or another form of liberation. These themes dominate the preaching and the collective agenda of the congregation. Social action has its place. Some, like Professor Glaude, might even call for more action rather than less. Nevertheless, social commentary and community action cannot sustain a church, nor can a church sustain such action indefinitely. The church that attempts to live by such commentary and action will inevitably suffer entropy.

In churches committed to the "prosperity gospel," the offering can crowd out the Bible for first place. Nigeria native, Femi Adeleye, describes this phenomenon in some West African churches:

> In the past the central part of the worship hour or two was the proclamation of the Word. Today in many churches the centerpiece is now the "offering time." Not a few churches have specially skilled and designated people to be masters of this significant ceremony. The popular saying is "Offering time is blessing time," not least because for many it is viewed as investment time. It is often regarded as a time to sow, while looking forward to significant returns. The Bible itself is often twisted to back the centrality of offering time and in some churches there is a mini-sermon to urge the congregation to give. Quite often there can be as many as five or six different collections taken in a single service. For example, in September 2008 I was at a church in Lagos where there were six different collections for various purposes, including freedom from fear. One cannot but feel a sense of the flock being fleeced bare.[17]

One can see similar scenes in some black churches in the United States. Elaborate appeals, pressure, and great promises consume large quantities of time during the worship service. Congregants make "seed offerings," drop quantities of cash on the rostrum while preachers preach, chant "money cometh," and wave money as an offering to God—all with the expectation of prosperity. The Bible is there, quoted and believed, but horribly misused and marginalized.

What Happens to a Church and a People Who No Longer Center Life on the Bible?

Does any of this really matter? So what if music and singing, offerings, or emotional exuberance become the centerpieces of black church life and worship? What harm is there if the Bible gets moved from the living room coffee table to the bedroom nightstand? If the Bible is still in use, what's the big deal?

Four significant problems arise when the Bible's influence on the congregation begins to wane. First, congregations lose the fear of the Lord. An inextricable relationship exists between a healthy fear or reverence for God and a right understanding of His Word. The preacher in Ecclesiastes 12:13 expresses this relationship well when he writes, "The end of the matter; all has been heard. *Fear God and keep his commandments, for this is the whole duty of man*" (emphasis added). All that God requires of His people might be summarized in terms of having a right heart toward God (fear or reverence) and having a right response to His Word (obedience). If a church centers its life on something other than the Bible, that church runs the great risk of eventually no longer fearing the Lord.

Second, congregations that no longer have the Bible at the center of their faith and life will lose the ability to discern the will of the Lord. The psalmist declares, "Your word is a lamp to my feet and a light to my path" (Ps. 119:105). The psalmist understands that without the Word of God his footing will be unsure and his path obscured. Deuteronomy 29:29 draws an even tighter connection between the Word of God and the will of God when it contends, "The secret things belong to the LORD our God, but the things that are revealed belong to us and to our children forever, *that we may do all the words of this law*" (emphasis added). The Lord hides some things in order to reserve them for Himself; but He openly shares other things so that we may possess them. Those things are found in His Word, things He gives to the faithful so that we may obey Him. One thinks of the Master's words in Matthew 28:19–20 as well: "Go therefore and make disciples of all nations, baptizing them in the name of the Father and of the Son and of the Holy Spirit, *teaching them to observe all that I have commanded you*" (emphasis added). Making disciples involves teaching them all that Jesus commands. But teaching disciples all that Jesus commands requires us to know both what His commands are and how to live our lives based upon them. When the Bible—which reveals for us the things that God desires us to know—loses its central place in the local church, we also lose the ability to truly make disciples that obey the Lord.

Third, a church that no longer makes the Bible central to its life and ministry runs the risk of altogether losing the gospel of Jesus Christ. Repeatedly the psalmist beseeches the Lord to "give me life according to your word" (Ps. 119:25, 107). The early church understood that spiritual life came by the Word of God. Recall Paul and Barnabas's rebuke of their Jewish contemporaries in Acts 13:46: "It was necessary that the word of God be spoken first to you. Since you thrust it aside and judge yourselves unworthy of eternal life, behold, we are turning to the Gentiles." The Jewish rejection or "thrusting aside" of the Word of God resulted in their being unworthy of eternal life. The Gentiles by contrast rejoiced to receive this Word which gives life (v. 48). The contrasting responses of early Jews and Gentiles teaches us that it is by "holding fast to the word of life" that the church avoids running or laboring in vain (Phil. 2:16). Undoubtedly, the early Jewish community did not consider itself in danger of forfeiting eternal life, nor was it likely that early Jews saw themselves as abandoning the Torah. But the Word of God was no longer central to their lives and they missed the day of their visitation. The same may happen in local churches that allow things other than the Scripture to drive its worship, faith, and practice. Such a church may lose the gospel of Jesus Christ.

Finally, a church built upon some foundation other than the Word of God will in time die. It will lose its life, for nothing can sustain a spiritual people other than spiritual food. The Devil tempted the very Son of God to live on some source of life other than the Word of God. But our Master replied, quoting the Scripture Himself, "Man shall not live by bread alone, but by every word that comes from the mouth of God" (Matt. 4:4). If the Savior's life depended upon the Word of God, how much more does our life? Can we be surprised that a church that looks to live by something other than the Word of God eventually dies? If the Black Church is dead, the chief cause will be the church's "thrusting aside" the Word of God, which is the Word of life.

A Vision for a Bible-Centered Black Church

What does a church centered upon the Word of God look like? It's fine to say the Bible should be central to the life of the church. Nearly all heads will nod in reflexive agreement. But how do we know when biblical centrality becomes the experienced norm rather than the spoken goal?

Jonathan Leeman provides one of the best analogies I've read to date. Leeman says, "God's Word gives life to a church like electricity gives power to a city." Here's how he further illustrates a Bible-centered church:

> Picture it. Electricity leaves the power plant and buzzes through power lines. Then it makes its way into street lights, grocery store freezers, office computers, and rows and rows of neighborhood homes. Lamps glow and refrigerators hum. In the same way, I'm contending that God's Word buzzes and hums through people and the local church, giving light to their eyes and hope to their hearts.[18]

To revive black churches, the Word of God must become as central to the life and activity of the church as a power plant is to the life and activity of our cities and homes. The Word must course through every aspect of faith and practice, giving energy and life to everything it touches.

Practically speaking, revival in black churches depends on a deep and wide ministry of the Word. Most black churches and most churches in general tend to limit the ministry of the Word to that portion of its worship service dedicated to the sermon. But that's like bottling the power plant's electricity inside the plant itself. The power plant may radiate with a blinding glow, but if the electricity never leaves the plant it does little good for the darkened, lifeless cities and suburbs that surround it. So it is with a Bible that's only preached or taught for a few minutes on Sunday morning. The pulpit glows and glimmers for a short time but little power and life reach the pew, much less the workweek.

But a deep and wide ministry of the Word means pastors and leaders teach the Bible in various settings and throughout the week. Certainly, the Bible commands attention during the sermon. But the entire worship service ought to be governed and informed by the Scripture. The congregation ought also sing the Bible, pray the Bible, and read the Bible in its gatherings. The Bible must also be taught, read, and studied in midweek Bible studies and small groups. With a wide ministry of the Word, persons meet together one-on-one to search the Scriptures and encourage one another. Pastoral counseling becomes another way to apply the truth of the Scripture to individual lives. And the members of the church take the Word of God into the workplace and community as they represent the Lord of the Word.

We might say that a church that centers the Bible in its congregational life will be filled with people who gossip the gospel. As the Word passes from lip to ear to heart, we may expect it to give spiritual life (Ezek. 37). As the Word of God goes forward into the world, we can confidently trust it will accomplish God's plans and purposes (Isa. 55:10–11). As the Bible is unleashed in the lives of saints and sinners, it will fall like a hammer and break up stony hearts (Jer. 23:29). Then revival comes to the Black Church.

Conclusion

Pastor, consider your leadership for a moment. Elder, reflect upon the lives of your members. Deacon and congregation, think about your meetings and your faith. Is everything done according to the Bible's clear teaching? Do people discuss the Word in smaller groups and one-on-one? Is the Word read privately? Do you gossip the gospel, or does it languish untold? Do you need the revival that comes from a church powered by the Word of God? If so, put the Bible and its message back at the center of everything. The life of your local church depends on the Bible being central and authoritative in everything.

CHAPTER 2

Reform Black Preaching, Part 1: A Case for Biblical Exposition

"Let the prophet who has a dream tell the dream, but let him who has my word speak my word faithfully. What has straw in common with wheat? declares the LORD. Is not my word like fire, declares the LORD, and like a hammer that breaks the rock in pieces? Therefore, behold, I am against the prophets, declares the LORD, who steal my words from one another. Behold, I am against the prophets, declares the LORD, who use their tongues and declare, 'declares the Lord.' Behold, I am against those who prophesy lying dreams, declares the Lord, and who tell them and lead my people astray by their lies and their recklessness, when I did not send them or charge them. So they do not profit this people at all, declares the LORD."
—JEREMIAH 23:28–32

Introduction

Days following the miscarriage of our first child, I sat at home in a mild depression. It was 10:00 a.m. on a Tuesday morning. Still wearing pajamas and a bathrobe, I should have reported to work hours earlier. My wife and I had just purchased a new home in anticipation of hearing the pitter-patter of little feet. Now, with its fresh white walls, spotless carpet, and shiny new appliances, the place seemed like a polished cave. I shuffled down the stairs, slumped onto the couch, picked up the remote, and turned to BET to watch music videos.

I expected to see "Rump Shaker" or some other hip-hop-inspired objectification of women, lust for money, or delusional claims to grandeur. Instead, my eyes and mind slowly focused on a short, square, balding brother entering a pulpit. He was serious, but not somber. He was purposeful but not anxious, prepared rather than flighty. I don't know why I continued to watch, but something held me—a gravity perhaps.

He announced that he would be continuing his series of sermons from Paul's second letter to Timothy. He read the text and opened the sermon with what I later learned was his customary way of beginning: "I want to lay down a systematic plan of development based upon the Word of God so that . . ." Then he began to slowly explain 2 Timothy 2:15: "Study to show thyself approved unto God, a workman that needeth not to be ashamed, rightly dividing the word of truth" (KJV). Phrase by phrase, this powerful petite preacher unfurled a vision for the Christian life—specifically the life of the Christian mind—and pressed his audience to pursue that picture. I sat engrossed with two thoughts: Who rewrote the Bible, and when did Christians begin thinking?!

Though not yet a Christian, at age twenty-five I had heard preaching of all sorts. I had heard the small-town Baptist preacher of my youth. He was a 'hooper and could send the church into flights of ecstasy. Later, as president of The Society for African-American Culture, I coordinated speaking invitations and visits to campus for many speakers and preachers. As a young Muslim convert, I travelled up and down the East Coast to hear Minister Louis Farrakhan speak to overflowing coliseums in the late 1980s. But I had *never* heard anything like the sermon I heard on television. Never had I witnessed such an understated man deliver such life- and mind-altering words from the Bible.

That Tuesday morning I sat with one determined response: I must hear more. But where to find it?

What Is Preaching?

We will hardly find powerful preaching unless we come to grips with what preaching is. What is it we propose to do when we enter the pulpit? What changes do we hope will result from all our proclamation?

Defining Preaching

Definitions of preaching abound. But for our purposes, three definitions from respected African-American preaching professors and practitioners illustrate the diversity in our thinking about preaching and consequently the difficulty in finding powerful biblical examples.

Isaac Rufus Clark, for twenty-seven years a professor of preaching at The Interdenominational Teaching Center in Atlanta, defines preaching as (1) divine activity (2) wherein the Word of God (3) is proclaimed or announced (4) on a contemporary issue (5) with an ultimate response to God.[1] By "divine activity," Clark means that in true preaching God does the actual preaching. The human instrument takes a secondary position; what matters is whether or not God speaks. The "Word of God" is not the actual words of the Bible, according to Clark, but a certain kind of revelation, a self-disclosure of God. That revelation must confront a "contemporary situation," the "relevant, existential context, the real-life situation to which the gospel is addressed."[2] Addressing people in their real-life context with the "Word of God" requires the preacher call for a response. Preaching has not happened until the preacher summons the hearer to reply to God's revelation.

Cleophus J. LaRue's *The Heart of Black Preaching* attempts to locate the central dynamic in powerful black preaching. LaRue profiles sermons from eleven prominent African-American preachers from the nineteenth and twentieth centuries. He concludes that the heart of black preaching combines (1) a particular view of God, (2) emphasis on the black sociocultural experience, and (3) practical and relevant application to black life. He explains:

> [P]owerful black preaching has at its center a biblical herme-
> neutic that views God as a powerful sovereign acting mightily
> on behalf of dispossessed and marginalized people. A belief in
> this God, an awareness of the sociocultural context of the black
> experience, and the creation of a sermon that speaks in a relevant

and practical manner to the common domains of experience in black life, when taken together, ultimately result in a powerful sermon that resonates in a potent and meaningful way with those listening in the congregation.[3]

Marvin A. McMickle defines preaching largely in terms of the task of the sermon. He writes, "Every sermon needs to make one clear, compelling, biblically centered and contextually relevant claim that sets some aspect of God's will and God's word before some specific segment of God's people. This is done with the hope that those people will be challenged, informed, corrected, or encouraged as a result of the word set before them that day."[4] Elsewhere McMickle elaborates on this definition:

> [The gospel] is what we should be preaching, and that is the claim that our sermons should be setting forth—what God wants to say to the church and to the world, as that message is found in the scriptures. Our task as preachers is to delve into that message, select one portion of it that will be the basis for a particular sermon, and then preach that message in a way that is clear and compelling. Our task is to be an instrument through which a word of ultimate significance claims our congregation in a transformative manner. And it is our task to do this week after week, every time we step into the pulpit.[5]

Each of these definitions takes for granted the need for sermons to be relevant and applicable to the lives of the hearer. Each definition also takes for granted the necessity of the sermon revealing some truth about the character and will of God in any given situation. And each definition places emphasis on the need for hearers to respond to the message preached. All of these emphases are good, necessary, and proper in their place. Without these characteristics, we could hardly call a public speech a "sermon."

However, what each definition fails to convey is the absolute centrality and urgency of the biblical text to the sermon preached. For example, Clark states that the sermon must proclaim the "Word of God." However, here his definition stumbles irredeemably. For Clark writes, "The Word of God is *not* the Bible, but God as God-self."[6] One wonders, then, why bother with the biblical text at all. Where will preaching's authority reside—in the preacher or the text?

While Clark flatly rejects the Bible as the Word of God, LaRue places emphasis on a particular hermeneutic rather than getting the actual biblical text correct. Of our sample definitions, McMickle comes closest to the goal when he calls for a "biblically centered" sermon and for the message to be "found in the scriptures." But even "biblically centered" may not be the same thing as "preaching the Bible."

Recently my wife attended a week-long series of meetings featuring a prominent African-American pastor and preacher. She attended the meetings hoping to hear a powerfully preached and applied sermon from the Word of God. Midway through the week she shared with me a nagging uneasiness with the preaching. The preacher was witty and engaging. He said true things and nothing unorthodox. But there was something "not quite right" with the preaching. By week's end she recognized the problem. The final night he preached an exposition of a text where he carefully unfolded the meaning of the biblical text in its context and insightfully applied it to the hearers. The difference between the first five nights and the final night was clear. In the first five nights this preacher skimmed over the biblical text like a flat rock skipping across the surface of a pond. But on the final night, he dunked the audience's heads into the text for a long, deep, refreshing drink of sacred Scripture. There was authority, insight, and power in the last sermon because the sermon emerged from the text, not the preacher's true but loosely connected musings.

"Rock-skipping" preaching appears to be the norm in far too many churches. Even many "good" preachers treat the text lightly. This is why so much preaching—in churches of every ethnic context—lack power. This is why that short, stout, understated preacher amazed me so on that Tuesday morning. *He actually believed the Bible to be the very Word of God and his preaching method manifested his belief in the Bible as the Word of God.* Where the Bible is not believed and where the preaching does not manifest belief in the Bible, then preaching itself dies an ignoble death. And if the pulpit dies the pew won't be long in joining it.

Expositional preaching takes seriously the Bible as the Word of God. Moreover, biblical exposition is the only preaching method that inherently communicates to the congregation that the preacher believes the Bible to be the Word of God. E. K. Bailey, late pastor of Concord Dallas, understood this truth. Bailey defines exposition as "a message that focuses on a portion of scripture *so as to clearly establish the precise meaning of the text*, and to poignantly motivate the hearers to actions or attitudes *dictated by that text* in the power of the Holy Spirit."[7] John Stott summarizes this truth well when he writes: "In expository preaching the biblical text is neither a conventional introduction to a sermon on a largely different theme, nor a convenient peg on which to hang a ragbag of miscellaneous thoughts, but a master which dictates and controls what is said."[8]

For the Black Church to be revived and for black preaching to be reformed, the black pulpit needs a master to control it. Only the Bible may master the pulpit without destroying the preacher and preaching. Power in preaching comes from unleashing the Bible in faith.

What Is Wrong with Preaching Today?

People frequently ask, "Where can I find good preaching?" Or, "Do you know of any good churches in my area?" It seems the prophet Amos's prediction has come to pass: there is a famine for the Word of God in the land (Amos 8:11). And it's no local famine. From what I can tell having preached from Canada to Brazil, in the Caribbean to Southern Africa, in the United Kingdom and the United States, God's people everywhere appear to be hungering for the solid meat of the Word. That hunger raises the question: What's gone wrong with preaching? The departure from true exposition results from four significant problems.

More Gravy than Meat: Style over Substance

I'm not the only one to write about problems in black preaching, and I'm certainly not the first to observe the hunger for solid biblical preaching. Over twenty years ago, Henry H. Mitchell, one of the "deans of black preaching," put his finger on one problem afflicting so much preaching in traditional black churches:

> The cardinal sin of the Black pulpit is probably that of irrelevant celebration—gravy that does not match the meat, so to speak. Good gravy is always made of the essence of the meat to be served, and the same is true of the good gospel feast. When the celebration is about something else, the real message is lost, while the celebration, if it has any substance at all, is recalled.[9]

Overall, Mitchell remains a champion of the virtues of black preaching. But even the casual observer can see the truth of Mitchell's critique. All too often we have heard a rousing sermon only to leave the service unable to tell our neighbor what the sermon was about. The preacher swaggers and swings, whoops and hollers, moans and mouths a torrent of words, but in all the gestures and speaking there doesn't seem to be any lasting power or content. The congregation bathes in gravy but finds no meat.

Or, as former Interdenominational Theological Center professor Isaac Clark put it, "For the most part, not every part, but for the most part, for the predominant part, preaching is 'shallow and in the shadows.'" Clark goes on to state that "much of so-called preaching today is not getting at the deep, fundamental, serious questions of life that people are concerned about." Contemporary preaching in too many African-American churches "is often lacking divine depth and human depth. There is often no profound impact on the thinking and behavior of people in their living today." As Clark graphically paints it, "Much of today's preaching is about as deep as a single dewdrop on the desert sand at high noon."[10]

If Mitchell and Clark correctly diagnose the preaching prevalent in African-American churches—high on style and low on substance—then we cannot be surprised that so many people have become impatient and disdainful toward preaching. But the people cannot be blamed. Many of them have never actually heard true biblical preaching.

Needs-Based and Man-Centered

There is, however, another problem with much contemporary preaching. The problem is subtle but has profound impact on the nature of preaching and the preacher's task. Recall LaRue's description of the heart of black preaching as combining a belief in a God that acts on behalf of the marginalized, awareness of the sociocultural context of black people, and a relevant address to some domain of black life. According to LaRue, the task of preaching then requires the African-American preacher to maintain certain sensibilities. LaRue writes:

> Black preachers approach the text with two fundamental questions in mind with respect to the creation and organization of their sermon: (1) How do I demonstrate to God's people this day through the proclamation of the Word the mighty and gracious acts of God on their behalf? And (2) How best shall

I join together scripture and their life situations in order to address their plight in a meaningful and practical manner? The first question *initiates the search for that portion of scripture that will conform to the template* growing out of their sacred story; the second question helps the preacher to *focus on a particular aspect of black experience.*[11]

What's the problem with this description of the black preacher's approach? Notice that it begins *not* with the biblical text but with an assumption about God and our social situation. LaRue's comment turns the preacher into a man with a sermon in search of a text.

We find at the center of this approach the assumed aspirations of the community rather than the carefully developed and explained meaning of the Bible itself. The Bible functions as a source for saying what the preacher *wants* to say rather than as the determining limit and guide to what the preacher *must* say. In the end, the preacher gives an exposition of the people's perceived situation rather than an exposition of God's Word in the Bible. According to LaRue, "A certain type of experiential brooding occurs in the embryonic stage of the sermon *prior to actual exegesis of the text*. This deliberate, subliminal musing is an essential ingredient in the creation of the black sermon."[12] LaRue maintains that "the starting point for the traditional black sermon is seldom a specific theological formulation but rather the concrete life experiences of those who make up the listening congregation."[13] He also argues that an understanding of the broad domains of black life "afford an endless resource of ideas for the content of the black sermon."[14]

In other words, the traditional black sermonic approach is needs-based and man-centered rather than text-driven. Henry Mitchell states the case plainly:

> Black preaching at its best has remained focused on problems that people confront daily and feel real needs in meeting. People who are oppressed are often preoccupied with problems. The Black preacher has had to give strength for the day's journey, the guidance and vision for extended survival in an absurdly trying existence.[15]

While it is undoubtedly true that black preachers have to give a sustaining word to their people, the contention that the experience of the people should be the *focus* and *material* out of which the sermon arises simply raises some important questions. Should not the Bible itself be the "endless resource for ideas" for the preacher's sermons? Does not the Bible speak directly into the various problems and situations of life? Is Scripture not relevant already? Are there any difficulties in a preacher predetermining the sermon prior to exegeting a text? Is there a danger of having the black experience (past or present) replace the biblical text as the distinctive and authoritative note in black preaching?

Hegemony, History, and Irrelevance

The problem becomes more apparent when we realize that the proponents of such preaching define "the black experience" exclusively in terms of marginalization and oppression. Referring to several nineteenth-century preachers in his study, LaRue proclaims that "all were shaped by the same sociocultural experience of marginalization and powerlessness that affected the whole of the black race."[16] LaRue assumes this same experience of marginalization and powerlessness for his late twentieth-century subjects as well.

We find this assumed monolithic black experience guiding the work of Black Theologians in general.[17] They take for granted the oppression of African-Americans and argue for liberation. The preacher's task becomes the proclamation of liberation to the oppressed. James H. Evans Jr. even speculates that "the relationship between faith and freedom is, perhaps, the most pressing theological problem of our time."[18]

But few seem to have stopped to ask how the changing social, cultural, and political situations of African-Americans should affect preaching. The continuing assumption of universal marginalization across every era of African-American history actually flattens the African-American experience and contributes to the increasing irrelevance of black preaching. What do I mean?

The experience of African-Americans in 1830 could fairly be characterized as near universal enslavement, oppression, and marginalization. Few would deny that. But how should we describe African-Americans in 1930? Should we consider life in the New Negro or Harlem Renaissance North equivalent to the sharecropping experience of the South? It would be fair to say that a great many, the majority, still suffered social and political marginalization and disenfranchisement even though slavery was over. The gains of Reconstruction half a century earlier had been successfully rolled back. However, by 1930, it would also be true that growing numbers of African-Americans were becoming middle class and educated. The rise of a distinct black middle class surely should affect how we characterize the black experience in America. Moreover, the 1930s seem like a lifetime ago for African-Americans born around 1980. The experience of 1980s-generation African-Americans is so different from previous generations that a burgeoning number of books dare to argue for a "post-Black" self-understanding.[19]

Any monolithic understanding of black experience crumbled long ago under the shifting weight of African-American progress and hard-earned victories. Those advances and the diversifying realities of black life have opened up possibilities unimaginable even fifty years ago, including the possibility of rethinking "blackness" itself. Yet most books published on black preaching continue to argue that the black preacher should assume a context of social and political marginalization similar to that of the 1800s and early 1900s as the starting point for the preaching task. Little wonder that black preaching might be seen as entirely irrelevant to black life today. The preacher faces unprecedented diversity and desperately needs the timeless word of God to determine his preaching.

False Teaching and Materialism

There's yet another problem confronting preaching in African-American and other communities. When we combine (1) a loose interpretative approach to the Bible such that the Bible is used to provide support to an idea or sermon already conceived by the preacher with (2) a focus on the assumed needs of the African-American audience rather than the meaning of the biblical text and (3) the shifting and diversifying social, economic, and political fortunes of African-Americans, we open the church pulpit to unsavory, self-interested, and materialistic preachers and teachers.

Have you ever wondered how "prosperity preachers" became so popular? How could a teaching largely unknown one hundred years ago gain the ascendancy so quickly? The short answer must be that the teaching and the teachers were able to exploit weaknesses already present in the church. The most basic weakness was the loose hermeneutic and interpretative practices already used in black preaching. If the same number of black preachers had long played loose with the text by importing figurative meanings, it would be easy for "prosperity preachers" to take advantage of the same looseness to spread their message.[20] And if black preaching has a long history of addressing the social situation of black audiences, is there any wonder that with the rise of the black middle class some audiences might actually have "itching ears" wanting to hear how they could get their "comeuppance"? The materialism of the 1980s provided a historical opening for the wider acceptance of "prosperity theology" even in churches with a longer history of working for social justice. Getting wealthy became the new social justice in a highly individualized social situation no longer dependent on black unanimity for self-protection and advancement. As a measure of progress and affluence, many prosperity preachers would even style themselves as respectable "teachers" over and against the traditional whoopin', sweatin', "backward" preachers of earlier generations.

What many traditionally regarded as strengths of the black preaching tradition actually became openings for the corruption of preaching and teaching itself. We have reached a pivotal moment in time where the future life of the African-American Church depends upon a thorough reform of its preaching. The reformation has to start with a rededication to preaching the Scripture in such a way as to release the Bible's own power to convert and convict, engage and edify, direct and deliver, instruct and inspire.

What Kind of Preaching Do We Need?

But what kind of preaching does the Black Church need? What characteristics would typify healthy biblical proclamation? The reform of black preaching must include five aspects—call it the "five Es" of biblical preaching.

1. Exposes the Meaning of the Biblical Text

The truest biblical preaching and the kind of preaching that needs reclaiming in the church today—of every ethnicity—is biblical exposition. By "expository preaching" I mean the kind of preaching that exposes the meaning of the text of Scripture and applies that meaning to the hearer. When the main point of the text becomes the main point of the sermon, then you have expository preaching. I could not agree more with H. B. Charles Jr. when he justifies his commitment to expositional preaching by writing, "I am convinced that the Bible is God's self-revelation. Therefore, to misinterpret the text is to misinterpret God. So the stakes are high. And the preacher must be extremely disciplined if he or she is to prepare at least fifty sermons a year without lying on the Scriptures. . . ."[21]

However, many things pass as biblical expositions that give expository preaching a bad name. Expository preaching ought not be confused with an academic lecture, or a running commentary with no application, or just plain boring preaching. Exposition is *not* contrary to emotion and passion in preaching. Nor is expositional preaching limited to consecutively working through books of the Bible, though for many reasons I contend that sequential exposition through books of the Bible provides the best overall spiritual diet for a congregation.

The expositor is the man who stands with a lump of coal in his hand, hammering that dark resistant rock with the hammer of his mind until it reveals the diamond buried inside. The expositor comes to the Bible believing that God's people need God's Word in order to live God's way. He knows that man does not live on the preacher's word but on every word that comes from the mouth of God. The fervent desire to preach the whole counsel of God drives him deeper and deeper into the meaning of the Word as the Divine and human authors intended. He lifts that meaning for all to see, exposes it to the light of the mind and the fires of the heart, and calls the people into its truth or pushes that truth down into their souls. He twists the Word of God like a screw into their heads, down into their hearts and out through their hands. That's the kind of preaching we need. Preaching that exposes the meaning of the Bible, then applies it.

2. Exalts the Biblical Jesus

Jesus has more makeover artists than any other personality in history! Throughout the ages men and women have fashioned and refashioned the Lord Jesus into their own image, making Him to say and do the things that please them. But the Jesus revealed in the Bible steps on every man's toes, towers over every man's head, and demands every man's worship. True expositional preaching exalts the Lord Jesus Christ, the Son of God, *as He is found in the Scripture.*

The expository preacher aims to make the true Jesus of the Bible known to his hearers. The expository preacher understands that exposition is one means of heeding the words of Psalm 34:3 (NIV)—"Glorify the LORD with me; let us exalt his name together." The expositor discovers through his study of the Word and sermon preparation that Jesus exists as a multidimensional God. He cannot be reduced to one attribute or one action in the world. He exists in variegated glory. For that reason, preaching must be designed to bring the hearer into contact with the living, reigning, glorious Redeemer. Such contact only happens as the expositor allows the text of Scripture to determine the shape and content of the sermon and as the expositor commits himself to preaching Jesus Christ through whole books of the Bible and portions of Scripture that he may naturally be inclined to ignore.

3. Exultation in the Biblical Jesus

But not only must Christ Jesus be exalted or lifted up, the hearer must also *exult* in Christ. The Lord Jesus draws out this very point in a brief parable He shared with the disciples. "The kingdom of heaven is like treasure hidden in a field. When a man found it, he hid it again, and *then in his joy* went and sold all he had and bought that field" (Matt. 13:44 NIV, emphasis added). Notice, "in his joy" the one who finds the kingdom of heaven sells all to purchase the treasure. Christ Jesus is that Treasure and those who find Him must exult or rejoice in Him.

As the prophet Isaiah declared, "In the LORD all the descendants of Israel will be found righteous and *will exult*" (Isa. 45:25 NIV, emphasis added). What is this exulting? To exult in the Lord means to feel a lively or triumphant joy, to be highly elated or jubilant, to delight, glory, or revel in the Person and work of Jesus. That is, the Christian must be brought to treasure and adore the Lord Jesus Christ.

Black preaching has long boasted an ability to celebrate the work of Jesus in the lives of His people. Most traditional black sermons conclude with a celebration wherein the pulpit and the pew aim to exult in Christ. However, the primary point I am making here has to do with what exactly produces the exultation. Is it the preacher's rhetorical flair and genius, the organ or keyboard harmonically accompanying the sermon, *or the truth of the Word of God explained and exalting Jesus*? The style becomes secondary. Is there an *exposition* present that informs the mind and then inflames the heart? Does the very form of teaching help to create sustained worship and adoration of the Savior? Or, as Henry Mitchell puts it, does the celebration amount to savory gravy without meat? We need preaching that leads the hearer to exult in Jesus *as a consequence of* having exposed and exalted Jesus from the very Word of God.

4. Edifies the Church

The natural consequence of preaching that exposes, exalts, and exults ought to be preaching that edifies the church. True proclamation of the Scripture builds up the people of God. Again, this should not be surprising since nearly everything the Lord gives or commands in the church He gives and commands to build her up—spiritual gifts (1 Cor. 14:12), apostolic authority (2 Cor. 10:8; 13:10), love (1 Cor. 8:1), gifted leaders (Eph. 4:11–16), and encouragement (1 Thess. 5:11). The Lord intends to spiritually build up His church. But what do we mean by "edification"?

Shall we equate edification with temporary feelings of happiness? Or, should we define edification in terms of the relief of suffering and hardship? Does edification involve or depend upon entertainment or education? Genuine edification may involve any of those things—increased happiness, relief from pain and suffering, entertainment, or education. But true edification does not *depend* upon those things and is not limited to them. For example, biblical edification also includes correction and reproof, which can hurt for a time.

The term *edification* comes from the root word "edifice." An edifice is a structure or building established on a foundation. When we speak of preaching that edifies we're speaking of sermons that build people deep and strong. The preacher should follow the apostle Paul's example with the Ephesian elders when he said, "Now I commit you to God and to the word of his grace, *which can build you up* and give you an inheritance among all those who are sanctified" (Acts 20:32 NIV, emphasis added). Do you see the connection between "the word of his grace" and the ability of that word to "build you up"? The ministry of the Word is the main way the Lord builds His church. The Word rightly preached puts load-bearing walls and beams into the structure of our lives so that we stand and face the world with the strength that comes from God. We desperately need that kind of preaching.

5. Evangelizes the Lost

The preacher has not properly exposed the meaning of a biblical text until he moves naturally from the particular text—whether Old Testament or New Testament—to the message of Jesus Christ and Him crucified, buried, and resurrected to save sinners from the wrath of God. Indeed, Jesus Himself understood that all of Scripture pointed to Him. I wish I could have heard that Bible study the Master held with the disciples on the road to Emmaus in Luke 24. They had hoped Jesus would be the promised Messiah. But the crucifixion had dashed their hopes just a couple days earlier and left them defeatedly shuffling back to Emmaus. Jesus appeared to them, but they did not recognize Him at first. They explained the recent events, including the crucifixion and the empty tomb, but they did not yet understand. Then Luke tells us, "And beginning with Moses and all the Prophets, [Jesus] explained to them what was said in all the Scriptures concerning himself" (Luke 24:27 NIV).

A little while later, the Lord Jesus appeared to His disciples, who were so overjoyed they could hardly believe it was Jesus even though He showed them His nail-pierced hands and feet. As the Savior ate with His followers, He taught them the Old Testament Scriptures concerning Himself.

> He said to them, "This is what I told you while I was still with you: Everything must be fulfilled that is written about me in the Law of Moses, the Prophets and the Psalms." Then he opened their minds so they could understand the Scriptures. He told them, "This is what is written: The Christ will suffer and rise from the dead on the third day, and repentance and forgiveness of sins will be preached in his name to all nations, beginning at Jerusalem. You are witnesses of these things. I am going to send you what my Father has promised; but stay in the city until you have been clothed with power from on high." (Luke 24:44–49 NIV)

The "Law of Moses, the Prophets and the Psalms" refer to the entirety of the Jewish Scriptures, the Old Testament. Jesus makes the audacious claim that centuries-old Jewish religious literature actually pointed to His mission to suffer, die, and rise for the forgiveness of sins! He commands His disciples to preach this message in all nations and sends them with the promise of the Holy Spirit.

If black preaching is to be apostolic preaching in the best sense of the phrase, then every exposition should include the proclamation of this good news! The preacher has not properly understood the text unless he has explained it in light of Jesus' death, burial, and resurrection as an atoning sacrifice for sinners and called his congregation to repent and believe for the first time or to continue believing this message.

In saying the preacher must explain the text in the light of the Person and work of Christ, I am not advocating that a short "gospel appeal" be tacked onto the end of every sermon as part of a ritualistic "altar call." Such appeals may do more to inoculate sinners against the gospel message than we realize. Another approach may be more effective. Since Jesus is the subject of the Bible, every sermon should explore the organic relationship between the text and the life and work of the Messiah. Either the Lord fulfills biblical prophecy (for example, Isaiah 53), comes as the true Israel or Son of God (Mark 1:1; Luke 1:35), fulfills even the pattern of Israel's history (Matt. 2:13–15), completes the types and figures of the Old Testament (1 Cor. 5:7; Heb. 7), or satisfies the righteous demands of the Law (Matt. 5:17–21). In these various ways, determined by the text of Scripture, the preacher should expose the Person and work of Christ for His hearers to see, knowing that if Christ is lifted up He will draw all men to Himself (John 12:32). In this way, every sermon ought to be an evangelistic sermon.

Exposition Changes Our Definition of "Good Preaching"

When the preacher exposes, exalts, exults, edifies, and evangelizes using the Word of God, we may be certain that God's power will rest upon such preaching. This means also that both preachers and congregations must learn a new metric for evaluating preaching. We must measure the sermon in terms of its substance, not primarily its style. We must learn to look for spiritual growth, not numerical growth alone. The people of God must value faithfulness to the text over the feelings that can be excited. And we must esteem sermon depth more than we disdain sermon length.

For our part, pastors and preachers must seek to be faithful as stewards of God's message. That's what God requires of us (1 Cor. 4:1–2).

We are ambassadors and heralds who must represent the message as the King and Sender requires us. We have no liberty to play with the message. We must joyfully embrace the constraints of God's Word, believe God's Word, and preach the entirety of God's Word as though souls depended upon it—for they do!

For their part, congregations must learn to listen to God's Word. If pastors must master expositional preaching, congregations must master "expositional listening." Expositional listening involves learning to listen to the preached Word for the meaning of the text of Scripture and learning to apply that meaning to our lives as listeners.[22] As John Stott rightly contends, "a deaf church is a dead church."[23]

Moreover, congregations must learn to encourage men who faithfully expound the Scripture accurately. Teaching and preaching the text demands a lot from the preacher. Honor such men. Encourage them for letting the Word speak. Give them specific words of appreciation after the service; let them know in detail how the Lord spoke to you through the text. If expositional preaching is as countercultural as some would have us believe, then those faithful expositors must not be taken for granted but greatly encouraged in their work.

Conclusion: Will Such Preaching Work in the Black Context?

In this chapter, we have seen that significant challenges confront preaching in the Black Church context. I have maintained that expository preaching—with its emphasis on exposing the meaning of the biblical text, exalting the Lord Jesus Christ, exulting in the glory of the Lord, edifying the church, and evangelizing the lost—represents the truest form of preaching and the only way to expect true power to rest upon black preaching.

But there remains one question to answer. Will expositional preaching work in the Black Church context? Is black preaching so culturally determined that exposition will not fit the needs and tastes of predominantly African-American congregations? In the next chapter, we turn our attention to some common objections to expositional preaching.

CHAPTER 3

Reform Black Preaching, Part 2: A Defense of Exposition in Nonwhite Contexts[1]

Therefore, since through God's mercy we have this ministry, we do not lose heart. Rather, we have renounced secret and shameful ways; we do not use deception, nor do we distort the word of God. On the contrary, by setting forth the truth plainly we commend ourselves to every man's conscience in the sight of God.
—2 CORINTHIANS 4:1–2 (NIV)

Introduction

May I never forget an opportunity to travel to Dubai to serve with my good friend John Folmar. I had the privilege of preaching at his church for the two Friday morning services. I'd just preached my heart out in the first service and made my way to the back of the church to greet people as they filed away. Most people greeted me in some kind way, thanking me for coming, thanking me for the sermon, asking me about the Cayman Islands. It was a pleasure to briefly fellowship with the many Christians from some sixty nations who worshipped together at the United Christian Church of Dubai.

As I greeted the morning's worshippers, I noticed one couple standing off to the side, waiting to speak with me as others finished their greetings. They were "lurkers"—those folks who know they have too much to say so they give room for others to go first.

When the line dwindled, they came over, introduced themselves (they were white Americans), and thanked me for the sermon. Then with a knowing smile he said, "But . . . I thought you would preach like a *black* preacher."

Awkward silence. Crickets chirped.

I played country dumb, though I knew what they meant. He went on to explain that he'd been looking forward to my coming so they could hear "some good ol' black preaching—whipping the people up."

If you're an African-American, and you are committed to exposition, chances are you have had someone say something like this to you: "You preach like a white man."

"You're not a preacher, but you are a good teacher." Or even, "You'd make a fine Sunday school teacher."

These comments reveal an implicit and sometimes explicit critique or rejection of exposition in some non-white contexts. It's my hope in this chapter to examine that critique or rejection and respond with what I hope is a biblical case for expositional preaching in those very contexts where the critiques arise. As we maintained in the previous chapter, expositional preaching is the form of preaching that best treats the Bible as the Word of God and thus brings reviving power to the Black Church.

Some Objections to Expositional Preaching

In nonwhite contexts, there are at least three implicit and sometimes explicit objections to the kind of preaching I have been advocating in this book.

Exposition Is Culturally Inappropriate Preaching

The first objection contends that biblical exposition is culturally inappropriate or out of place. Most African-American commentators on preaching assume that cultural context and cultural considerations reign supreme in preaching preparation and delivery. Here's how one African-American writer, a dean of black preaching, puts it:

The real message of this cultural consideration, then, is not the promotion of a particular culture, but the insistence that the preacher affirm and work within the culture of the congregation. Whatever that culture may be, it is utterly fruitless to try to communicate effectively outside it. The preacher should also remember never to fight a war with or engage in frontal attack against the surrounding culture; it is too well entrenched and one could get uselessly wasted. And besides, if the preacher were to succeed on a large scale, it would be disastrous for the hearers to see so much of their survival kit destroyed. *They could very well become pathologically disoriented, requiring institutional care.*[2]

Mitchell rightly recognizes that all preaching occurs in a cultural milieu, a milieu that has to be respected. However, Mitchell goes beyond simply respecting the cultural milieu to suggesting that cultural considerations are impervious to "frontal attack" or efforts to change. Moreover, according to Mitchell, if the cultural milieu and expectations could be changed, "it would be disastrous for the hearers." If we don't preach in the cultural expectations of our congregations, then the people won't be able to cope and they'll go crazy! "They could very well become pathologically disoriented, requiring institutional care." That's the kind of argument sometimes encountered in preaching texts written by and for African-Americans. To the extent people believe exposition to be contrary to cultural forms of preaching, this argument assumes exposition to be the enemy of effective communication within African-American culture.

But it's not just African-Americans who make those kinds of arguments. One Asian-American Christian, David Ng, suggests, "The church needs to support the search for and the recovery of ethnic and cultural identity and values. . . . Asian North American Christians believe that their identity, culture, language, religious heritage—their whole way of life—is good and is where God is present and at work." Ng's perspective resembles that espoused by Henry Mitchell. However, Ng goes further than simply saying culture is important to address. We're told that God is present and at work in the Asian North American culture. Is God not present and at work elsewhere? Is the Lord's presence and work limited to that culture?

Ng continues: "Asian American pastors *must preach in a style that is unique to our culture so that our messages will connect with the minds and hearts of bicultural Asian American souls.* By combining methodical biblical exposition with the exegesis of our Asian American listeners, we can present sermons with timeless Scriptural truths in a contextualized, personal, ethnic, and cultural style."[3] Though the writer mentions "methodical biblical exposition," he insists on a "contextualized, personal, ethnic, and cultural style." He does not clarify what he means by such a style, but we easily see where arguments for cultural appropriateness tend to go. Sermonic style becomes the second objection or reason for believing exposition will not work in non-white settings.

Exposition Is the Wrong Style of Preaching

The culturally appropriate argument inevitably emphasizes sermonic style over biblical substance. Even where proponents rightly call for biblical content and sensitivity to one's audience, the most potent feature appears to be cultural form or fashion. We might see this objection at work in calls for three examples of culturally preferred styles of preaching: whoopin', hwyl'n, and whinin'.

Whoopin'. The *sine qua non* of African-American preaching is the "whoop." Known by various names, the "whoop" is the crescendo of call and response to which the traditional black sermon builds. One writer describes traditional black preaching as beginning in a sunny calm, letting the distant thunder roll, bringing the winds and the rain, and then leaving the people in a perfect storm of ecstasy. Some identify this cadence as the aim of preaching itself.

> No matter how misused by some or criticized by others, *the celebration at its best is the goal to which all of the Black sermon is moving.* In sermon preparation, it is often the celebration that is chosen right after a text and purpose have been selected. *It is on the basis of the final celebration more than any other element that the sermon will be judged.* If the sermon is remembered, then it will be because *the text was etched by ecstasy* on the heart of the hearer.[4]

In other words, the traditional black sermon aims in part at emotional response. According to this respected author, we want to leave people with the cathartic "whoop" or "celebration."

Hwyl'n. Historian Iain Murray records an interesting anecdote regarding the cultural preaching context in which Dr. Martyn Lloyd-Jones began his preaching career. Among Welsh preachers of the 1900s, there existed the accepted and revered practice of preaching with "the hwyl." Murray explains, in the words of a newspaper of the time, that "the hwyl" was a "combination of ecstatic emotion and of musical intonation which has held vast congregations absolutely spellbound with its mesmeric effect." That same columnist declared that "the hwyl" was "the distinctive and exclusive characteristic of Welsh preaching."[5] Welsh audiences initially expected Lloyd-Jones to pay homage to this preaching style. I read this biographical anecdote and found myself amused with the thought, *Man . . . Lloyd-Jones was a black preacher preaching like a white man!*

Whinin'. Martyn Lloyd-Jones served in Wales in a different cultural context. We don't have to go that far to find someone objecting that exposition is the wrong style. Henry Mitchell reminds us that white congregations and preachers closer to home also express style preferences akin to some African-Americans. "The White Separatist Baptists in the South devised their own preaching tone; they called it the 'holy whine.' Decades of African American seminary students have been surprised and delighted to learn that what they know as a 'whoop' had—and still has, in a few areas—parallels in some White pulpits."[6]

For many people, "whoopin", hwyl'n, and whinin' are the dominant stylistic requirements for the pulpit. Most do not readily envision exposition fitting the stylistic preference.

Exposition Is Not Relevant to the Needs of Black Communities

Some also contend that preachers committed to exposition fail to raise important questions facing black communities. These questions have to do with politics, justice, poverty, liberation, or personal, emotional, and psychological needs. Critics claim that commitment to sequential exposition dooms the congregation to antiquated information removed from the real stuff of black life.

Exposition Is Too Intellectual

Finally, some critics maintain that expositional preaching may be too intellectual a form of preaching for the Black Church context. In their view, the expositional preacher heavily taxes the listening and reasoning capacity of his hearers. People can't understand exposition. The preaching is too theological, too abstract, too erudite. It belongs to an educated middle class who has long forgotten the everyday exigencies of black life and faith. This objection is quite old. For example, the famous preacher and churchman Richard Allen, founder of the first African-American denomination, says he became a Methodist because he found that others preached with "too high-flown a doctrine."[7] Allen thought their expositions and orations were too far above the head of the people. Many today continue to hold Allen's view of doctrinal and expositional sermons.

A Biblical Example and Warrant for Expositional Preaching

Surely some of these problems really *do* exist and poor exposition *does* fail to serve the spiritual and practical lives of a congregation. One must honestly admit that *bad* exposition suffers many of these diseases. So how do we answer these objections? Where do we find warrant for and examples of expositional preaching to make our case? As we might expect, we turn to the Bible itself.

It would be difficult to name someone who had a greater political and social leadership task than the Old Testament reformer Nehemiah. Nehemiah participated in the rebuilding of the city and temple following Israel's exile and oppression in Babylon and Persia. In Ezra 1, we're told of God's great power, demonstrated in turning King Cyrus's heart to proclaim throughout the realm that God told him to build a temple at Jerusalem and to allow Israel's return to Jerusalem for that purpose. Cyrus commanded citizens of the Persian Empire to provide the Israelites silver, gold, goods, livestock, and freewill offerings to rebuild the temple.

In Nehemiah 1, Nehemiah receives word about the progress in Jerusalem. He learns that the wall in Jerusalem has not been rebuilt. So he petitions Artaxerxes for permission to rebuild the wall. Again, God turns the heart of a pagan king to support the completion of his work. The Lord makes the enemies of His people the servants of His cause. Despite the opposition that arose in the days of Ezra and Nehemiah, Israel finally completes the wall.

When the wall is rebuilt and we come to Nehemiah 8, we read of the people's response:

> All the people came together as one in the square before the Water Gate. They told Ezra the teacher of the Law to bring out the Book of the Law of Moses, which the LORD had commanded for Israel.
>
> So on the first day of the seventh month Ezra the priest brought the Law before the assembly, which was made up of men and women and all who were able to understand. He read it aloud from daybreak till noon as he faced the square before the Water Gate in the presence of the men, women and others who could understand. And all the people listened attentively to the Book of the Law.
>
> Ezra the teacher of the Law stood on a high wooden platform built for the occasion. Beside him on his right stood Mattithiah, Shema, Anaiah, Uriah, Hilkiah and Maaseiah; and on his left were Pedaiah, Mishael, Malkijah, Hashum, Hashbaddanah, Zechariah and Meshullam.
>
> Ezra opened the book. All the people could see him because he was standing above them; and as he opened it, the people all stood up. Ezra praised the LORD, the great God; and all the people lifted their hands and responded, "Amen! Amen!" Then they bowed down and worshiped the LORD with their faces to the ground.
>
> The Levites—Jeshua, Bani, Sherebiah, Jamin, Akkub, Shabbethai, Hodiah, Maaseiah, Kelita, Azariah, Jozabad, Hanan and Pelaiah—instructed the people in the Law while the people were standing there. They read from the Book of the Law of God, making it clear and giving the meaning so that the people understood what was being read. (vv. 1–8 NIV, 2011)

How did Israel respond to the completion of the wall? In a word, the people respond with *preaching*. In *two* words, the people responded with a *preaching conference*. In *three* words, the people responded with an *expositional preaching conference*. "[Ezra] read [the Book of the Law of

Moses] aloud from daybreak till noon as he faced the square before the Water Gate in the presence of the men, women and others who could understand. And all the people listened attentively to the Book of the Law" (v. 3).

Verse 8 records the process of exposition used in the assembly on that day. First, they read God's Word. Second, they made God's Word clear or translated it. Third, they gave the meaning of God's Word. Finally, they aimed primarily to impact the understanding of the people. Here we find a pretty straightforward model of biblical exposition that any preacher can follow.

We cannot underestimate the importance of preaching to first impact the understanding of the congregation. New England Puritan preacher and theologian Jonathan Edwards (1703–1758), who when accused of emotionalism and excess defended the Great Awakenings of the mid-1700s, wrote eloquently about the aim of preaching. Edwards asserted that, "The main benefit that is obtained by preaching is by impression made upon the mind in the time of it, and not by the effect that arises afterwards by a remembrance of what was delivered." Historian George Marsden interpreted Edwards's comments, writing:

> Preaching, in other words, should be designed primarily to awaken, to shake people out of their blind slumbers in the addictive comforts of their sins. Though only God can give them new eyes to see, preaching should be designed to jolt the unconverted or the converted who doze back into their sins (as all do) into recognizing their true estate.[8]

This is not to minimize emotion and passion in preaching. It is, rather, prioritizing the head such that the heart moves with reason. When God's people need to be awakened, God sends preachers. And when preaching successfully awakes the slumbering, it is biblical exposition—reading, explaining, and applying the Word of God—that does the work.

What Are the Results of Expositional Preaching?

Notice the result that attended Ezra's exposition of the Book of the Law. The people in Ezra's day were not unaffected. They were deeply moved. We notice two reactions in the text: weeping and celebration.

Weeping and Celebration

First, we notice in verses 9–12 weeping and celebration among the people.

Then Nehemiah the governor, Ezra the priest and teacher of the Law, and the Levites who were instructing the people said to them all, "This day is holy to the LORD your God. Do not mourn or weep." For all the people had been weeping as they listened to the words of the Law.

Nehemiah said, "Go and enjoy choice food and sweet drinks, and send some to those who have nothing prepared. This day is holy to our Lord. Do not grieve, for the joy of the LORD is your strength."

The Levites calmed all the people, saying, "Be still, for this is a holy day. Do not grieve."

Then all the people went away to eat and drink, to send portions of food and to celebrate with great joy, because they now understood the words that had been made known to them. (NIV)

Those who object to biblical exposition in favor of black preaching's tendency to produce celebration need to consider Nehemiah 8 for an illustration of the power of exposition to excite the passions of God's people. We may produce emotional celebrations through a variety of means. But if the preaching that excites emotional replies is not exposition, then we must ask, "What are the people weeping and celebrating over?"

Verse 12 tells us quite plainly what aroused the affections of God's people on that day. They went away "to celebrate with great joy, *because they now understood the words that had been made known to them.*" The preaching improved their understanding of the Word and their improved understanding of God exposed in His Word provoked great joy. Do we want our people to be happy in God? Then we ought to expose or reveal God to them as He is found in His Word. Set the Lord clearly before the people by explaining both what He is like and how they must respond to His truth. Some have mistakenly criticized emotion as the problem. Emotional response is *not* the problem; emotional response *disconnected from the truth of God's Word* is the problem.

The priests in Ezra's day did an interesting thing. They said, "Don't weep. Celebrate." "Don't weep; celebrate." The Black Church—every church—should do that every Lord's Day, every time we open the Scriptures. Why? Because preachers have the indescribable privilege of proclaiming that God has most clearly revealed Himself in His Son, His Last Word who became flesh, and spoke the last word upon the cross—*It is finished!* As songwriter Horatio Spafford puts it in his classic hymn, "It Is Well with My Soul":

> My sin, oh, the bliss of this glorious thought!
> My sin, not in part but the whole,
> Is nailed to the cross, and I bear it no more,
> Praise the Lord, praise the Lord, O my soul!

We may preach in such a way that people weep over their sins—and they should. But we're not finished until they also cry tears of joy over what God has done about their sin through His Son. He has nailed our sins to the cross, punished His Son in our place, satisfied His holy wrath, raised us together with Christ, freed us from guilt and condemnation so that we may live in the fellowship of His love. The cross says to sinners, "Have your weeping in repentance, but come with joy to Jesus."[9]

Reformation and Joy

The second response produced by God's Word was reformation and joy. We see this in Nehemiah 8:13–18.

> On the second day of the month, the heads of all the families, along with the priests and the Levites, gathered around Ezra the teacher to give attention to the words of the Law. They found written in the Law, which the LORD had commanded through Moses, that the Israelites were to live in temporary shelters during the festival of the seventh month and that they should proclaim this word and spread it throughout their towns and in Jerusalem: "Go out into the hill country and bring back branches from olive and wild olive trees, and from myrtles, palms and shade trees, to make temporary shelters"—as it is written.
>
> So the people went out and brought back branches and built themselves temporary shelters on their own roofs, in their court-yards, in the courts of the house of God and in the square by the Water Gate and the one by the Gate of Ephraim. The whole company that had returned from exile built temporary shelters

and lived in them. From the days of Joshua son of Nun until that day, the Israelites had not celebrated it like this. And their joy was very great.

Day after day, from the first day to the last, Ezra read from the Book of the Law of God. They celebrated the festival for seven days, and on the eighth day, in accordance with the regulation, there was an assembly. (NIV)

The Word of God reformed the life of the people. They read the Word, applied the Word, and lives and customs began to change. The Word is a reforming Word—but only where it is understood and applied. The best way to understand the Word and apply the Word is to expound the Word.

Think of all the reforms we may wish to see among God's people. If we're pastors, we have a front-row seat for viewing the great weaknesses and problems our people face. Consider the major social problems we face. Formulate a list of some of the people in your church facing difficulty, sin, and weakness. There is not a single person who may not be sufficiently and thoroughly helped and delivered by God's Word. The Scripture preached line upon line, precept upon precept, will have its intended effect (Isa. 55:10–11). The people and the pastor will be reformed by it. And that will bring very great joy.

How Does Expositional Preaching Address Cross-Cultural Objections

While we have used Nehemiah 8 as a representative sample of biblical exposition from the Bible itself, we have not yet addressed all the objections that may be raised.

Exposition Is Indeed Culturally Appropriate for Christians

First, the assumption that exposition belongs to white culture is quite incorrect. The people of Nehemiah 8 are Jewish—not "white" as we understand them today. When we dismiss exposition as "white preaching," we tend to have in mind modern notions of "whiteness." But ancient Israel was not a "white" nation by any modern standards of "whiteness." When Ezra expounded the text of Scripture, no one said to him, "You preach like a white man." Nor does anyone assume Ezra ought to preach that way because of the color of his skin and the social assumptions we make about "whiteness."

To the contrary, the Scripture here demonstrates that exposition is not the province of white culture. It's transcultural. Are you from an Asian background? What are you to do with your cultural heritage? Are you from an African-American background? What are you to do with your heritage? Hispanic? Dutch? Rural Appalachian? You may be asking, "What am I to do with my culture?"

If I might answer a question with a question: Are you a *Christian*? Are you a part of the new humanity Jesus creates in His body (Eph. 2:14–15)? Then, what culture has God given you as a part of this new spiritual ethnicity called "Christian"?

Christians are the "spiritual ethnicity" for whom exposition is most appropriate. Exposition flourishes best in the Word-centered culture God gives His people in the church. The variegated cultural assumptions and shibboleths of the world simply cannot reign where God's Word determines the content of our preaching. Cultural assumptions and practices will certainly be present, but they cannot be allowed to rule. We must cast down everything that exalts itself against the knowledge of God. Everything! Including cultural preference.

Exposition Frees Us from the Tyranny of Style Preference

One necessary goal of all communication is clarity. Without clarity we simply fail to communicate. However, with clarity we are able to convey ideas, receive information, process meaning, and enter the thought world of others. We might say clarity is transcultural. Therefore, the clarity that comes from exposition diminishes the seeming importance of style.

Clarity also defeats the objection that exposition is "too intellectual." If we wish to communicate up, down, and across the economic, social, cultural, educational, and intellectual ladder, we must study to be plain and clear in preaching. Such clear content will be the currency we trade in when attempting to communicate across certain boundaries. Lucidity becomes the *lingua franca* of preaching and must become the measure of the sermon, not style.

When we bind ourselves to the text with the purpose of making the Bible clear to our hearers, we find ourselves liberated from artificial style requirements. We find freedom to accept Lloyd-Jones's definition of preaching: *Preaching is logic on fire.*[10] One thing absolutely essential to effective preaching is that the preacher be himself in the pulpit, clothed not in King Saul's armor but in his meager shepherd's clothing and slingshot if necessary. Preaching is mediated by personality, not by cultural norms and dictates.

In freeing us from contrived stylistic impositions, biblical exposition frees us from that false eloquence about which the apostle Paul chided the Corinthian church (1 Cor. 1:17; 2:1). Exposition eliminates sophistry—or at least it should. Exposition eliminates cleverness, cuteness, and puffed-up but ultimately empty words. Power attends preaching when eloquence is eliminated as the goal and revealing God through His Word takes center stage. Real power—not emotional manipulation.

Expositional Preaching Is Relevant because It Expounds the Always-Relevant Word of God

God's Word rightly explained always remains relevant to His people. The Scripture's relevance cannot be bound by class and education. Remember—Ezra preaches to *exiles*—the poor and the oppressed. And yet, He does not preach liberation, politics, social justice or mercy ministries. He preaches the Word clearly and that clear preaching reforms the lives and outlook of the people. The Word does the work.

I pray that Lloyd-Jones's attitude would come to characterize more and more handlers of the Word of God. Murray tells us that "Dr. Lloyd-Jones viewed [the hwyl] as an artificial contrivance to secure effect, just as he did the multitude of illustrations and anecdotes which the preachers had taught the people to expect. In contrast to this, his sermons were closely reasoned, with the main theme carefully analyzed. He was certain that true preaching makes its impact, in the first instance, upon the mind."[11]

Yet Lloyd-Jones was not merely an intellectual preacher. He intended from the onset to engage the "average man" and to preach with unction. In his own words, Lloyd-Jones describes his basic approach:

> I am not and have never been a typical Welsh preacher. I felt that in preaching the first thing that you had to do was to demonstrate to the people that what you were going to do was very relevant and urgently important. The Welsh style of preaching started with a verse and the preacher then told you the

connection and analysed the words, but the man of the world did not know what he was talking about and was not interested. I started with the man whom I wanted to listen, the patient. It was a medical approach really—here is a patient, a person in trouble, an ignorant man who has been to quacks, and so I deal with all that in the introduction. I wanted to get the listener and then come to my exposition. They started with their exposition and ended with a bit of application.[12]

Do you see? Intellect and exposition *do* belong together. The preacher's intellect is for the benefit of his hearers as he makes the Scripture's meaning clear. And as the preacher makes the Word clear, the people's intellectual grasp of the Scriptures should improve. Joy in Christ will be the ultimate result.

While we do not need imitators of Lloyd-Jones, we do need more men who think carefully about their approach in the pulpit. What are we doing there? Who are we speaking for, and who are we speaking to? And for what effect?

Conclusion: Will It Preach in Your Context?

You may have been reading this chapter as a bystander, thinking the chapter is about non-white contexts. Perhaps the chapter's subtitle isn't quite correct. Maybe we should subtitle this chapter "Exposition in Subcultural Contexts."

Many readers of this chapter worship and serve in subcultures that have objections to expositional preaching similar to those outlined here. You may return to an overly politicized evangelical subculture that insists that you preach political sermons week after week.

One pastor friend in a high-profile case faced disgruntled members who, in part, thought he failed to include enough political sermons in the church's preaching diet. They exerted pressure to have him removed from his post.[13] You may be facing a very similar thing. Recognize that subcultural orientation may express itself in opposition to exposition, but the preaching pastor's fundamental calling to stand in the gap and expose this glorious God has not changed. A yearning for political and culturally determined sermons is just another kind of "itching ear" (2 Tim. 4:3). Don't scratch those ears.

Can exposition be applied in non-white contexts? Will it preach? Exposition is the only form of preaching that can cross boundaries of time, place, people, and culture. Will it preach? Beloved, nothing else is preaching.

CHAPTER 4

Recover the Gospel

Jesus returned to Galilee in the power of the Spirit, and news about him spread through the whole countryside. He taught in their synagogues, and everyone praised him.

He went to Nazareth, where he had been brought up, and on the Sabbath day he went into the synagogue, as was his custom. And he stood up to read. The scroll of the prophet Isaiah was handed to him. Unrolling it, he found the place where it is written:

"The Spirit of the Lord is on me,
because he has anointed me
to preach good news to the poor.
He has sent me to proclaim freedom for the prisoners
and recovery of sight for the blind,
to release the oppressed,
to proclaim the year of the Lord's favor."

Then he rolled up the scroll, gave it back to the attendant and sat down. The eyes of everyone in the synagogue were fastened on him, and he began by saying to them, "Today this scripture is fulfilled in your hearing."
—LUKE 4:14–21 (NIV)

Introduction

The village of Mufutuli stood a far distance from the center of the kingdom and the king. No paved roads could wind their way to the village. Surrounded by dust, clay, and bramble, the people of Mufutuli barely remembered there was a king or a kingdom. No dignitaries ever visited the villagers. In fact, no one alive could ever remember hearing any news from the king.

Listless and nearly lifeless, the people languished in poverty. They had little hope and even fewer dreams. Once, a long time ago, someone mentioned "a better place." But everyone laughed that riotous laughter that makes everyone else to know they should never hope again or mention their dreams out loud. Life in Mufutuli ran on as one long, hot, dusty day.

One day a visitor came to Mufutuli. As he entered the village, the people blinked intentionally, as if trying to wipe the dust from their eyes and erase the mirage of a man before them. The visitor claimed he was sent by the king. He announced to the villagers that the king himself would one day visit and see to it that their lives were wonderfully and radically changed. He told the villagers they had not been forgotten. The messenger spoke of the greatness of the king and the life he would create. "But," the messenger said, "this new life isn't what you would expect. For one thing, it's a life that never ends and the best parts come after your current life." Many of the people grew excited. Some scoffed. Others withheld opinion lest their dreams be trampled by thousands of laughing earth-dusted feet.

About that time another messenger entered the village. He, too, announced that he had come from the king. He proclaimed to the villagers that the king would end their poverty. "However, the king might or might not come," he said. "But in the meantime you all should get to work on making sure no one is ever poor and that everyone is free to live as they want." The villagers puzzled over this second message. Many liked it, but some wondered how it could be that both messengers were correct.

Confusion and debate raged when a third messenger entered the village. Like the others, he claimed to have been sent by the king. He told the people that the king would make their lives better *now*—richer than they ever imagined. They wouldn't have to work to end poverty but would immediately receive more than they could imagine if they simply believed in the king. "The king does not want you poor," he assured them. "He thinks of you as his children and will give you all the riches of his kingdom if you believe."

The villagers were now completely befuddled. Some chose this messenger, others that. They argued from time to time but mostly cast disdaining glances as they passed one another to gather with those who agreed with them.

One day a child asked, "But which one really delivered the king's message?"

The Question Facing the Black Church: What Is the Gospel?

Thus far, we have argued that reviving black churches depends upon re-centering the Word of God, the Bible, in the life of the local congregation. No church can live that does not nourish itself on the living life-giving Word of the Lord. And in order to provide that sustenance, we have argued that preachers in the African-American church must reform their preaching such that the main point of any biblical text must be the main point of their sermons. Hopefully we have seen that biblical exposition does the best job of honoring the Word of God, exposing its meaning, and providing the congregation with the Word of life.

However, we might ask one further question about re-centering the Bible and reforming preaching. If the Bible's content occupies the central position in the life of the church and the preacher commits himself to preaching the message of the Bible, what would be the message heard by the congregation? To borrow the question from our fictional introduction, "What message has the King really sent by His messengers?"

Even though we have argued the Bible should be central to all we do, we have not yet said enough about what that means. There exists in the Black Church varying contentions about what precisely the Bible teaches. Of course, the Black Church is not the only quarter of the church world experiencing this debate. But if we're going to revive black churches we must settle this issue in the black church context. At the heart of the matter is one question: What is the gospel?

Rival Claims in the Black Church

Broadly speaking we find three answers to the core question, "What is the gospel?" Each of these answers makes reference or allusion to the biblical text, but each offers a very different worldview and ethical implication for the Black Church. While there are some points of commonality, in the final analysis these views cannot be easily reconciled. The Black Church faces a critical dilemma: What is its core message and what implications does that have for its mission? We turn now to three answers to the question, "What is the gospel?"

The Evangelical Gospel

The oldest answer to the question, "What is the gospel?" adopted by African-Americans is what we might call the "evangelical gospel." This is the gospel message that slaves encountered as they listened to the preaching of many white evangelists, itinerants, and preachers in the 1700s. Henry Mitchell points to evangelist George Whitefield as perhaps the itinerant most influential among enslaved Africans. Mitchell writes:

> It would be hard to overestimate the influence of George Whitefield, for it was he more than any other who gave the once isolated colonies something which bound them together enough to throw off the British yoke. It was Whitefield more than any other who not only revived a dying Protestantism but also built the bridge over which it could travel to a spiritually hungry and brutally oppressed people from Africa.[1]

In addition to the popular appeal and influence of forceful and emotional preachers like Whitefield, many African-American preachers, exhorters, and pastors received their training through apprenticeships with white clergymen. No doubt their training would have included immersion into the evangelical assumptions of the broader white church. Even those early African-Americans who were largely self-taught likely would have come into contact with white evangelical preachers and resources. This does not mean African-Americans adopted wholesale whatever was being taught by white preachers. But the historical record clearly establishes that from the earliest generations until the present an evangelical gospel tradition has existed in the Black Church.

What is "the gospel" according to black evangelicals? We can summarize the view in four points. First, black evangelicals believe the gospel begins with the truth about God. Evangelicals hold that God created the universe and that as Creator He owns the universe. God is holy, righteous, and good. He rules the universe with justice for His own glory and the highest happiness of His creatures.

Second, black evangelicals believe the gospel tells us the truth about the nature and future of humanity. God made humankind in his own image and likeness for an unending fellowship with Himself (Gen. 1:26–27). All men were created equal with common capacities. As God's vice-regents on the earth, mankind was to "subdue the earth" and fill it with God's glory. However, our first parents, Adam and Eve, rebelled against God by breaking His command not to eat of the tree of the knowledge of good and evil. When they disobeyed God, sin entered the world and corrupted the originally good creation, including every person ever born. Now, instead of enjoying fellowship with a loving God who provides all our needs, God cuts mankind off from Himself because of our sin and pronounces the curse or judgment of death against sinful humanity (Gen. 3). But the worst part is that because of our sin, every person faces the coming eternal wrath of a holy, righteous, and all-powerful God against sin. If we find no escape from His wrath, God will rightly and perfectly condemn every sinner to judgment in hell (Rom. 1:18–32; Rev. 20:11–15).

Third, the evangelical believes that God has made a way of escape from His wrath. Man is unable to save himself, and because of his sin unwilling to pursue God's righteousness (John 1:13; 6:44). Humankind is "dead in trespasses and sin" and "children of wrath" (Eph. 2:1–5). But God has done what no man could do for himself. In His love God sent His Son, Jesus, into the world, born of a virgin, fully God and fully man, sinless and perfect, to be righteousness for us (1 Cor. 1:30) and to become a curse for us so that sinners through faith in Jesus could become the righteousness of God (Gal. 3:13–14). The crucifixion of Jesus accomplishes the reconciliation of sinners with a holy God. The crucifixion satisfies the wrath of God against all those who have faith in Christ and proves God's love for sinners (Rom. 5:8) just as the resurrection proves God's acceptance and justification of Christ and those who trust in Jesus (Rom. 4:25).

Fourth, African-American evangelicals believe that this "good news" about the righteous life, atoning death, and justifying resurrection of Jesus demands a response from those who hear it. When this news was first preached by the New Testament apostles and disciples, they called on their hearers to do two things: repent and believe (Acts 2:38; 8:12). The Lord Jesus called His disciples to make the same response of repentance and faith when He announced the in-breaking of the Kingdom (Mark 1:15). By "repent," the Lord and His apostles simply meant to turn away from sin, to change their minds about pursuing sin and instead turn to follow Jesus as Master and God. By "believe," they intended their hearers to put their complete trust and reliance in Jesus alone to provide the righteousness and salvation that He promised. According to evangelicals, all that Jesus is and did is credited to the sinner when by God's Spirit they are given the gifts of repentance and faith in Jesus. Those who turn from sin and follow Jesus, trusting His promise of righteousness and eternal life, are forever joined to Jesus and His life now becomes theirs (Gal. 2:20).

This view of "the gospel" centers on the reconciliation of fallen humanity with a perfectly holy God angry about our rebellion in sin. This view of the gospel emphasizes the atoning work of Jesus Christ on the cross and the vindication of Jesus as the Son of God through the resurrection (Rom. 1:4; 4:25). The "good news" according to this view is that everyone who repents of sins and trusts in Jesus will be saved from God's coming wrath and enjoy the love of God for eternity in God's coming kingdom. African-American Christians have believed this message from the earliest days of their contact with gospel preachers in the colonies. Other views of the gospel must in some way use the language of this oldest view and respond to it.

The Liberation Gospel

A second view of "the gospel" in some black churches is what we might call the "gospel of liberation." Though widely attributed to the pioneering writings of Dr. James H. Cone, professor of systematic theology at Union Theological Seminary in New York, Cone and many proponents of the liberation gospel see plentiful evidence of liberation themes in the writings and speeches of black Christians since the 1800s.

In the late 1960s, with the publication of his book *Black Theology and Black Power,* Cone spawned and began to codify liberation theology in the black context. Though Black Theology exerts its influence primarily in academic settings, advocates actively seek to see its influence spread more widely in the Black Church.

Many people had never heard of Black Theology or a gospel of liberation until prime-time news programs flashed across television screens fiery images of Rev. Jeremiah A. Wright Jr. calling God to "damn America" for various historical and contemporary acts of oppression. Wright, former pastor of Chicago's Trinity United Church of Christ and then pastor to presidential hopeful Barack Obama, made Black Theology and the gospel of liberation a hot topic across the country.

But what is "the gospel" according to Black Theology?

Perhaps the easiest approach to defining a liberation gospel would be to allow Cone's early work to speak for itself. Writing in the aftermath of 1960s race riots in major U.S. cities, Cone sought to provide theological ballast to the protests and turmoil of the day. He especially sought to answer the question, "What does the Christian gospel have to say to powerless black men whose existence is threatened daily by the insidious tentacles of white power? Is there a message from Christ to the countless number of blacks whose lives are smothered under white society?"[2]

Cone's answer, like the evangelical view of the gospel that preceded it, centered on the person of Jesus Christ. However, Cone adopted a decidedly different definition of Jesus and His work. He wrote, "[Jesus] is God himself coming into the very depths of human existence *for the sole purpose* of striking off the chains of slavery, thereby freeing man from ungodly principalities and powers that hinder his relationship with God."[3] One of the foundational texts for Cone and adherents of Black Theology is Luke 4:18–19, cited at the opening of this chapter. They hear in Jesus' appropriation of Isaiah's prophecy a message about human liberation— "preach the good news to the poor," "proclaim release to the captives and recovering of sight to the blind," "set at liberty those who are oppressed." Cone comments on this passage and Jesus' announcement of the kingdom of God in Mark 1:14–15 this way:

> On the face of it, this message appears not to be too radical to our twentieth-century ears, but this impression stems from our failure existentially to bridge the gap between modern man and

biblical man. Indeed, the message of the Kingdom strikes at the very center of man's desire to define his own existence in the light of his own interest at the price of his brother's enslavement. It means the irruption of a new age, an age which has to do with God's action in history on behalf of man's salvation. It is an age of liberation, in which "the blind receive their sight, the lame walk, the lepers are cleansed, the deaf hear, the dead are raised up, the poor have good news preached to them" (Luke 7:22). This is not pious talk, and one does not need a seminary degree to interpret the message. It is a message about the ghetto, and all other injustices done in the name of democracy and religion to further the social, political, and economic interests of the oppressor. In Christ, God enters human affairs and takes sides with the oppressed. Their suffering becomes his; their despair, divine despair. Through Christ the poor man is offered freedom now to rebel against that which makes him other than human.[4]

God's righteousness was not so much the perfect obedience of Jesus credited to those who believe in Him but "the divine decision to vindicate the poor, the needy, and the helpless in society."[5] According to Cone, unless Jesus is in the world working for the liberation of the oppressed, "then the gospel is a lie." But Cone asserted confidently that "Christianity is not alien to Black Power; it is Black Power."[6] The resurrection, then, becomes a political event wherein the poor are "granted freedom while they are still poor," find out that "their poverty is a contrived phenomenon, traceable to the rich and the powerful in this world," and are required to "practice political activity against the social and economic structures that make them poor."[7]

Cone recognized that the kingdom of God had already broken into the world but that its full consummation was not yet accomplished. But rather than conceive of the Kingdom's in-breaking primarily in terms of spiritual liberation from sin and sin's bondage as earlier evangelicals had, Cone thought of the kingdom of God in terms of black people's social, political, and economic liberation from oppression. "The kingdom is not an attainment of material security, nor is it mystical communion with the divine. It has to do with the *quality* of one's existence in which a person realizes that *persons* are more important than property."[8] According to

Cone, "The Good News is that God in Christ has freed us; we need no longer be enslaved by alien forces."[9] He argues:

> To participate in God's salvation is to cooperate with the black Christ as he liberates his people from bondage. Salvation, then, primarily has to do with earthly reality and the injustice inflicted on those who are helpless and poor. To see the salvation of God is to see this people rise up against its oppressors, demanding that justice become a reality now, not tomorrow. It is the oppressed serving warning that they "ain't gonna take no more of this [expletive], but a new day is coming and it ain't going to be like today." The new day is the presence of the black Christ as expressed in the liberation of the black community.[10]

In the final analysis, "the gospel" in Black Theology focuses on the right-now liberation of black people from all forms of oppression.

A second generation of Black Theologians have extended Cone's premise beyond the Black Power concerns of the 1960s to address a range of other concerns, including the liberation of women, freedom struggles in the so-called Third World, and the inclusion of homosexuals in black church life.[11] They contend that women and homosexuals suffer marginalization and oppression at the hands of black male patriarchy. If the gospel means liberation right now, then these writers tell us it must mean liberation from all oppression—political, racial, gender, and sexual. In Black Theology, "the gospel" functions as a call to social justice and group solidarity against oppression. Like the second messenger in our opening parable, preachers of Black Theology and a gospel of liberation have come to the village proclaiming that the King wishes the people to fight to end poverty and remove every form of oppression. That, they tell the people, is "the gospel."

The Prosperity Gospel

The "prosperity gospel" represents a third view of the gospel found in some black churches. Like the liberation gospel, prosperity gospel adherents use the language and themes of the older evangelical gospel but call for the definition of the gospel to be expanded to include physical, emotional, material, social, and financial prosperity in this life. Champions of the prosperity gospel exercise considerable influence in local churches through their dominance on television and through their networks and conferences across the country.

Stephanie Y. Mitchem has identified three streams of prosperity preaching in the Black Church.[12] "The old school prosperity preaching," as Mitchem labels it, included New Thought cult leaders like Daddy Grace and Father Divine, Black Nationalist leaders like Marcus Garvey, and James Forman. Many of these leaders taught a version of the prosperity message that sometimes kept an eye on the well-being of the black community and opposed racism. The second stream according to Mitchem is the "Hagin/Copeland school" of prosperity preaching. Mitchem names this stream after the men many regard as the popularizing teachers of the movement they inherited from E. W. Kenyon: Kenneth Hagin and Kenneth Copeland. Since Hagin and Copeland are white, Mitchem contends that this stream of prosperity teaching is not indigenous to African-American communities. Third, Mitchem points to a stream of prosperity preaching associated with the New Age and metaphysical teaching of leaders like Johnnie Colemon and Barbara King, and science of the mind cult leader Reverend Ike.

Of these three streams of prosperity preaching, the Hagin/Copeland school easily stands out as the most widespread in black churches. Well-known African-American leaders like Creflo A. Dollar Jr., T. D. Jakes, Leroy Thompson, Eddie Long, and Fred K. C. Price represent this variety of prosperity preaching. Through their television shows, conferences, books, and online resources, prosperity gospel preachers have become arguably the most significant movement impacting the Black Church since the Civil Rights movement.

But what is "the gospel" according to these prosperity preachers?

I recognize that not every preacher of the prosperity gospel would be in complete agreement with all other preachers—that's true in almost any school of thought. But there are some themes representative of most people who teach and preach a prosperity message. In many ways the teaching of Creflo A. Dollar Jr. is representative. Dollar's brand of prosperity preaching combines traditional evangelical ideas with the distinct emphases of prosperity theology.

Dollar, like many prosperity advocates, teaches some things consistent with evangelical views of the gospel. For example, in his book *Not Guilty: Experience God's Gift of Acceptance and Freedom,* Dollar writes:

"Our righteousness in Christ is the centerpiece on which Christian faith is built. Everything God's Word promises us hangs on it, and the entire structure of our salvation is built upon it. If we are going to walk in the joy of our salvation and the power of the promises we have in Him, we must understand our righteousness in Christ."[13] Most evangelicals would state something similar about the centrality of the righteousness of Christ to the Christian faith.

However, Dollar also distances himself from evangelical witnesses. He writes, "When Christians hear the word *righteous*, nearly all of us think we understand what it means. The biggest part of the problem is that very few understand. We only *think* we do. Often, our religious traditions have distorted our understanding of righteousness. Consequently, the authority that God intended for us to have has been rendered totally ineffective."[14] Dollar continues, "The watered-down traditions that have resulted have seduced many into powerless, ineffective forms of religious thinking instead of the vital, dynamic faith that really can move mountains."[15]

The departure comes not so much in the facts of the gospel or with redefinition of the Person and work of Christ. Prosperity gospels depart from both evangelical and liberation gospels by including *in* the work of Christ *more* than either of those rival views include. For Dollar, Christ's righteousness includes both an ability to stand forgiven before God through faith plus a right to all forms of prosperity. He writes:

> Righteousness is the ability to stand before God without the sense of guilt or inferiority. It is the ability to stand before God and talk to Him as a child to a Father, expecting His response, and knowing that we have a right to receive what we ask because of what He has declared over us.[16]

He lists the rights this righteousness supposedly conveys:

> I am righteous; therefore, I can be healed. I am righteous; therefore, I have angelic protection. I am righteous; therefore, I will always triumph in Christ Jesus.
>
> Every promise in the Bible hinges on my acceptance of the righteousness of God. By simply realizing His righteousness in me, the wrong in my life can be fixed. If I am poor, I have a right to prosperity. If I am sick, I have a right to be healed. If I

am in bondage, I have a right to be delivered. Everything can be received through God's righteousness.[17]

Dollar writes: "Our prosperity is a reflection of God's righteousness in our lives. We should speak of our well-being and wholeness in all areas of our lives daily. Total life prosperity belongs to those who receive the righteousness of God and everything else that the blood of Jesus provides. The fact that someone has wealth is not proof that he is walking in God's righteousness."[18] Later he promises, "If you walk in your righteousness, you will never be broke another day in your life. You will never be without the power of God or His blessing."[19]

In the final analysis, according to prosperity teachers, "the gospel" functions much like a mantra to change reality or a doorway into affluence. The "good news" includes not only individual spiritual salvation but also individual temporal prosperity. Like the third messenger in our opening parable, the prosperity preacher comes to a people needing a word from the King and announces, "You're the King's kids and He wants you rich. Just believe and you will receive."

Not Every Gospel Is Good News

In the evangelical view, righteousness before God includes a right legal standing before the bar of His judgment. The righteous are those declared "not guilty" before God by God's grace through faith in the perfect life, sin-atoning death, and glorious resurrection of Jesus Christ. In the liberationist view typified by James Cone, righteousness before God dealt primarily with God's vindication of the poor and oppressed and their fight for liberation as a class of people. In prosperity teaching like that of Creflo A. Dollar Jr., righteousness before God gives rise to individual prosperity and blessing in this life.

This all raises a question: Who is bringing the true "good news" from the King of heaven?

The Liberationists and Evangelicals Critique the Prosperity Preachers

Writers promoting each of the views have at times offered critique of the others. For example, in an essay honoring Dr. Samuel DeWitt Proctor, Jeremiah Wright Jr. took an opportunity to criticize prosperity teaching as a betrayal of the cultural legacy of African-Americans and the Black Church. Wright wrote:

> Dr. Proctor taught that the gospel we preach could not be cut off from the culture that produced it or the culture that produced us. That part of the Proctor legacy becomes extremely important in an age of "prosperity preachers," who operate as if we live in a cultural vacuum. The garbage being proclaimed as the gospel by the prosperity-pimps preaches capitalism as being synonymous with Christianity. It also preaches the philosophy of Adam Smith as if Smith's philosophy were the theology of an almighty Savior!
>
> Capitalism as made manifest in the "New World" depended upon slave labor (by African slaves), and it is only maintained by keeping the "Two-Thirds World" under oppression. That heresy has nothing to do with the message of the man from Galilee, a Capernaum carpenter who had no place to lay his head, and that heresy is completely oblivious of the culture that produced the gospel and the culture of the Africans living in the American diaspora.[20]

Wright points in the general direction of the primary deficiency in prosperity theology and the prosperity gospel—it's slippery hermeneutical principles, which allow interpreting the Scripture in ways clearly contrary to the plain meaning of the text.

Pentecostal and evangelical theologian Gordon D. Fee argues that the most problematic weakness of prosperity theology and the prosperity gospel "is the purely subjective and arbitrary way they interpret the text."[21] In terms reminiscent of Jeremiah Wright, Fee delivers a strong condemnation of prosperity gospels:

> [S]uch an Americanized perversion of the gospel tends to reinforce a way of life and an economic system that repeatedly oppresses the poor—the very thing that the prophetic message denounces so forcefully. Seeking more prosperity in an already affluent society means to support all the political and economic programs that have made such prosperity available—but almost always at the expense of economically deprived individuals and nations.[22]

Mitchem posits that the prosperity gospel finds traction among African-Americans because of historic African-American longing for full economic and social justice and inclusion in the American experiment.[23]

In calling the prosperity gospel a "heresy" and a perversion of the gospel, these writers—both evangelical and liberationist—use the strongest terms possible to indicate the bankruptcy of prosperity teaching. They tell us that the "prosperity gospel" cannot save and therefore is not good news.

Evangelicals Critique the Liberation Gospel

But the same has also been said about the liberation gospel. With its focus on social, economic, and political enfranchisement now—an often defensible goal—the liberation gospel fails to answer man's most basic and serious need—escaping the wrath of God and reconciliation with God. At best, proponents of a gospel of liberation turn biblical themes like wrath, hell, and righteousness into political ideals and symbols in the quest for justice. At worst, some proponents of Black Theology simply deny the relevance and reality of these biblical concepts.

In his review of Black Theology, Bruce L. Fields points out that a "foundational Christian identity is the only thing that will insure the future of Black Theology as a contributor to the African-American church and ultimately to the African-American community."[24] Fields acknowledges that there are many passages in the Bible that "demonstrate God's demand for justice on behalf of the powerless." But he warns, "[O]ther characteristics of the God of the exodus must be considered, otherwise the emerging picture of God is one of a mere force for change and relationship with this force degenerates into a social program. Such a view borders on idolatry."[25]

Fields offers a trenchant critique of Cone's view of the cross. He finds much to commend in Cone's two-fold emphasis on the cross as the divine defeat of sin and satanic power and an act of solidarity with humanity. However, Fields notes a crippling flaw in the liberation gospel of Cone.

Cone's definition of the cross robs the cross of both its endurance of suffering force and its substitutionary nature. As I intimated above, I do not wish to suggest that there is not a multiplicity of meanings properly proposed for the single event of Christ's death on the cross. I am arguing that some understandings lie outside of biblical parameters, and are therefore non-Christian. Not all interpretations of the atonement offered in the name of constructing a relevant understanding of the event and driven by a unique set of experiences may be called Christian.[26]

In other words, simply pointing to Jesus and pontificating about His cross does not make a theology Christian. The meanings must be substantiated and warranted by the Scripture itself. Anything outside the biblical text, rightly interpreted and summarized, fails to qualify as the true message sent by the King.

Anthony Carter summed up nicely the evangelical critique of both prosperity and liberationist gospels. He writes:

> What was once the treasure chest of the church—namely, the person of Christ and the message of the gospel—has been exchanged for social expedience and financial gain. What has been lost, indeed forfeited, is an uncompromised, orthodox, biblical view of Jesus and the message of the gospel that saves sinners from the death that is due to all of us because of our sin. What has been lost is the unique message and calling of the church.[27]

If Carter is correct, then the losses have been too great and the gains too minimal to justify continuing in the direction of either liberationist or prosperity teaching. We need a recovery of that true gospel that gives light and life to every person who believes it.

Liberationist and Prosperity Critiques of the Evangelical Gospel

Strikingly, liberationist and prosperity preachers offer the same general critique of the evangelical gospel. Both liberationists and prosperity teachers charge the evangelical gospel with being irrelevant to the needs of people.

James Cone contends that "abstract theological disputation and speculation . . . serves as a substitute for relevant involvement in a world where men die for lack of political justice." Cone filed that charge against the many whites he saw hiding behind intellectual analysis. However, one can readily imagine this critique extended to black evangelicals as well. Cone continued this theme of (ir)relevance by asking, "Unless there is a word from Christ to the helpless, then why should they respond to him?

How do we relate the gospel of Christ to people whose daily existence is one of hunger or even worse, despair? Or do we simply refer them to the next world?"[28]

Much to Cone's chagrin, I'm sure, Dollar sounds a similar albeit more individualistic note. Having already intimated his critique of historic evangelical confession by calling it "watered-down traditions that have seduced many into a powerless, ineffective form of religious thinking instead of the vital, dynamic faith that really can move mountains,"[29] Dollar goes on to ask questions about the relevance of traditional evangelical positions. Dollar writes, "People often say that because there are people around the world who need to hear about Jesus, there is no need to teach about prosperity as often as I do. But why would anyone want to hear about a Jesus who is broke and unable to lead them to a successful life? What would a person hope to attain in this life if nothing changes once they receive Jesus into their hearts? What is the point?"[30]

For vastly different reasons—one for political and economic liberation for the oppressed and the other for social, emotional, and financial prosperity for individuals—both Cone and Dollar look to evangelicals and ask, "What is the point? Why bother? If these earthly goals are not met then how can your Jesus and His cross be relevant?"

Will the Real Gospel Please Stand Up?

The greatest virtue of Black Theology and the prosperity movement is their tendency to ask two excellent questions. Black Theology forces us to consider whether Jesus Christ offers any way of overcoming black oppression. The prosperity movement prompts us to ask whether God wants good for black people. Any thinking, feeling, African-American must surely recognize our interest in those questions. In some respects, these questions represent the pressing theological concerns for the entirety of African-American history. Though these schools of thought raise important questions, they fail to answer the questions biblically. They, in fact, mishandle the Bible or set it aside for answers that end up contradicting the basic truths of the faith.

One wonders why Cone, Dollar, and those who hold their positions have not heard the Lord Jesus Himself answer such questions. "What good will it be for a man if he gains the whole world, yet forfeits his soul? Or what can a man give in exchange for his soul?" (Matt. 16:26 NIV). We can hardly miss the fact that Jesus values the soul of a man well beyond all the riches and benefits this world has to offer. Nothing of any value approaches the worth of the eternal human soul. This means the salvation of souls far outranks liberation and prosperity in this life. Jesus says as much when He teaches the counterintuitive and eternal-life-changing truth, "For whoever wants to save his life will lose it, but whoever loses his life for me will find it" (Matt. 16:25 NIV). Losing our lives through Christian discipleship means finding eternal life with Christ. Jealously clutching or saving our life in this world leads to death; prosperity and liberation "gospels" offer a short-term solution to a long-term problem.

The highest reward comes to the faithful when the Savior returns in glory, not during this earthbound life. This is why Jesus grounded His teaching with the statement, "For the Son of Man is going to come in his Father's glory with his angels, and then he will reward each person according to what he has done" (Matt. 16:27 NIV). The gospel gives us eyes that look with hope beyond this life to a far greater reward and joy. Many mock this as "pie-in-the-sky" and irrelevant. But how would you answer Jesus' question? What does it profit *you* to gain the whole world and lose your soul?

Only the evangelical gospel—that old, old story that holds out the hope of eternal life to dying sinners—results in the salvation of souls. That evangelical message is the true message sent by the King of heaven to that far-off country where sinners languish lifeless and hopeless. To lose the gospel is to lose all hope, truth, and mission. As Anthony Carter points out, "There are infinite ways to lose your soul. There is only one way to save it."[31]

The recovery of the gospel of Jesus Christ is the most urgent need of the hour. Without the evangel all is lost. In fact, everything we have discussed to this point—the re-centering of the Bible and reforming black preaching—have this one indispensable aim: to get the true biblical, evangelical gospel correct. All other "gospels" are counterfeits. The recovery of the gospel gives the church life.

Conclusion: Does Getting the Gospel Correct Really Matter?

Getting the gospel correct matters immensely. When we distort the gospel, we distort our lives and our view of the world. The story of Sean

DeMars illustrates this well. In his twenties, DeMars was an avid follower of a major prosperity preacher. He recounts the heart of his story in an e-mail to me:

> The prosperity gospel nearly killed me. Literally. I was so sick I was on the verge of death. I was lying in a hot bath with a temperature of 96 degrees, way beyond dehydrated, and literally dying with mercury poisoning. My mother was crying over my naked body, begging me to go to the hospital for treatment. "NO!" I insisted. How could I put faith in a doctor? "God is my ultimate healer! In him alone will I place my faith!"
>
> I did eventually receive treatment, but I was still being ravished by this heresy. When I married my beautiful wife, Amber, I taught her (with the Bible of course), that there would be no taking of medicine in MY HOUSE! We would be faithful. When we were dead broke I refused to get a job because "God had promised me (through Canton Jones, no less) that I would be a business CEO, Fortune 500, of course. How could I not have faith in that word of prophesy?
>
> And there were a hundred other things that nearly destroyed my life and marriage.[32]

DeMars would not blame all his decisions on the particular preachers he followed. But we must not miss the point: Believing a false gospel of prosperity resulted in tremendous real-life consequences for him and his family. He nearly lost his life because he believed untrue things about God and our relationship to Him. DeMars was one of millions of individuals negatively affected.

But distortions of the gospel also produce negative effects on the church's understanding of her mission in the world. The liberationist gospel, at best, confuses the gospel message itself with certain entailments or implications of the gospel. Every Christian should recognize the Bible's radical call for Christians to love one another (John 13:34–35), to love their neighbors as themselves (Luke 10:27; Rom. 13:9), and to even love their enemies (Matt. 5:43–45). Love becomes the very sign of discipleship (John 13:35), and without love we are nothing (1 Cor. 13:1–3). But those ethical commands cannot, without destroying the faith, take the place of the good news of Jesus' life, death, and resurrection to rescue sinners.

The church finds herself pursuing many noble and necessary pursuits while leaving aside the one thing that only the church can do—proclaim the gospel of our salvation to a perishing world. Other agencies will assist the poor or battle injustice, but no other agency will preach the gospel. Though the church must do her part to alleviate poverty and oppression, such efforts should never become the main function of the church. If they do, the church will indeed die a terrible death.

If we want our churches to live, we must make every effort to ensure we protect and proclaim the gospel of Jesus Christ. The gospel is our life.

CHAPTER 5

Rejoice in the Truth
(Worship)

Our churches are where we dip our tired bodies in cool springs of hope, where we retain our wholeness and humanity despite the blows of death.[1]
—RICHARD WRIGHT

Introduction

Worship wars devastate churches. Conflicts over instruments, contemporary or traditional hymns, and even the use of screen projectors claim more casualties in Christian churches than nearly anything else. Former friends divide over preferences. Congregations split into separate services or divide altogether. Denominations battle over hymnals. Proponents of various views write book after book recommending and defending their perspective. Opponents offer counter-perspectives. And on it goes. The wreckage piles high with everyone assured they're offering the truest praise to God.

In many respects the African-American church has avoided the worst of these "wars." We've seen our share of tension and conflict, but by and large the African-American church seems united in its basic philosophy of music and singing: make it good! If the Black Church does one thing well, it's sing!

In a book on reviving the African-American church, one might not expect to see a section on congregational praise and music. Joel Gregory cites dynamic worship as one indication of the church's vitality.[2] What could be wrong with the Black Church's singing that it needs attention or adjustment?

The answer may surprise you. It's not musicianship. By and large the church *produces* musicians. It's not singers. Nearly every *bona fide* black superstar singer boasts a beginning in a church. It's not style. The church exudes rhythm, expression, and even "cool." So what's the problem?

Pastor Anthony J. Carter of East Point Church in Atlanta, Georgia, describes the problem well.

> Unfortunately, in the majority of churches in America, particularly predominantly African-American churches, the Bible is nothing more than a prop or an institutional icon. It is present, but we rarely read it, we sporadically preach it, we hardly pray it, *we sparingly sing it,* and we reluctantly see it. Recovering biblical worship in our churches will begin with the recovery of the Bible as the guide for worship.[3]

If God's Word is to be central to the life of the church as we've been arguing, then it must be central to the singing of the church. Most every Christian church devotes a significant portion of its gathering to praising God in song. But few, it seems, have given sufficient attention to thinking through the place of the Bible in determining, shaping, and informing what we sing. Fewer still place emphasis on *understanding* what we're singing. As a consequence, if we're going to see the Black Church revived and thriving, we will need to have our congregations rejoice in the truth of God's Word through song.

The Substance of Singing: The Word of Christ

The writers of the New Testament give very little attention to singing in Christian gatherings. The paucity of instruction could lead us to think singing is insignificant were it not for the Psalter in the Old Testament and the occasional historical references to singing in the New Testament (Matt. 26:30; Acts 16:25; Rev. 5:9, 12–13). Apart from these few historical references, only two passages totaling three verses *instruct* us in Christian singing. Only three verses in the entire New Testament! But those passages hold tremendous value for informing our singing and reviving our churches.

The first appears in a letter written by the apostle Paul to the church in Colossae. Nestled near the end of the letter, Paul writes, "Let the word of Christ dwell in you richly as you teach and admonish one another with all wisdom, and as you sing psalms, hymns and spiritual songs with gratitude in your hearts to God" (Col. 3:16 NIV).

The basic command of the verse is, "Let the word of Christ dwell in you richly." "The word of Christ" refers to the gospel message. Paul uses the phrase again in Romans 10:17, where we read, "Faith comes from hearing the message, and the message is heard through the word of Christ" (NIV). Paul's burden for the Colossians is that the gospel, which gives and nourishes faith, should *dwell* richly in them. We must be roommates with the gospel of our Lord so that our faith may be nourished and strong. That message must reside or live *richly* in our hearts or souls. This is no light grasp of the truth, but strong, tight, deep embrace. The gospel message, or "word of Christ," is not something we hear once, believe, and then never consider again. It's meant to live in us.

Paul goes on to state that the richly dwelling word of Christ enters the heart in two ways. First, the word dwells in the church "as you teach and admonish with all wisdom." That's the primary way the word of Christ enters and lives in the human heart. It happens as the teachers of the church explain the Word of God and as church members "admonish" or correct each other with wisdom. Paul makes this his apostolic ambition in Colossians 1:28: "We proclaim him, admonishing and teaching everyone with all wisdom, so that we may present everyone perfect in Christ" (NIV).

Second, the word of Christ dwells in the church "as you sing psalms, hymns and spiritual songs." We cohabit with the gospel when we sing the gospel. The word of Christ must be the substance of our hymns, psalms, and spiritual songs. When we say the word of Christ must be the substance, we mean it must be the content, intent, and extent of our singing. The lyrics we lift up to God must be an exploration and exposition of what God has done for us in His Son Jesus Christ. Melva Wilson Costen, former professor of worship and music at the Interdenominational Theological Center in Atlanta, gets to the crux of the matter when she writes, "The New Testament understanding of liturgy, which has suffered loss in translation, is that Christ's life, death, and resurrection are, in fact, the epitome of liturgy."[4] We're not truly worshipping if we're not touching upon the redemption we have through the Person and work of Jesus Christ as it is revealed in God's living Word. What Anthony Carter writes about preaching is no less true of singing: "The predominantly black church has not lacked men with style; what has been lacking, however, is substance. We have not been in need of better technique, but we have been in need of content—theological, biblical content."[5]

I wonder how often we think of singing as a method for creating a rich dwelling for the gospel in the congregation's heart? I suspect we think of this far less often than we ought. This is why thinking of Christian singing primarily in terms of emotion or entertainment eventually denigrates and degenerates Christian worship. God does not intend emotional experiences and entertainment to sustain the soul. That's the place of His Word, and that's why His Word must hold center stage in our singing.

When the Word Gives Way in Song

One of the most significant worship decisions pastors and worship leaders make is the decision to place the Word of God at the center of the lyrical content the people sing Sunday to Sunday. Conversely, the most pernicious danger is having that Word-centered content displaced by other things, however good.

In many churches the danger arises from the pressure to entertain congregations in order to attract and keep larger crowds of attendees. Sometimes the pressure may be hardly noticeable, partly because African-American culture places a lot of value on music, songs, art, and style. So, the danger lurks in a cultural blind spot. One writer, expressing appreciation for spirited singing, illustrates the blind spot well:

> It is possible to have church without outstanding preaching, *but not without good singing*. It can fill the vacuum of a poor sermon. *Good singing is impassioned, intense, emotional, and spiritually powerful*. This is due to the conviction about what sermon the soloists and choir are delivering in song.[6]

The writer clearly appreciates singing. Undoubtedly she captures what a lot of church attenders feel—good singing makes the service. Further, "good singing" features powerful cathartic qualities. The author rightly identifies the fact that the soloist and choir deliver a kind of sermon in the singing. They are communicating something. But the well-intentioned author terribly overemphasizes the place of singing as well as the importance of feeling in singing. It's good to feel and to feel deeply. But does she not give the *central* place to feeling rather than God's Word? She believes that the sermon—the *main* way in which God's Word is transferred to God's people—can be poor but not the singing. "Good singing" ought to be defined by good theology, "the word of Christ," and powerful feeling ought to arise from that good word.

After reflecting on the importance of freedom in black Christian worship, Melva Wilson Costen identifies the chief dangers of taking such an emphasis on freedom too far. She writes:

> [C]ongregations might find themselves "enjoying the Lord" so much that they assume that this is to happen only when one gathers to worship informally. Another danger is that congregations might assume that all services of worship must be jubilant in order for authentic worship to take place. There is always the possibility that Christ has entered the space with a whip to drive out the thieves and money changers—those who have allowed ritual actions to become empty.[7]

Wilson contends that it is entirely possible to mistake a good time in the gathering with genuine worship. We may come to equate such good times with the never-ending joyful feelings of public praise, and in doing so may actually mistake Jesus' message to us. If Jesus calls us into times of celebration, we will know it through His Word. If the Lord enters to drive out falsehood with a whip, as Costen suggests, we will know that too by the Word preached and sung. The text drives the content of our praise. That's why the word of Christ—the gospel—must determine what we sing.

The Spirit of Singing: Thanksgiving

Threaded throughout Paul's call to singing the Word is a corresponding call to thanksgiving. In Colossians 3:15–17 the apostle steps back to survey the sweeping work Jesus has completed in the lives of believers and the heart response believers should express to the Lord. For the peace we have in Christ, we find the simple command, "And *be thankful*" in

Colossians 3:15. Then the apostle explains that such thankfulness should characterize our praise also. Sing . . . "*with gratitude* in your hearts to God" (3:16 NIV, emphasis added). Finally, we receive notice that all our practices in the Christian life ought to be performed with Godward thanksgiving—"whatever you do, in word or deed, do everything . . . *giving thanks* to God the Father through [the Lord Jesus] (Col. 3:17 ESV, emphasis added).

In these three short verses the apostle gives us a tour of what Christ achieves for us (peace), what Jesus inspires in us (praise), and what God in Christ accomplishes through us (practices in word and deed). For all that the Lord Jesus is and does, the appropriate response is thanksgiving. Peace, praise, and practice bloom in the hothouse of gratitude. Peace without thanksgiving crumbles into a numb *détente*. Praise without gratitude amounts to mere formalism. Christian practice and lifestyle minus thanksgiving hollow into empty hypocrisy. Without gratitude we falsify all that Christ Jesus has done.

The New Testament describes the gathered singing of the congregation as "giving thanks always and for everything to God the Father in the name of our Lord Jesus Christ" (Eph. 5:20). "Always" and "for everything" defines the times and scope of our praise to God. Our celebrations of God's goodness ought to pervade our lives. No time exists when the gathered people of God should fail to express gratitude to God. No situation—however small or great, whether good or bad—exists when thanksgiving is inappropriate for the faithful. In our suffering and our success, we owe God our heartfelt and genuine thanks for who He is to us and for what He has done, is doing, and will do for us.

Such thanksgiving is Christ-centered, not man-centered. It looks to Christ's rule in our hearts, to His Word dwelling in us, and to His service in the world. Such praise defies our circumstances by daring to see God's goodness at all times. Singing with the spirit of thanksgiving celebrates God's redemption in the past and looks with hope to His deliverance in the future. Thanksgiving turns the church's lament songs into cathartic sacred blues songs that exult in the triumph to come. The soul looks back and wonders how it got over. Then it answers, "If it had not been for the Lord who was on our side, where would we go?" And the entire family of God discovers fresh wells of gratitude to sustain its praise.

But we need to add a word of caution. It's possible to enjoy great times of thanksgiving and celebration and miss the deeper things of God. It's possible to have public gatherings full of joyful music, gratitude, and catharsis but fail to root those responses and emotions in the Word of God itself. When that happens we may find that emotional displays become the root of our ministry philosophy instead of the fruit of deeply embracing the truth. We may find that our services drift toward emphasizing entertainment rather than the more substantial work of edification. We can even find our gatherings becoming manipulative in the name of the Spirit rather than allowing the Spirit of God to use the truth we sing to produce different and appropriate emotional responses in individuals. We can reduce "freedom" to permission to be expressive instead of the necessity of individuals to respond differently depending on the state of their hearts and the state of their lives.

The only safeguard against imbalance is a constant return to the living Word of God to shape and anchor our responses to the gospel truth we sing.

The Subjects of Singing: The Congregation

The Scripture defines and delimits the substance and the spirit of the church's singing. But it also says something relevant about *who* should sing and *to whom* we should sing.

Of course our praise is offered up to God. The Father receives our song offered through Jesus Christ our High Priest and the Holy Spirit our Comforter. Our hearts make music and melody to the Lord.

However, the Bible teaches that all Christians in the church's gathering are responsible to sing and that they should sing *to one another* in addition to singing to God. We "speak to one another in psalms, hymns and spiritual songs" (Eph. 5:19 NIV). Christian singing is both *congregational* singing and *conversational* singing. True congregational singing does not merely mean everyone sings at the same time; it also means that everyone "speaks to one another." Our songs become discourse. Singing becomes dialogue between the church and God as well as between saint and saint.

The traditional African-American call-and-response is one form of congregational and conversational participation in singing. Black folks

talk back to singers! We express our appreciation, join in the refrains, and
sometimes take over the soloist's lines as we join in praise together. The
Bible calls us to do this not just between choir loft and the pew, but also
from pew to pew, person to person, heart to heart.

I well remember leading a staff of white brothers to a service at
my home church in North Carolina. Most of the large staff of young
men had never been to a black church service. We arrived a little late
and church was packed. So ushers guided us to the first two rows in
the church, historically the "mourners' bench" used during times of
response. As a staff, we had spent considerable time discussing the
importance of congregational singing. Some had even taken the view
that choirs were "unbiblical" because they made the congregation "pas-
sive" rather than engaged in singing to one another. That line of reasoning always seemed odd to me because in the Black Church we almost
always had choirs *and* we always sang as a congregation. That Sunday
morning was no different.

After the service, we visited my mama's house for barbecue and there
shared our reflections and appreciations for the service. One brother who
previously thought choirs were anathema to congregational singing con-
fessed that hearing the congregation sing so expressively along with the
choir had changed his view of what counts as "congregational." The choir,
though important, was incidental to the congregation's praise. A dialogue
took place in song and the body built itself up in love.

That morning my white brothers experienced a different form of
congregational praise. They tasted what Pastor Anthony J. Carter so
wonderfully describes of the congregational and conversational nature of
Christian singing:

> When we gather for worship, one of the important realities is
> that we testify to our being there for one another. We exhort one
> another. We edify one another. We challenge one another. We
> admonish one another. We pray for and with one another. We
> share with one another our time, our treasures, and our talents.
> We teach one another. And we equip one another. Therefore, I
> must be reminded that I do not go to church for myself. I go to
> church for all those who have come to church for me. The most
> selfish act a Christian can do is stay away from the gathered body
> of Christians. To stay away is to deny my brothers and sisters the

fellowship and encouragement only I can give. God has designed the church in such a marvelous way as to have us intricately interdependent upon each other for his glory. This is a reality that takes place whether we realize it or not.[8]

According to Carter, singing should foster a healthy interdependence. We should gain from our brother or sister in the pews around us a lyrical and melodic exhortation to continue in faith, hope, and love. Rather than always closing our eyes and lifting our arms heavenward in solitary devotion, we should find ourselves making brief eye contact with those around us, smiling knowingly, nodding confidently, and receiving a spiritual lift from the affirmation of the saints as we sing the truth. Singing the Word of God *to* one another—not just *with* one another—stirs and revives the body of Christ with fresh life from Sunday to Sunday.

How to Make the Word Central

Yet, churches do not sing the Word of the Lord by happenstance. It doesn't happen randomly or without forethought. A well-ordered service driven by and filled with the Word of God requires planning and intentionality. Pastors and worship teams that invest the time to structure the service such that the Scriptures take center stage will have the joy of seeing the Word of God bless and sustain the saints every week. Several steps may help with building Word-centered gatherings of the saints. Of course, the liturgy from church to church may vary, so this is not a one-size-fits-all recommendation. What's important in the following recommendations and framework is the fundamental principle that the Word of God must provide the context and content of our public praise. This is one approach for centering the Word in our singing and our services.

Frame the Order of Service as a Conversation

First, leaders should teach the congregation that public gatherings of the church are not one-way affairs. The church does not gather to solely lift our voices to God; God also speaks back to us in the service. Typical orders of service reflect the dialogue between God and His people.

Call to Worship. Generally services begin with a call to worship. The service leader perhaps introduces and reads a passage of Scripture that summons God's people to meet with Him and praise Him. That call to gather comes through the human service leader but it comes from God because it comes from God's Word. God speaks first and His sheep know His voice and follow Him.

Congregational Singing. Many services then follow the call to worship with one or more songs. As we've stated earlier, Christian singing is a conversation between the people and God and also the people with one another. Our time of singing comes as a response to God's invitation to worship Him. We lift up our voices to declare the mighty works of God and to have His Word dwell in our hearts richly.

Scripture Reading. From this point most traditional services will feature the reading of one or more passages of Scripture. Again, God speaks to the congregation through the reading of his Word. The reading addresses the heart and prepares the congregation to come closer to God in response.

Corporate Prayer. The time of prayer continues the conversation between the Savior and the saved. Perhaps the reading of the Law ushers the congregation into a time of confession, or the reading of a psalm introduces a prayer of praise. Having heard His Word read, we now "think God's thoughts after Him" in prayer.

Assurance of Pardon. Many churches will use an assurance of God's pardon following the prayer of confession. That assurance or guarantee of forgiveness usually comes from a promise in God's Word, reminding the congregation that the removal of sin and guilt are not wishful thinking but a matter of God's divine work and word. The Lord's promises are to be embraced and trusted for He is faithful even when we are faithless. After God's Word searches the heart and believers grieve over the week's sin, such assurance cleanses the conscience and restores the saints in hope. Often the congregation responds to God and to each other with another round of singing so that the word of Christ dwells in the people's hearts.

Sermon. In most Protestant services the bulk of the congregation's time is given to hearing God speak through the preaching of the Scripture. This is especially the case among those churches that take seriously the Word of God. God speaks most authoritatively and clearly in the exposition of His Word. The congregation lives by every word that proceeds from His mouth. So, above all, the church is to be a listening community. Though we have the privilege to speak to God in songs and prayer, our greatest privilege is hearing from the God who speaks and whose Word never returns empty (Isa. 55:10–11).

Response. Following the sermon, most churches provide another opportunity to respond to God's Word. It may be a moment of silent reflection or of corporate prayer. Members may remain in their seats or gather with the leaders around the pulpit. Either way, the believing community takes the opportunity to commit themselves afresh to God and to hide His Word in their hearts.

Benediction. Finally, the service leader or pastor brings the assembly to an end with the benediction. Benedictions are words of blessing spoken over the congregation. The words represent God's final comment before the church departs to serve the community and live out the faith. Just as the Lord opened the gathering with words of invitation, He now closes the gathering with words of blessing and encouragement.

Keeping in mind the dialogical nature of the public service helps us appreciate the centrality of God's Word in the gathered life of His people. The Lord is present with His people by His Spirit and His Word. Worship, then, is the active and thoughtful response to His presence in His Word. We want congregations trained to recognize that Christ inhabits the praises of His people and speaks to us in public praise through His Word. Such a congregation will stand in glad awe as they commune with their God.

Plan Services from Biblical Text to Biblical Themes

Second, we should work to ensure the service "hangs together" on a central theme or thought. Nothing defeats the understanding and engagement of God's people quite like a service that feels chaotic or incoherent. So, pastors and worship leaders should work to make sure each Sunday gathering has an overarching point or theme that everything else supports and clarifies.

The best way to do that is to let the Word dictate the focus. An increasing number of preaching pastors are planning their sermon schedule months and in some cases a year in advance. This practice gives direction to the preaching ministry of the church and allows for thoughtful advanced planning by the worship leaders. Those responsible for planning the services should begin with Sunday's text in mind. Read the passage several times until the main thought of the passage emerges.

You might try to isolate the main thought about God and His character as well as the main thought about man and his character. Those main thoughts derived from the text become the thematic truths about God and man.

For example, assume the sermon text will be 1 Thessalonians 2:10–12, which reads, "You are witnesses, and so is God, of how holy, righteous and blameless we were among you who believed. For you know that we dealt with each of you as a father deals with his own children, encouraging, comforting and urging you to live lives worthy of God, who calls you into his kingdom and glory" (NIV). After several readings, the team may focus on the omniscience of God, who "witnesses" (v. 10) the life and ministry of His servants. The team may also focus on the faithfulness required of ministers who care for the family of God. The omniscience of God and the faithfulness of believers become the God-centered and man-centered themes that shape the service. If we were to ask a congregant, "What was the service about?," they should be able to give us these main ideas derived from the morning's text.

Move from Text and Themes to Readings

Third, along with the sermon text, our two themes should guide our selection of readings for the service. The call to worship might pick up on the theme of God as witness with a text like Jeremiah 42:5 or the call to faithfulness with 1 Corinthians 4:1–2. We may pair an Old Testament reading about the omniscience of God (e.g., Ps. 33) with a prayer of praise and later pair a New Testament reading about faithfulness (Matt. 24:36–51) with a prayer of confession. The readings provide broader biblical context for our focus and begin to pastorally address the congregation on our themes from God's perspective. These themes ought to also guide the selection of our assurance of pardon. The assurance can come from one of the selected readings (say, Ps. 33:18–19), or it can be a separate text embodying our hope of salvation and our theme (2 Tim. 2:12–14).

From the sermon text we move out to biblical themes to the other texts to be read during the service. God's Word provides a spine for attaching the other "bones" of the service together.

Let Readings and Themes Inform Prayers and Songs

Fourth, the collection of readings and themes ought to inform our prayers and our singing. For example, songs that celebrate the omniscience of God ought to lead to the prayer of praise. Likewise, songs that call the congregation to faithfulness and perseverance can lead into the prayer of confession. The truths of such songs should prepare the heart and mind to extol God in prayer for His infallible knowledge of all things. Those who lead in prayer should use the Scripture readings and truths from the songs to spur the content of their prayers. The prayers need not be written, but those who lead in prayer should prepare their hearts and minds in advance to lead the congregation in soulful reflection on the truth read and sung.

Conclusion

God places great power in song. He gives the church song so that the church may be built up in the faith, strengthened by grace. Our singing teaches and admonishes, so our singing requires the very best biblical content we can give it. Given how little instruction the New Testament gives the church for singing, it's striking that God should choose to tell the church, "Let the word of Christ dwell in you richly . . . as you sing." The ministry of the Word—the gospel—includes singing. Reviving a local church depends upon singing the Word of life.

PART II

Revive with Godly Leadership

CHAPTER 6

Restore Biblical Models for Pastoral Ministry

To the elders among you, I appeal as a fellow elder and a witness of Christ's sufferings who also will share in the glory to be revealed: Be shepherds of God's flock that is under your care, watching over them— not because you must, but because you are willing, as God wants you to be; not pursuing dishonest gain, but eager to serve; not lording it over those entrusted to you, but being examples to the flock. And when the Chief Shepherd appears, you will receive the crown of glory that will never fade away.
—1 PETER 5:1–4 (NIV, 2011)

On some high moor, across which at night hyenas howl, when you meet him, sleepless, far-sighted, weather-beaten, armed, leaning on his staff, and looking out over his scattered sheep, every one on his heart, you understand why the shepherd of Judea sprang to the front in his people's history; why they gave his name to their king, and made him the symbol of Providence; why Christ took him as the type of self-sacrifice.[1]
—G. A. SMITH

Introduction

Rev. Dr. F. D. Betts's eyes yellowed with age. His hair whitened with experience. His voice rasped and moaned with use. But he seemed to me a tireless older man. Always dressed well, he drove a Cadillac and lived in a small home next to the church. He smelled of an aromatic but perhaps too generous aftershave. Outside the pulpit he seemed a gentle and sweet man, caring and available. In the pulpit he appeared twenty years younger, in black gown, soaring above the congregation with oratorical crescendos that could as easily bring tears as shouts of acclamation.

For most of my young life, I knew Rev. Betts as my grandmother's and my mother's pastor. I attended the church but he seemed too old to really be my acquaintance. I made sure to be seen and not heard when he was around—not because he was stern or unkind but because I suffered a child's timidity around men of importance. I didn't know much about what it meant to be a pastor, but I knew that a pastor must be a respected and important member of the community.

Whenever Rev. Betts found me and some of my playmates about the community, he would often pull us aside and joke with us. His main joke was a promise to "talk to the man up town" to get us jobs on the back of a garbage truck. Somehow we believed he could do it. So we all turned up our noses, ewwed, and shouted, "No way!" With those yellowing eyes he'd peer down on us and say, "But son, that's an honest job." Two points needled their way into our little heads: we were capable of doing more if we worked hard, and yet there was nothing at all wrong with blue-collar, smelly, honest work.

I came to appreciate Rev. Betts most when I was arrested some years later as a rising junior in high school. Along with some older men, I had agreed to steal some goods from the local department store where I worked. It was the dumbest thing I'd ever done to that point in life (other dumb things would follow!). There was no reason to steal the items since I had a pocket full of money and a generous employee discount. I could have purchased anything in the store several times over. But in the stupidity of sin, I cast my lot with these young men and in God's mercy was arrested.

Charged with a felony misdemeanor, everything about my young life seemed to be over. I didn't know it at the time, but Rev. Betts visited my mother to see what he could do. On the day of my trial, he appeared in the courtroom minutes after the proceedings began. The judge immediately acknowledged him and asked if he would approach the bench. I don't know what was said, but I gather Rev. Betts spoke on my behalf. After a couple minutes, the judge dismissed him and I caught a whiff of that too-sweet aftershave as he passed by, flashing a sad smile with those yellowing eyes. A few moments later the judge gave me a short admonition and informed me that my judgment had been suspended.

I couldn't believe it, but I was free to go. My mom and I saw Rev. Betts in the courthouse lobby when we exited. He wasn't waiting for us. He was waiting to put in a word for someone else from the community. We greeted him and thanked him—too faintly for my part. Rev. Betts served our church from 1951 until his death in 1995. Years after going to his reward in heaven, the things I remember most about Rev. Betts are the oft-repeated garbage worker promise and his showing up on my behalf in the courtroom.

When You Hear the Word "Pastor," What Comes to Mind?

What comes to mind when you think of a pastor's role in the church and the community? Most of us have rather long lists of expectations and hopes for pastors. It is difficult to imagine any one profession or calling that requires more of its occupants than pastoral ministry. Some of the expectations come from outside the church, from community members in need and critics enraged. Other expectations come from the members inside the church. And all of these expectations pile atop those the pastor already has for himself. No wonder so many pastors labor under a crushing load of guilt, inadequacy, exhaustion, stress, and brokenness!

I'm convinced that the church's health and strength depends a great deal on restoring to the church a biblical model of pastoral ministry along with a corresponding set of biblical expectations. But before we turn to healthier models, perhaps it's worth taking a moment to consider some traditional and contemporary models of pastoral ministry prevalent among black churches.

Traditional Models of Pastoral Ministry

Many of our expectations of local church pastors emerge from our historical and social situation. "Social isolation and the struggle to survive in America made mutual dependence a practical necessity for black life."[2] Consequently, the local church played a pivotal role in assembling and caring for the wider African-American community. As Homer Ashby puts it, "the black church has been engaged in the survival business for a long time."[3] We often hear it said that "the black church was the only institution independently owned and controlled by black people." Some today debate this claim, or at least the extent of its truth. But whether the centrality of the church was a reality or a revisionist myth, it cannot be doubted that the perception of the church's historical and social centrality produced certain expectations for the men who led them.

In broad categories, the African-American pastor is expected to exercise both a priestly and a prophetic ministry. Ashby, drawing on the work of C. Eric Lincoln and Lawrence Mamiya, summarizes these two traditional aspects of black pastoral ministry:

> Lincoln and Mamiya define the priestly function of the black church as a maintenance function, a function that addresses the worship and spiritual needs of its members. The prophetic function, on the other hand, leads to involvement in more political concerns and participation in the affairs of the larger community. [T]he priestly functions . . . focused on survival and the prophetic function on liberation. The black church is always engaged in both survival and liberation; at any given moment in its history, though, the black church may be more concerned with survival or liberation.[4]

One recognizes in this prophet/priest framework an allusion to the Old Testament offices of Israel and, if we're Christocentric in our understanding of Scripture, an allusion to two of the three offices the Lord Jesus Christ fulfilled in His Person and ministry. Those priestly and prophetic functions, as Ashby summarizes, play out in a range of roles traditionally expected of African-American pastors.

Spiritual Leader. Congregations primarily expect their pastor to provide spiritual leadership and nurture. The pastor teaches God's Word, cares for souls, and guides members into spiritual truth. He certainly provides more, but the spiritual or priestly dimension is of first importance. Samuel DeWitt Proctor articulately captures the importance and centrality of this aspect of the pastor's role when he writes:

> The pastor stands alone, different from the politician, the social worker, the entrepreneur, the engineer, the physician, and the jurist. All these deal with a segment—a significant segment—of the human enterprise, but the pastor—alone—steps back from it all, examines it from God's perspective, and tries to give it all meaning, purpose, and direction. And he accomplishes this without physical power or civil authority. The pastor has only the power of example, the power of trust, the power of respect, and the power of the love of God shed abroad in Jesus Christ.[5]

So, above all things, African-American pastors are expected to provide spiritual nurture, care, and direction in an often hostile world.

Community Organizer. Though their spiritual role is paramount, congregations and communities also expect pastors to play many of the prophetic roles Proctor cites. For example, some view the pastor as a community organizer and leader. Sometimes the most educated African-American in the community, the pastor is called upon to negotiate the needs of the community with an indifferent-to-belligerent wider society. As community representative, the pastor brokers important relationships and decisions. Some whites expect the pastor to "control" or "influence" black communities on behalf of white agendas and concerns. Meanwhile, African-Americans look to the pastor to champion their cause and articulate their defense as situations require.

James Cone helps us to understand how these first two roles— spiritual leader and community organizer—blend together in traditional notions of black pastoral ministry:

> Ministers are both priest and prophet. They care for the souls who are wounded by personal loss and hurt, and they fight for justice for the people who have been wronged in society. The Black community has survived both spiritually and physically because we have had prophetic ministers who have stood before courageous crowds facing a hostile government in order to proclaim: let justice roll down like waters and righteousness as the mighty stream.[6]

The pastor stood between these two competing and combative worlds providing leadership and organizational genius in service to the community's aspirations.

Social Worker. From time to time, the pastor also serves as a kind of social service worker. When members need clothing, shelter, or food, they oftentimes call on the local church pastor for help. Familiar with the resources available in the community and among church members, the pastor occasionally works to supply material and practical needs. Pastors sometimes make valiant efforts to keep families together when circumstances threaten to split them up.

Counselor. In addition, the pastor provides counseling in a range of situations. In many respects, the mental health of the community depends upon the ability of the pastor to provide emotional, social, and spiritual comfort, direction, and healing "to give it all meaning, purpose, and direction," as Proctor put it. For the longest portion of the African-American experience, the only professional counseling available to the community came from faithful pastors, men to whom people could go to talk out their problems.

My first pastor, Rev. Betts, a good man, fit squarely into this traditional model. Indeed, many of the expectations listed above were demonstrated in his kind and generous help to me in my moment of need.

Contemporary Models

Still other models arise out of more contemporary concerns and opportunities. The traditional roles are still played. But in the ever-changing information age of opportunity in which we live, pastoral models expand to include other aspects of leadership and organizational expertise. Some leaders refer to these roles as the "kingly" roles of the ministry, alluding to the third major role in Old Testament Israel and embodied in the Person and work of Jesus Christ.

CEO. For example, increasingly we see pastors functioning as CEOs in the local church. Such pastors may view themselves as leaders in a business venture as much as they view themselves as spiritual guides. Church is big business and many people unashamedly or uncritically embrace current business practices and models to define pastoral ministry. Pastors legally incorporate "ministries" using their personal names and appoint boards of directors to direct its business affairs. Many pastors at the helm of such organizations receive significant salaries and benefits from their nonprofit corporations. Indeed, the CEO-lifestyles of some pastors have attracted the attention and investigation of U.S. Senators and the Internal Revenue Service.[7]

Entrepreneur. Another contemporary model of pastoral ministry views the pastor as an entrepreneur. Some pastors labor to create, package, and distribute products for wide commercial consumption and simply list "pastor" as the last in a long list of titles and descriptions like "entrepreneur," "change agent," or "catalyst." The titles imply that pastors ought to bring novel and innovative ideas, approaches, services, and products to market. This model appears to attract many new pastors and pastors of new church plants. They tend to see themselves and their ministry as largely dependent on innovation rather than the Word of God.

Motivational Speaker. The motivational speaker represents yet another contemporary model of pastoral ministry. Pastors adopting this model or aspect of ministry think of their role in wider terms than simply preaching, teaching, and leading in local churches. They think it important to motivate people to reach higher goals and feel or think better of themselves. As "life coaches," they aim to inspire and to equip their listeners with practical tools for living better lives. Some do this in an overtly biblical way, using the Scripture as source materials for motivating, while others place light emphasis on the Scripture and more emphasis on positive thinking.

Many of the most high-profile pastors and preachers in the Black Church now adopt one or more of these paradigms of ministry. Moreover, many young men entering the ministry aspire to these models. Even though the overwhelming majority of pastors will serve congregations of three hundred or less, their ambition will often be to become the next megachurch CEO, entrepreneur, or motivational speaker.

Some Problems with Traditional and Contemporary Models

As we can see from this partial list, competing models of pastoral ministry abound. However noble many of these roles are we ought to stop and ask a couple of questions. Are these approaches taught or suggested in Scripture? Do these expectations and models for pastoral ministry pose any significant problems? Are these harmless or even necessary approaches to black church life? It seems to me three potentially fatal weaknesses arise.

Secularization and Mission Drift

Both traditional and contemporary models assume that black pastors must play an active part in the community and secular concerns of black people. It would be difficult to deny that many pastors have shown dual concern for both the sacred and the secular. But can such a dual concern be sustained? And is this focus healthy for the Black Church?

Two esteemed veterans of black church pastoral ministry, Dr. Samuel D. Proctor and Dr. Gardner C. Taylor, have pointed to the difficult tension created by an overly secular view of pastoral ministry. They write:

> In our own culture, the black preacher has always been, or was supposed to be, involved in the secular problems of the people. The great danger that has come out of this is that many young preachers have lost the central purpose of their mission. They have made more or less secular pursuits their primary aim, perhaps as a misappropriation of the model left for us by Martin King. This was not Martin King's intention. On the contrary, he wanted very much to be a preacher, and he succeeded magnificently. Nonetheless, the influence of that era has taken us away from our central goal.[8]

Proctor and Taylor rightly recognize the threat of mission drift in traditional paradigms. Mission drift occurs whenever the pastor begins to pursue secondary goals over the primary goal of pastoral ministry. Some secondary goals may be very important and worthwhile pursuits. But the importance and worthiness subtly seduces the pastor away from the *most* needful things, which sometimes are the most difficult things.

If the pastor takes his eyes off his *primary* mission—to preach and teach God's Word and shepherd the sheep—he may find himself importing models and expectations of leadership that ultimately weaken the ministry itself.

Superman and Burnout

Moreover, many of the traditional and contemporary models of pastoral ministry assume that pastors must be supermen, Renaissance men, capable of excelling at every possible venture and need of the church. To the extent that these models overlap, they require the pastor to have or develop expertise well beyond biblical requirements or educational experience.

Consequently, the social, mental, physical, and spiritual health of pastors and their families suffer. According to one survey, only 23 percent of pastors report being happy and content in Christ, in their church, and in their home.[9] Ninety percent of pastors surveyed report working between 55 to 75 hours per week. Seventy percent feel grossly underpaid. Fifty percent feel unable to meet the demands of the job.

When it comes to training and preparedness, surveyed pastors report similarly disturbing situations. Ninety percent feel they are inadequately trained to cope with ministry demands and said the ministry was completely different than what they expected before they entered.

This affects the health and well-being of pastors and their families. For instance, seven out of ten pastors surveyed constantly fight depression. One-half of pastors reported feeling so discouraged that they would leave the ministry if they could but have no other way of making a living. Eight out of ten pastors believe pastoral ministry has negatively affected their families, and eight of ten spouses feel the pastor is overworked while spouses themselves feel left out and underappreciated by church members.

Relationships with others in the church also suffer under inordinate demands and expectations. Seven out of ten pastors surveyed do not have someone they consider a close friend in the church. Forty percent report serious conflict with a parishioner at least once a month. The number-one reason pastors reported for leaving the ministry is the congregation's unwillingness to pursue the same direction and goal as the pastor. Without close friends, without broad support from their people, and facing regular conflict, many pastors find themselves torn between what they believe to be a God-given direction for the church and a resistant people.

Not surprisingly, fifty percent of new ministers will not continue in the ministry just five years later. Only one of every ten ministers will actually retire in some ministry capacity. Each year an estimated four thousand new churches begin and each year approximately seven thousand churches close. Monthly more than 1,700 pastors left the ministry and more than 1,300 pastors were terminated by their local church, many without cause.

That's a sad and alarming picture of pastors and churches, isn't it? Work long hours in a job with too many demands for too little pay, with the wrong skills amidst taxing expectations. Families are pressured and battered. Pastors are discouraged and depressed. No friends, serious conflict once a month, and people who will not follow. Is it no wonder so many quit so soon? Inordinate and extra-biblical expectations might be faulted for a great deal of this distressing situation. Pastors are not supermen, and recalibrating our expectations will undoubtedly help wherever church revival is needed.

Pastor-Dictators and Congregation Abuse

If it is true that black churches sometimes expect too much from their pastors by requiring them to play more roles than humanly possible, then it is also true that black congregations can find themselves under the dictatorial control of highly charismatic figures. There may be a surprising relationship between embracing traditional and contemporary models of pastoral ministry and welcoming autocratic and abusive leaders. The church's embrace of highly charismatic and variously gifted individuals can open her to overdependence upon the pastor and controlling leadership styles. In the worst-case scenarios, leaders abuse the people they are supposed to shepherd.

Ronald Enroth's *Churches That Abuse* highlights past and present cases of church abuse. He identifies nine characteristics of abusive churches, including: a control orientation to leadership, manipulation of members, rigid insistence on certain lifestyles and behaviors, a combination of feeling superior to and persecuted by other churches, disallowing questions from members, and making it difficult or painful for members to leave the church.[10] Often control-oriented leaders display dogmatic, self-confident, arrogant, and self-centered behaviors. Such leaders position themselves in the center of the congregation's life with all the programs and activities orbiting them. Questioning such a leader becomes tantamount to questioning God. Even if other ministers and elders serve in the church, charismatic and control-oriented ministers tend to exercise complete rule and receive little to no accountability. In such situations, pastors become dictators and, rather than feed the sheep, they fleece and beat the sheep.

That is the worst-case scenario. Not all churches suffer such poor leadership. But even if most church leaders do not become abusive, it may still be the case that a local church's model of leadership assigns too much authority and control to the leader. If we care about the vitality of the Black Church, then we must be concerned with the quality and accountability of black church leadership. For even milder models of overreliance and power-concentration can weaken the overall health of the pastor and the congregation.

What Model of Pastoral Ministry Should Black Churches Embrace?

Given the serious weaknesses of some models of ministry, it seems wise to ask another question: Are these traditional and contemporary leadership models even biblical? To what extent are local church pastors to embrace prophet, priest, and king roles ultimately fulfilled only by the Lord Jesus? After all, if the church must be centered on God's life-giving Word, then "no church should embrace a ministry model that cannot demonstrate its biblical rationale."[11] What, then, does the Bible teach us about the qualifications, expectations, and roles of pastors?

Qualifications

First, the Bible teaches that pastoral ministry requires a certain kind of man, not certain kinds of activities. We'll turn to the biblical responsibilities of pastors in a moment. But we must emphasize what the Bible emphasizes regarding church leadership: character. In the apostle Paul's first letter to Timothy, the veteran church leader outlines for his young apprentice the qualities that must be present in any pastor or elder of the church.[12] Paul writes:

> The saying is trustworthy: If anyone aspires to the office of overseer, he desires a noble task. Therefore an overseer must be above reproach, the husband of one wife, sober-minded, self-controlled, respectable, hospitable, able to teach, not a drunkard, not violent but gentle, not quarrelsome, not a lover of money. He must manage his own household well, with all dignity keeping his children

submissive, for if someone does not know how to manage his own household, how will he care for God's church? He must not be a recent convert, or he may become puffed up with conceit and fall into the condemnation of the devil. Moreover, he must be well thought of by outsiders, so that he may not fall into disgrace, into a snare of the devil. (1 Tim. 3:1–7)

A full exposition of this text lies beyond the limits of this chapter,[13] but a few key observations seem warranted. First, consider the nobility of the pastoral office. Some men have tarnished the office by their misbehavior and corruption. But God considers pastoral service a "noble task" whose only worthy occupants are "above reproach." To be "above reproach" means to be blameless, to live a consistently spiritual and moral life that itself frees a man from the illegitimate charges of others. Paul does not advocate perfection here. Rather, "above reproach" is an omnibus characteristic that includes the remainder of the list and describes a general habit and consistency of life that others find unimpeachable. Only such men can rightfully hold the office of overseer.

Second, notice that, with the exception of "able to teach" (v. 2), every qualification Paul lists has to do with Christian character and maturity. Nowhere does the apostle include entrepreneurial skill, visionary leadership, or political savvy. The apostle recommends brown paper bag Christian character. In fact, every attribute aside from "able to teach" and "not a recent convert" applies to all other Christians elsewhere in the Bible. The distinguishing mark of a Christian leader is not unusual talent and gifts but consistently mature spiritual living evident in their lives.

Which leads us to a third observation: The pastor's character ought to be demonstrated in his personal, public, and paternal life. His personal example should include internal characteristics like "the husband of one wife [literally, one-woman man], sober-minded, self-controlled, respectable, hospitable" (v. 2). Peacemaking and gentleness must mark his public life. He is "not a drunkard, not violent but gentle, not quarrelsome, not a lover of money" (v. 3). And the overseer's paternal life, his family life—the most important place of all, prerequisite to public service—demonstrates his leadership and his caregiving ability. As Paul puts it in verses 4–5, "He must manage his own household well, with all dignity keeping his children submissive, for if someone does not know how to manage his own household, how will he care for God's church?" The pastor or bishop must prove himself a person of godly character in every sphere of life and relationships.

Notice finally that the selection of appropriate pastors or elders is a matter of spiritual warfare. Inexperienced men are susceptible to pride and "fall into the same condemnation of the devil," which either means the same judgment that befell Satan may come upon the arrogant pastor or that the puffed-up pastor is vulnerable to the devil's slander (v. 6). Moreover, the pastor's reputation with "outsiders," those not involved with the body of Christ, can be the source of Satanic entrapment and shame. How can a man effectively serve as the leader of God's people if even those who do not know God find him blameworthy and morally deficient?

Reviving the Black Church requires restoring godly character to its rightful determinative place in selecting and following spiritual leadership. "The usefulness of an elder will depend in the long run more on his character than on his gifts and knowledge."[14] Without godliness the pastorate crumbles. Without a godly pastorate the church dies.

Roles and Responsibilities

Though the Bible teaches that congregations should search for godliness as the chief requirement for pastoral ministry, the Bible also gives us a definite set of responsibilities for church leaders to play. Traditional pastoral theologies have emphasized prophetic and priestly roles, while more contemporary notions have stressed kingly functions. These roles place the pastor in the position of emulating the three-fold office of prophet, priest, and king fulfilled by the Chief Shepherd, Jesus Christ. While this framework provides a helpful rubric for understanding pastoral ministry, it is perhaps too general to protect the local church pastor from inordinate expectations and extra-biblical roles. It seems that a lot of things *not* required by the Scripture end up on the pastor's plate using this three-part approach.

So, the critical question to ask is: What responsibilities does the Bible assign the local church pastor? Again, Paul's letters to Timothy provide guidance.

Pray. The apostle Paul informed young Timothy that he desired "that in every place the men should pray, lifting holy hands without anger or quarreling" (1 Tim. 2:8). If Paul envisioned all the men of the church committing to prayer, then it stands to reason he especially wanted the pastors to be men of prayer. Indeed, during a pivotal point of need and division in the early church, the apostles committed themselves to the ministry of prayer rather than personally attending the injustice or physical need (Acts 6:4).

Prayer may be one of the most difficult yet necessary duties of pastoral ministry. One nationally representative survey of Protestant pastors revealed that very few ministers are satisfied with their prayer lives. While pastors over sixty were most likely to be satisfied with their prayer lives, pastors on average only prayed some thirty-nine minutes per day![15] Can we be surprised that the church appears dead or ineffectual when so few of us pray at any length or with any fervency? If we would see revival in the church, we need fewer pastors marketing their sermons or books and more pastors marking their knees in prayer. Unless we abide in Christ we can do nothing, but if we abide in Him—prayer being one means of doing so—we can bear much fruit (John 15:4–7).

Preach and Teach. Above all, the pastor must preach and teach God's Word. Like the apostles of the early church, he cannot leave the ministry of the Word in order to wait tables if the church is going to thrive and grow as God intends (Acts 6:2, 7). The pastor must "devote [himself] to the public reading of Scripture, to exhortation, to teaching" (1 Tim. 4:13). He must "preach the word; be ready in season and out of season; reprove, rebuke, and exhort, with complete patience and teaching" (2 Tim. 4:1–2). He must carry on this responsibility with a singular and heavenly devotion, as one charged "in the presence of God and of Christ Jesus, who is to judge the living and the dead, and by his appearing and his kingdom."

Nothing a pastor does surpasses in importance the ministry of the Word. If the Word gives life to the church, then pastors must give their lives to the Word. I have a friend who interviewed some time ago for a senior pastor vacancy at his local church. When asked what he would focus on if called as the new pastor, he told the congregation he would be happy to see every other ministry in the church fail if it meant the ministry of the Word flourished. Of course he didn't want any good work to suffer, but he made the point. His great and consuming priority would be the teaching of God's Word. So it ought to be with all God's men. As Scottish pastor William Still observes: "The greatest failure is that you fail to minister the Word of God in any effectiveness or fullness to the people."[16]

Disciple Other Teachers. The apostles intended that their ministries be replicated in the lives of their followers and their followers' followers. "You then, my child, be strengthened by the grace that is in Christ Jesus, and what you have heard from me in the presence of many witnesses entrust to faithful men who will be able to teach others also" (2 Tim. 2:1–2). We should think of pastoral ministry and the teaching ministry in particular as a relay race. One pastor passes what he has learned on to the next runner who in turn does the same. In a very real sense, if a pastor or group of elders neglects to train other men to teach God's Word, then they fail at the most essential and basic task for extending the life of the church beyond themselves and beyond their generation.

In many African-American churches, the lone teaching pastor hoards the teaching ministry to himself. Rather than develop other men, they may keep aspiring ministers on hold, perpetually waiting for opportunity. I've been a member of and visited many other black churches with a gaggle of young "ministers" and "associates" who seem to have no other function than sitting in the pulpit area along with the pastor. They are seen but not heard. The failure to deploy these men in active teaching settings impoverishes the church. They ought to be able to open the Word in Sunday school, midweek Bible studies, small groups, and in morning and evening services on occasion. Sharing the pulpit and providing teaching opportunities help to make the church less pastor-centric, grow men in their teaching gifts, edify the body, and more effectively discern preparedness for more substantial ministry. In the final analysis, it is the church that trains men for the ministry. The best preparation comes at the feet of faithful elders who pass on their experiences of success and failure along with the word of God. The life of the church depends upon a warm and joyful embrace of this critical pastoral responsibility.

Shepherd the Sheep. Shepherding lies at the heart of the pastoral calling. "The care of the Lord for his people is to be reflected in those whom he calls to lead."[17] The Lord Himself is the Chief Shepherd (1 Pet. 5:4) and His pastors serve as under-shepherds. To shepherd the flock requires that pastors attend to at least four key responsibilities. First, shepherding requires pastors to watch over the flock—protecting and guiding them in the Word of the Lord. Second, shepherding requires setting an example for the flock to follow "in speech, in conduct, in love, in faith, in purity" (1 Tim. 4:12). Third, shepherding includes visiting the sick and healing those with spiritual wounds as well (James 5:13–16). Fourth, shepherding involves seeking after erring sheep and those entangled in sin in order to correct, restore, or remove them from the church for their spiritual well-being (Matt. 18:10–20; Gal. 6:1–2).

True shepherds do this "not under compulsion, but willingly, as God would have you; not for shameful gain, but eagerly; not domineering over those in your charge" (1 Pet. 5:2–3). The true shepherd lays down his life for the sheep; he does not slaughter the sheep for his own life's sake. "All who are called to be elders are called to the sheep-intensive work of shepherding."[18]

How Will We Know We Are Successful?

Moving to a biblical paradigm for pastoral ministry requires not only a restoration of biblical qualifications and responsibilities but also restoration of a biblical measure of pastoral performance. An old adage in the field of organizational development says: What you measure is what you get. Measurement criteria drive behavior. If hours worked becomes the standard, then employees will focus on punching in and out of work at appropriate times. If rate of production becomes the criteria, then employees will seek to match rate expectations. Measurement and reward often determine the effort and direction of the worker.

The same truth holds when it comes to pastoral ministry. Most pastors labor under a heavy burden to be "successful." Even "successful" pastors find themselves ensnared by the "success syndrome."[19] Success drives the ministry and appearing successful provides the minister's sense of self-worth. Consider again the various models of contemporary pastoral ministry—CEO, entrepreneur, motivational speaker. Each of those paradigms suggests high-profile success and achievement. And if we read further into the biographies of ministers using such titles, we'll find a steady emphasis on numbers attending their churches, the size of their church budgets, numbers of programs and ministries, and a host of other measures designed to communicate "success." Ask nearly any pastor about their church and the first replies will likely be numerical measures of growth or size. Why does that happen? It happens usually because "success" has become the measuring rod for pastoral service.

But is "success" the Bible's criterion for evaluating pastors and ministries? The short answer is "no." In fact, far from describing elders, bishops, or pastors with lofty titles or dazzling stats, the New Testament apostles and pastors used what many today would regard as lowly descriptions for church leaders. Jesus Himself set the framework by rebuking His disciples for jostling for position between themselves, saying, "You know that the rulers of the Gentiles lord it over them, and their great ones exercise authority over them. It shall not be so among you. But whoever would be great among you must be your servant, and whoever would be first among you must be your slave, even as the Son of Man came not to be served but to serve, and to give his life as a ransom for many" (Matt. 20:25–28). Self-exalting behavior belongs to Gentile unbelievers, not Christians. We're not "lords" and "rulers" but "servants" and "slaves" to our brothers and sisters. The apostle Paul described himself and other apostles as "the scum of the earth, the refuse of the world" (1 Cor. 4:13 NIV). When's the last time you saw "slave," "servant," or "scum of the earth" on a business card or website?

How does one evaluate servants and slaves? The Bible points to faithfulness as the criteria. The apostle Paul wrote to a Corinthian church filled with factions clamoring to follow their favorite leaders. He reminded them that the human agents were nothing to exalt and were, in fact, serving in the same ministry of planting and watering (1 Cor. 3:5–9). Then he teaches the Corinthians how to rightly evaluate them. "This is how one should regard us, as servants of Christ and stewards of the mysteries of God. Moreover, it is required of stewards that they be found trustworthy" (1 Cor. 4:1–2). Trustworthiness or faithfulness with the Word of God is the proper standard for appraising a gospel worker.

It matters little whether a man is entrepreneurial or creative because the steward or slave must only do what the master commands. Men cannot boast of their productivity or church growth because "neither he who plants nor he who waters is anything, but only God who gives the growth" (1 Cor. 3:7). Even when a servant fulfills his commission, he has no cause for boasting. The Lord tells us that "when you have done all that you were commanded, say, 'We are unworthy servants; we have only done what was our duty'" (Luke 17:10). Whether the Lord tends our ministry with unusual blessing or difficult labor in barren fields, He calls us to remain faithful until the end. "Successful" ministries built on unfaithfulness will perish with the wind while the unfaithful servant is beaten with many blows (Luke 12:47). Faithful servants with seemingly unsuccessful ministries earn a great reward (1 Tim. 3:13) and "receive the unfading crown of glory" (1 Pet. 5:4).

Conclusion

The critical questions for the life of the black church are: Does each local black church have qualified leaders leading them? Do we have the correct expectations regarding their roles? And, are her pastors and elders faithful to the charge given by God as found in the Word of God? The church will need to be revived by godly leadership.

CHAPTER 7

Realign Authority with the Proper Office

Remember your leaders, those who spoke to you the word of God. Consider the outcome of their way of life, and imitate their faith.

Obey your leaders and submit to them, for they are keeping watch over your souls, as those who will have to give an account. Let them do this with joy and not with groaning, for that would be of no advantage to you.
—HEBREWS 13:7, 17

Introduction: A Tale of Pastors, "Mothers," and Committees

Now in her sixties with regal gray hair, Karen grew up in the church. Her father was a white evangelical pastor who left her a rich spiritual legacy. But she came of age in the segregated South, which afforded her little opportunity to worship in the Black Church.

I remember her returning to the office one Monday morning, asking if I had some time to talk. She explained that a longtime friend had died and the funeral was held that weekend. Her friend attended a black Pentecostal church. Karen's voice filled with wonder as she recalled the hours-long homegoing celebration. She spoke of the singing, the shouting, the heat and the church fans, and the various women in white—so many in white. "Why were there nurses in a church service?" she asked. "Who were the other ladies dressed in white off to the side of the pulpit area?" "And," she continued, "several women let out these loud yells and began to dance and tremble and jump during the service. What was that all about?"

Karen's first visit to a black church funeral must have felt like a spiritual "field trip." A sweet and gracious woman, usually filled with a child's wonder, she had been transported to another world altogether. She was introduced to a world of worship that most white Americans will never encounter, except in movies and sitcoms designed to caricature the Black Church. She witnessed some practices and roles indigenous to many black churches but relatively unknown in other settings.

Karen's experience reminded me of my own childhood growing up in and around Files Chapel Baptist Church. I remember the nurses in white and the "church mothers." They were the older women of the church, influential in the life of the congregation. We had nurses, too, because we were not a "dead" Baptist church. Every once in a while someone started "having church" and needed to be attended. Who knew when the Spirit might "fall" on someone?

Then there were the many committees that carried out the work of the church. The deacons were older, grave men who seemed to run the church's business. And there was Rev. Betts who seemed to sit on all the committees, negotiated with the deacons, and gave attention to the mothers of the church.

Looking back, it's difficult to imagine how he did it all or to see how anything ever got done with so many layers of sometimes competing structure and authority.

In the last chapter, we considered the need to reform the model of pastoral ministry in local churches. We argued for a return to the biblical call for mature Christian character as qualifications for the office; the spiritual activities of prayer, preaching and teaching, making disciples, and shepherding; and an embrace of faithfulness as the criteria for judging the effectiveness of a pastor's ministry. While all those reforms are necessary and vital, they will be hindered if there isn't also a return to biblical distributions of authority. Most black church pastors can tell horror stories about convoluted committee processes, runaway deacons, and unclear lines of authority. Many members can share similar stories of dictatorial leaders. So, to strengthen and revive the church, we need to realign biblical authority and leadership structures to support the reform of pastoral ministry. The right people in the wrong structures can kill a local church.

Realign Authority with the Correct Office

I didn't know it as a little boy, but by having "church mothers," our Baptist church was borrowing an innovation from black Pentecostal groups like the Church of God in Christ, who officially recognize "church mother" as an office in the local church.[1] In retrospect, it seemed also that our times of singing and praise were more Pentecostal in flavor than the reserved "Baptist" style of some sister congregations.

But one thing seemed to be deep-fried Baptist—committees! There were committees for everything: pastor's aid, willing workers, kitchen and hospitality, and so on. With all the committees we maintained, you would think there was a "Book of Committees" in the Bible. But there isn't. And to be honest, a number of practices in the Black Church—practices that without doubt have at one point been important to the ministry of the church—find no warrant or justification in the Scripture. Many of these structures have outlived their usefulness and have sometimes become the cause of much strain and strife. So returning to biblical structures holds promise for strengthening and reviving the Black Church.

Two Offices: Elders and Deacons

The New Testament reveals that the early church maintained two enduring offices: elders (pastors) and deacons. These two offices provided for both the spiritual and physical care and leadership of the congregation. Persons filling these offices were to meet the character qualifications of 1 Timothy 3 and Titus 1.

Deacons. The New Testament dedicates less space to the role of deacons than it does to the role of elders. However, one should not underestimate the importance of deacons to the unity and strength of the church. If we assume Acts 6 to be paradigmatic for the deacon's role in the church, we may say that while elders give general spiritual oversight and leadership to the church, deacons attend to the practical and material needs. The deacons' focus on the congregation's material needs free up the ministry of the Word and preserve the unity of the church. Acts 6:1–7 provides the backdrop for this view of diaconal ministry:

> Now in these days when the disciples were increasing in number, a complaint by the Hellenists arose against the Hebrews because their widows were being neglected in the daily distribution. And the twelve summoned the full number of the disciples and said, "It is not right that we should give up preaching the word of God to serve tables. Therefore, brothers, pick out from among you seven men of good repute, full of the Spirit and of wisdom, whom we will appoint to this duty. But we will devote ourselves to prayer and to the ministry of the word." And what they said pleased the whole gathering, and they chose Stephen, a man full of faith and of the Holy Spirit, and Philip, and Prochorus, and Nicanor, and Timon, and Parmenas, and Nicolaus, a proselyte of Antioch. These they set before the apostles, and they prayed and laid their hands on them. And the word of God continued to increase, and the number of the disciples multiplied greatly in Jerusalem, and a great many of the priests became obedient to the faith.

Inequity or perceived inequity threatened the unity of the church. There appeared to be unfair treatment along ethnic or cultural lines. The church's commitment to justice was called into question right at its infancy. Faced with explosive growth, with increasing demands and needs from the people, the apostles had to make an important decision. Should they leave the spiritual oversight and leadership of the church (prayer and the ministry of the Word) to personally attend the justice and material needs of the congregation? They decided instead, "It is not right that we should give up preaching the word of God to serve tables" (v. 2). They charged the congregation with identifying seven men to serve the material, unity, and justice needs of the assembly. These men were ordained with prayer and laying on of hands and given the responsibility to attend to the widows' distribution.

Many regard Acts 6 as the birth of the office of deacon and the apostles as paradigmatic for the role of elders. If so, then the apostles' decision resulted in a broad division of labor and authority between deacons and elders. Deacons served the practical physical needs of the church.

Elders. Meanwhile, elders served the spiritual leadership needs of the congregation. The apostle Peter put his finger on both the elders' shepherding and oversight responsibility when he addressed his fellow elders in 1 Peter 5:1–3. Peter wrote, "So I exhort the elders among you, as a fellow elder and a witness of the sufferings of Christ, as well as a partaker in the glory that is going to be revealed: shepherd the flock of God that is among you, exercising oversight, not under compulsion, but willingly, as God would have you; not for shameful gain, but eagerly; not domineering over those in your charge, but being examples to the flock." The main charge Peter gives is to "shepherd," further defined as "exercising oversight." He also specifies the attitude and spirit in which this is to happen—"not under compulsion, but willingly . . . not for shameful gain, but eagerly; not domineering."

The writer of Hebrews also understood the elders to have oversight authority for the spiritual benefit of the congregation. He commands the church members to "Obey your leaders and submit to them." Then he states the reason for such submission: "for they are keeping watch over your souls, as those who will have to give an account. Let them do this with joy and not with groaning, for that would be of no advantage to you" (Heb. 13:17). The elders receive the congregation's support and obedience only insofar as they faithfully watch over the souls of the saints. In turn, the elders must also keep in mind that their leadership position requires them to submit to and obey the Lord to whom they "will have to give an account." The Lord designs this chain of submission and oversight, joyfully and willingly undertaken, for the advantage or benefit of the church.

Moreover, the elders must exercise this oversight responsibility with full dedication. Near the end of his life and ministry, the apostle Paul traveled through the city of Ephesus, where he once labored to establish the church. On his way to trial for preaching the gospel, Paul called the elders at Ephesus to meet and pray with him. The apostle reminded them of his ministry among them, how he "did not shrink from declaring to [them] anything that was profitable, and teaching [them] in public and from house to house" (Acts 20:20). He announced to the elders, "imprisonment and afflictions await me." Luke tells us, "There was much weeping on the part of all; they embraced Paul and kissed him, being sorrowful most of all because of the word he had spoken, that they would not see his face again" (Acts 20:23, 37–38). In the middle of the teary scene, Paul charged the elders to "Pay careful attention to yourselves and to all the flock, in which the Holy Spirit has made you overseers, to care for the church of God, which he obtained with his own blood" (v. 28).

That's what elders are called to do: to pay careful attention to themselves and the flock. They receive this assignment from God the Holy Spirit. And they are to care for the church fully appreciating that Christ bought her with his precious blood, a price far costlier than all the world's silver and gold. It was a call to full dedication as overseers.

The Relationship between Elders and Deacons. Though both offices perform important tasks in the local church, realigning authority between offices requires understanding how elders and deacons relate to one another. In many churches—of all ethnicities—elders and deacons function like two branches of government. Imagine the Senate and the House of Representatives in the U.S. Government. Both the Senate and the House have a part to play in crafting legislation and leading the government. Together they form a system of checks and balances. Many people see elders or the pastor in a similar relationship with deacons in the church.

However, while both offices remain vitally important, the Bible does not teach that elders and deacons are two halves of a bicameral legislature, each exercising equal authority. Nowhere does the New Testament assign authority of this sort to deacons or call congregations to submit to them in the way they are to submit to their elders or pastors. For the church to receive the leadership and care God intends, leadership authority must be assigned to qualified elders. In some cases this means slowly and carefully redefining the role of deacons.

Many deacon boards that misunderstand this have created hurtful and sometimes divisive situations inside the church. Pastors sometimes find themselves embattled as they attempt to lead the congregation in particular directions. Deacons, meanwhile, can feel overlooked and underappreciated as their input gets pushed aside. Part of the difficulty lies in not maintaining the broad role distinctions that the New Testament seems to present.

One pastor friend illustrates the different yet complementary roles of elders and deacons with a road trip analogy. In his illustration, elders determine the destination and attend to the passengers in the car, including the deacons. Once the elders communicate the destination, deacons have responsibility for plotting the course, getting the gas, and perhaps maximizing seating arrangements. In this way, elders maintain their leadership and oversight authority while deacons maintain their focus on serving the practical needs of the congregation. The smooth operation of the church depends on this realignment of authority to the elders.

Realign Authority with Shared Leadership: The Plurality of Elders

Realigning biblical authority requires putting in place the two New Testament offices of elder and deacon. However, that's only one step in the restructuring. A second vital step involves creating a *plurality* of elders to share the governance of each local body.

Some black denominations have maintained the office of elder from their founding. However, other denominations, particularly Baptists, have typically been led by a single pastor. Sometimes this single pastor receives assistance from trainee or staff "ministers" and "associates." But traditionally everyone has understood that "*the* pastor" was the "real" elder in charge of the congregation. Even in denominations that feature multiple elders in a congregation, the lead pastor or bishop can sometimes function as the person with sole authority in the church. But is this how the Bible distributes authority in the local church?

The New Testament evidence indicates that the ordinary practice among the apostles was to establish multiple elders in each local church. As Benjamin L. Merkle points out:

> The concept of shared leadership is a common theme in the Bible. In the Old Testament, leadership was shared by the elders of Israel. In the New Testament, Jesus chose twelve apostles to lead the church. In addition, the early church appointed seven men to assist the apostles by caring for the church's widows (Acts 6:1–6). This pattern of plurality was continued with the establishment of the Christian eldership.[2]

Merkle continues:

> The first mention of Christian elders appears in Acts 11:30, which tells us the church in Antioch sent Barnabas and Paul to the elders in Jerusalem with money to aid in the famine relief. Later, in Acts 15, the elders are referenced along with the apostles in the context of the Jerusalem Council. Similar to the apostles, the elders formed a collective body of leadership.[3]

Nearly all references to elders in the New Testament occur in the plural (see, for example, 1 Tim. 5:17; Titus 1:5; James 5:14; 1 Pet. 5:1). The exceptions involve instances where individual elders are the focus of concern, as in qualifications for the office (1 Tim. 3:1), charges against an elder (1 Tim. 5:19), and a New Testament writer referring to himself as an "elder" (1 Pet. 5:1; 2 John 1; 3 John 1).

Collectively, this plurality of elders held responsibility for the oversight, teaching, and leadership of the church. Only in pioneering situations where churches were first being established did a lone elder or pastor lead the congregation. Titus found himself in such a situation in the church in Crete. Even so, Paul's main instruction to Titus was to "put what remained in order, and *appoint elders in every town as I directed you*" (Titus 1:5, emphasis added).

Merkle identifies several advantages to maintaining plural leadership in the local church, including: biblical accountability, balance, burden sharing, and a better representation of the nature of ministry. The *biblical accountability* of shared leadership helps protect a pastor and church from error, insensitivity, blind spots, and abuse. How else could Paul's charge to "Pay careful attention to yourselves and to all the flock" (Acts 20:28) be obeyed without the benefit of accountability and mutual care afforded by plural leadership? The need for *balance* indicates that no one man has all the gifts and ability necessary for shepherding an entire congregation. We need other leaders to help compensate for our weaknesses and to extend the reach of the ministry. The balance that plural leadership creates also makes possible the *burden sharing* required in the ministry. The significantly high burnout, depression, and resignation rates of pastoral ministry could be ameliorated if churches encouraged and supported true partnership in church ministry. Finally, Merkle contends that plural leadership *better represents* the "every member ministry" of the New Testament.

Plural eldership removes the perception that the church belongs to one pastor and that only the elite may enter the Lord's service. Shared leadership creates room for the expression of diverse gifts and abilities.[4]

But even in settings with plural leadership, I've watched men tire beneath the heavy load of pastoral ministry. It's a miracle that men who serve as long-term pastors aren't crushed more often and more completely than they are. I used to wonder how Rev. Betts maintained his busy schedule of committee meetings, board meetings, church events, and community demands. When I entered the ministry I found out. Without help there's only so much even the best pastors can do. Chances are Rev. Betts was sometimes forced to neglect some of the more important matters of the ministry: prayer, study, and teaching. Having biblically qualified men serve with him would have made the work of the ministry more effective and more joyful.

One wonders why more black churches don't move more quickly toward shared authority among multiple qualified elders. If we are to revive the church, we can no longer allow fear of change, possessive leadership, idolatrous attachment to "*the* pastor," lack of biblical knowledge, or a perceived lack of qualified men hinder the sharing of biblical leadership in the church.

Realign for the Proper Use of Authority

Black churches continue to be communities that honor and respect the authority of pastors to lead the congregation. Authority consists of the *ability* and the *right* to make decisions, take actions, and direct the affairs of the church. The Bible teaches that "elders who rule well [should] be considered worthy of double honor" (1 Tim. 5:17). We see plentiful evidences of such double honor in the typical Black Church in things like pastor appreciation dinners, congregational gifts to pastors, and historically the congregation's eagerness to supply food and other resources to their pastors. Honor for those in authority remains alive in the Black Church—even if such honor has waned in other parts of the world.

However, "our sinful tendency is either to abuse authority or to neglect its proper use."[5] So, before we proceed, we should outline what "proper use" of authority entails.

Dr. Timothy Witmer, professor of practical theology at Westminster Theological Seminary, sketches five key points regarding the appropriate exercise of leadership in the church.[6] *First, there must be the recognition that all human authority is derived.* Authority does not inhere in any individual; it is delegated. In the church, Jesus Christ is the only and sufficient Head of the church. Only Jesus' authority is underived. This means an elder must not act as if it is "his church," and members should avoid the tendency to think of the church as something belonging to the pastor. The church is not a sole proprietorship; it is not a business owned by any man. To treat it as such is really to reduce black people to owned commodities or slaves. We may be slaves to Christ, but we should never again be slaves to men—even if the men in question look like us. There must be the recognition that all true and final authority belongs to God.

Second, the elders' use of authority must serve the well-being of those under their care. God braids authority and love together. We see this principle in Hebrews 13:17. We see it also in the example of Jesus Himself, who "came not to be served but to serve, and to give his life as a ransom for many" (Mark 10:45). Elders do not "lord it over the flock." They use their position for the betterment of the sheep.

Third, God's Word must direct the use of authority. One pastor friend loves to say, "An elder without a Bible is an elder without authority." Since an overseer's authority is derived from the Lord Jesus, he cannot act in ways prohibited by or neglect actions required by the Scripture. He must conform to the Word of God else his "authority" oversteps its bounds and loses legitimacy. Elders must first be men under the authority of the Word, then they must lead others from beneath the Bible's rule.

Fourth, those who hold authority must give an account to the Lord. Every elder must "work heartily, as for the Lord" (Col. 3:23) and serve as "men who must give an account" (Heb. 13:17 NIV). Elders are really stewards, and stewards simply manage what belongs to another. A steward has no right to discharge things as he or she sees fit. Rather, they must answer to the owner who for a time allows them the privilege of managing. The elder who serves well can expect a great reward from the Chief Shepherd (1 Pet. 5:4). But the unfaithful steward will be judged strictly (Luke 12:45–47).

Fifth, the congregation is to submit to the proper exercise of authority. The apostles frequently enjoined submission to godly authority. Paul wrote, "We ask you, brothers, to respect those who labor among you and are over you in the Lord and admonish you, and to esteem them very highly in love because of their work" (1 Thess. 5:12–13). The Bible here requires the entire church to submit to the entire eldership. This is important because abusive situations often feature individual leaders taking advantage of individual members. But biblical authority doesn't work that way. Members thrive as they benefit from the collective wisdom and care of the team over them.

Much of the Western world distrusts and disdains authority of any sort. The bumper sticker slogan "question authority" typifies many churchgoers as well. When we adopt that attitude, we deny ourselves the blessing of loving leadership while denying our leaders the blessing of loving support that God intends us both to enjoy. Whenever we find godly and Bible-driven leadership, we should endeavor to strengthen them in their labors.

For the church to thrive, we need both leaders and members who understand the importance and proper use of authority. If one abuses or the other rejects God-ordained authority, the consequence will be pain and death for the local body of Christ.

Gender and Authority: The Role of Women in Church Leadership

One other aspect of realigning biblical authority deserves attention: the role of women. For nearly two hundred years, questions have arisen about the role of black women in the leadership of the Black Church. One of the earliest African-American women preachers was a woman named Elizabeth (1766–1867), who began to preach in 1796. Philadelphia Quakers published her story in 1889. Jarena Lee (1783–185?) offered the first official challenge to restrictions on black women preachers in 1809. Lee appealed to Bethel African Methodist Episcopal Church in Philadelphia for license to preach. Under the leadership of Richard Allen, Bethel refused to grant the request but Lee preached without it.[7]

No black denomination ordained a woman to either of the biblical offices of deacon or elder until the African Methodist Episcopel Zion (AMEZ) Church reversed the traditional stance. Mrs. Julia A. Foote received the double honor of serving as the first ordained deacon (May

1894) and later as the first ordained female elder (1900). Mary J. Small also received ordination as a deacon in 1895. Mrs. Foote and Mrs. Small "became the first women to achieve the rights of full ordination to the ministry by any Methodist denomination, black or white."[8]

Though the AME Church allowed for non-ordained female deacons beginning in 1900, the denomination did not ordain black women until 1948. The Christian Methodist Episcopal Church granted full ordination for women in 1954.

Among the major black Baptist denominations, none officially endorse women's ordination, choosing instead to leave the question of ordination to autonomous local congregations.[9] The largest black Pentecostal denomination, the Church of God in Christ (COGIC), maintains a firm policy against the ordination of women clergy.[10] However, this does not mean Baptist and COGIC congregations are without women pastors. For example, after the death of their male pastor, some COGIC congregations may call the former pastor's wife to continue the work of the ministry. And though National Baptist bodies have no policy on the full ordination of women, many local congregations have ordained black women to pastoral ministry. This practice of "loose coupling" allows denominations to adopt a public position of opposition while local congregations circumvent the policy.[11]

The Womanist/Liberationist Case for Women's Ordination

Should the Black Church reverse its historical opposition to the full ordination of women? Some womanist and liberation academicians and practitioners argue, "Yes." They develop their case along three lines.

A Matter of Justice. Advocates for female ordination consider female leadership a matter of justice and gender oppression yet to be faced by the Black Church. Marcia Y. Riggs, associate professor of Christian ethics at Columbia Theological Seminary in Decatur, Georgia, states the matter thus:

> While justice is a core value of the black church with respect to racist, capitalist oppression, that core value is subverted when men assert patriarchal privilege. Patriarchal privilege has "control of women" as its core value, and this value cannot exist in the same context in which justice is a core value without creating a context that breeds moral corruption.[12]

Demetrius K. Williams has written one of the most extensive treatments of the subject, examining the historical, theological, and exegetical case for female pastoral leadership. For Williams, the matter remains in part an issue of equitable reciprocity: "Are black women worth enough for black men to stand in solidarity with them around the issue of sexism, just as *they* have with us around racism?"[13] Williams thinks the Black Church's support or opposition to women's ordination boils down to consistency and integrity. "Since African American churches were organized and founded upon the biblical principle of 'the equality of all people before God,' which caused them to protest against slavery (classism) and race prejudice (racism), and in order for them to be faithful to their tradition as nonclassist and nonracist institutions (that is, their protest posture against race and class oppression), *they must also become nonsexist institutions.*[14]

An Argument from Historical Reconstruction. A second argument in favor of women's ordination concerns how Christians should read the history of the church over the centuries. Williams reads the history of the Black Church as a failure to live up to its ethic of liberation when it comes to women. Williams attempts to reconstruct the history of both the early church and the Black Church. His revision begins with representing Jesus and Paul as liberators of women and founders of an egalitarian community that later moved to patriarchy and oppression.

> What I have argued in my examination of Jesus and Paul is that their vision of human relations was rooted in a worldview that sought to equalize human social structures and relationships. Their view opened the possibilities especially for women, who in several early churches were considered equal to men: some were revered as prophets, and others acted as teachers, traveling evangelists, healers, priests, and even apostles. This was rooted in a paradigm based on the saying "in Christ . . . there is neither male nor female."[15]

Despite this start, Williams sees the church adopting suppressive practices toward women.

> But after 200 C.E. there is little or no evidence for women taking prophetic, priestly, and episcopal roles among proto-orthodox churches. This is an extraordinary transition from the earliest phase of Christian leadership patterns among women and

men because, despite the previous public activity of Christian
women, the majority of Christian churches in the second century
aligned with the burgeoning wing of "middle-class" leadership
in opposing the move toward equality. By the second century,
an increasing number of Christian communities endorsed as
canonical the Pastoral letters and household codes, which stressed
willing subordination to oppressive trends in society "out of love
for Christ." As I have argued, such views probably represented
neither Jesus' nor Paul's views. Nevertheless, the views of the
emerging proto-orthodox leaders were gaining ground and
were finding support in many "orthodox" communities. Yet
exceptions occurred.[16]

According to Williams's view, the problem occurred with a move
to what he calls "proto-orthodox" or "orthodox" positions. Though he
never defines what is meant by "proto-orthodox" or "orthodox," Professor
Williams sees a parallel move in the development of the African-American
church.

An important parallel now emerges between the early Christian
churches and African American churches. Faced with new
and difficult challenges of northern migration, pervasive racist
repression, and the need for ecclesiastical maintenance, Paul's
letters (especially the deutero-Paulines, the Pastorals) and legacy,
along with the household codes, receive a second life, that is, a
new assessment and appreciation in black churches. As in the early
church these texts are used in the process of institution building.
Black churches, like early Christian churches, required a source or
body of writings that could serve as a model for its institutional
endeavors. In addition, black churches were also trying to make a
favorable showing to those on the outside (cf. 1 Tim. 3:7; 1 Pet.
2:12). While there were egalitarian trends in early Christianity and
in the early black religious tradition that the black church could
have appropriated, they instead opted for a patriarchal model for
their ecclesiastical structure; authority in the church and family
rested squarely within the domain of males.[17]

According to Williams's historical-critical reading, the full ordination of black women would simply return the Black Church to the practices of equality and freedom founded by Jesus and Paul.

An Argument from Biblical Interpretation. A third argument in favor of women's ordination involves approaches to the reliability and interpretation of the Bible. How should the various biblical texts which seem to prohibit women pastors be regarded and handled? How do advocates for women clergy respond to these passages of Scripture? Most commentators recognize that Paul's writings present a thorny interpretive issue.

Demetrius Williams summarizes the range of approaches to relevant Pauline texts. "Some contemporary black biblical scholars and theologians have perceived almost unequivocal liberating potential in Paul's thought . . . while others have taken a *via media* with respect to the liberating potential of Paul's thought, recognizing his ambivalence and ambiguity in matters of class and sex. Others have viewed Paul's thought, at best, as conservative and useless to the cause of human freedom and hence to be dispensed without further ado." As Williams sees it, the difficulty occurs because "In both cases, one has to confront Paul's ambivalence on the important matters of human freedom and oppression."[18] In these approaches to the Scripture, people assume the freedom to discard portions of the Bible they think historically or culturally outdated or portions with which they disagree.

Some reject the authority and inerrancy of the Bible altogether. According to Dr. Daphne C. Wiggins, associate pastor and former assistant professor of congregational studies at Duke Divinity School, "Womanists are not wed to biblical authority that is predicated on the Bible's being inerrant or infallible."[19] For example, Renita J. Weems considers the Bible "a thoroughly political document" and calls for "an analysis of the biblical worldview, specifically its claim to be unique, different, and elect." Weems professes, "It is our stubborn faith that even our small, uncelebrated, but persistent acts of hermeneutical insubordination will eventually topple kingdoms," by which she means oppressive racial, class, and gender kingdoms in church and society.[20]

Another approach to interpreting the Bible involves dividing Paul against himself. In part, Williams uses this strategy in order to reconstruct what he considers to be the authentic and historical Paul. Relying heavily on biblical criticism and theologically liberal approaches to Scripture, Williams separates the Pauline letters into two classes: authentic and pseudo. He assigns all New Testament passages that support distinctions in gender roles to a period following the death of all the apostles and to an author unknown to Paul and the early church. Meanwhile, he attributes passages that support egalitarianism to the apostle himself. Dividing the Pauline corpus this way allows Williams to reject the texts that most clearly prohibit female leadership (1 Tim. 2:11–15 and 1 Cor. 14:33–36) while simultaneously casting Paul as an egalitarian liberator of women rather than an oppressor of women as often maintained.[21]

Based on a call for justice, historical reconstruction, and either a rejection or reinterpretation of biblical texts that seem to limit women's ordination, advocates of female church leadership call for a reversal of the Black Church's historical stance. But is that the proper Christian response to and use of the Bible?

Engaging the Womanist Perspective on Women's Ordination

Supporters of women's ordination raise many challenges that deserve reply. Many of the book-length arguments, like Demetrius Williams's fine work, deserve book-length responses in turn. While such a full response remains beyond the limitations of this book, we can outline a brief direction for resolving questions of gender and authority in the Black Church.

Responding to Justice Appeals. Without question, women have sometimes been abused and repressed in church settings and by professing Christians. The cause of justice for women *must* be upheld by God's people. Any attempt to restrict the legitimate freedoms and ministries of women must be met with honest, serious, aggressive, and loving rebuke and correction—sometimes including legal action. Christians, in the name of Christ, must oppose every form of injustice wherever and whenever we find it.

But ought we to think of the Bible's teaching on gender roles as necessarily oppressive and unjust? Many proponents of women's ordination think so. But are they representative of women in general? Daphne C. Wiggin's qualitative interviews with African-American women in two Southern congregations reveal female ambivalence toward the issue. Wiggins found that most "women are not taking an active role in instituting structural changes concerning women in their denominations." She documented "a general lack of preoccupation with the issue of female clergy among the group" and "no organized support among these women for female ordination." Wiggins concluded that "The absence of female clergy in the church is not regarded as a justice issue or a question of sexism. . . ."²² It would seem that proponents of women holding authority as pastors in a local congregation remain a minority, even among women. We should be careful not to automatically dismiss a concern because a minority of persons holds to it. Sometimes minorities have seen an issue more clearly than the masses. However, when, in this case, the claims to injustice are not even made by most of the group assumed to be oppressed, we should hesitate to reassign church authority on so slim a basis.

The argument from "justice" ignores several vital facts. First, if God exists as our Creator then He certainly has the right to order our lives and to determine who may serve in which capacities. The Holy Spirit sovereignly gives gifts as He chooses (1 Cor. 12:11). That God distributes His own gifts as He pleases ought not be regarded as unjust since He owns us and in Him is no darkness at all (1 John 1:5). Second, the appeals to justice seem to confuse *being* with *function*, ontology with role. A difference in role does not mean or even suggest a difference in value, belonging, or importance. Only one man can play quarterback on a football team, but that does not denigrate the ten others who play different roles. Most womanist and feminist appeals to justice make the mistake of regarding *any* distinction as inherently inferior. But that ignores the fact that while men and women are different, they are also equal. Distinction does *not* imply superiority or inferiority. We find the same reality in the Trinity itself. The Father, Son, and Holy Spirit play different roles in our redemption (Eph. 1), but each member of the Trinity is fully and equally God. Our differing gender roles reflect that basic intra-Trinitarian reality.

Responding to Historical Theories. Moreover, the attempt to rest women's ordination on historical reconstructions relies too heavily on human imagination. Consider, for example, the historical reconstruction from Demetrius Williams quoted earlier. Williams writes with certainty and clarity, but provides no footnotes, citations, original source material or evidence to support his view of history. The entire reconstruction depends on the existence of early Christian communities Williams *imagines* to be "behind" the text of Scripture. Not surprisingly, when scholars imagine such groups hidden "behind" the text, those communities happen to think and act a lot like the scholars themselves. With these kinds of reconstructions, there's always the danger of evoking a past that confirms our present positions, a kind of confirmation bias that simply serves our own interests. If such divergent communities existed in the early church, we would expect the biblical writers to address these factions since they spend so much time addressing factions and false teachers throughout the New Testament (see, for example, 1 Cor. 1–2; 1 Tim. 1; Gal. 1; and 1 John 4). We might especially expect this in the case of women's ordination given how often the writers define the role of women in the Scripture (for example, 1 Cor. 11:3–16; 14:33–36; 1 Tim. 2; and Titus 2). In the final analysis, imaginative reconstructions of history lack compelling evidence to justify ignoring or abandoning the biblical texts as we have them. Better to trust the eyewitness accounts of the Bible than to trust the undocumented theories of people who live two thousand years later.

Responding to Biblical Interpretations. Finally, we ought to consider the claims for women's ordination based on biblical teaching. Any attempt to simply discard the Bible, to challenge its integrity, or declare it irrelevant means that such persons or churches are not centered on the Bible. Attempts to divide the canon of Scripture between Pauline and so-called "deutero-Pauline" writings—even while privileging parts of Paul's letters—implicitly rejects the inspiration, integrity, and authority of the Bible as a whole. A hermeneutics of suspicion might best be regarded as simple unbelief.

Better to "Let God be true, and every man a liar" (Rom. 3:4 NIV) than to imagine ourselves more truthful and knowledgeable than our all-knowing Lord. Better to trust the Scripture and submit to it even when it's difficult, than to only trust and submit to the parts we find favorable. If we only embrace the favorable, we'll soon find ourselves embracing fewer and fewer texts because the "living and active" Word of God has a way of sharply piercing and judging "the thoughts and attitudes of the heart" (Heb. 4:12 NIV). Selective acceptance of the Bible is the slow path to a more complete rejection of God and His Word.

The authority of God's Word must remain unimpeached, including its authority to determine which persons may lawfully serve as pastors in the church. This means we need to rightly understand the meaning of particular texts and then order ourselves under those texts as servants to the living God. When we turn to specific texts of Scripture, the question of who can legitimately exercise pastoral authority in the church finds a clear answer. Let's examine two passages: 1 Timothy 2:11–15 and 1 Corinthians 11:3–16.

1 Timothy 2:11–15. The clearest text addressing women and authority in the local church is 1 Timothy 2:11–12, which reads: "Let a woman learn quietly with all submissiveness. I do not permit a woman to teach or to exercise authority over a man; rather, she is to remain quiet." The apostle's instruction has both a positive and a negative side. Positively, women are to learn as fellow disciples in the company of the entire church. Most contemporary debates of women's roles overlook the radical nature of this statement. We must note the positive inclusion of women in Christian discipleship. "Let a woman learn. . . ." The spiritual education of women was a Christian innovation, bringing greater attention to their spiritual needs. Yet, Paul specifically forbids women teaching or exercising authority over men, which should be understood as pastoral authority over the entire church. Under the inspiration of the Holy Spirit, Paul restricts pastoral authority—not to men as a class—but to *spiritually qualified men only* (1 Tim. 3:1–7). Women should learn, but they should avoid usurping authority over the congregation.

Some commonly think Paul's prohibition rests on first-century prejudices and attitudes. But Paul grounds his instruction not in the social conventions of his time but in the creation order itself. He writes, "For Adam was formed first, then Eve; and Adam was not deceived, but the woman was deceived and became a transgressor" (1 Tim. 2:13–14). In appealing to the very first man and woman, Paul bases gender roles in the church on an ideal that transcends time, place, and culture. This ideal has been distorted by man's fall into sin. But the New Testament's teaching on gender roles begins to restore the Edenic order and goodness of creation before sin entered the world (Eph. 4:23–24). This is not injustice; rather, it is the reclaiming of the goodness of manhood and womanhood as God originally designed it.

1 Corinthians 11:3–16. Perhaps 1 Timothy 2:11–15 helps us understand the knotty teaching of 1 Corinthians 11:3–16. In that passage, Paul addresses the public worship practices of the Corinthians, specifically the matters of head coverings, authority, public prayers, and prophecies offered by women. The apostle appeals to the relationship between the Father and the Son as well as the creation account to resolve the issue. He writes, in part:

> Now I want you to realize that the head of every man is Christ, and the head of the woman is man, and the head of Christ is God. . . . A man ought not to cover his head, since he is the image and glory of God; but the woman is the glory of man. For man did not come from woman, but woman from man; neither was man created for woman, but woman for man. For this reason, and because of the angels, the woman ought to have a sign of authority on her head. In the Lord, however, woman is not independent of man, nor is man independent of woman. For as woman came from man, so also man is born of woman. But everything comes from God. (1 Cor. 11:3, 7–12 NIV)

Verse 3 establishes the principle of headship and submission by appealing to the relationship of the Father and the Son, Jesus Christ. Verse 7 reminds us that headship and submission are tied up with honor or glory and its opposite, shame. In verses 8–9, Paul further reinforces this pattern of relationship by appealing to the order and purpose of creation—the man was created first and the woman came from man, and the woman was created as a helper for man. As a consequence a sign of authority should be maintained (v. 10), showing the woman's submission to and honoring of her husband. Nevertheless, this order of relationship and authority does not imply inferiority or independence. Rather, verses 11–12 establish the equality of worth and mutual dependence of man and woman. Though the first woman came from man, all men are born of women. And everyone comes from God who is Creator of all.

Efforts to reject these passages as irrelevent or outdated fail to honor and interpret the passages correctly. First Corinthians 11:3–16, and other passages like it, continue to be authoritative and relevant. New Testament scholar Anthony C. Thiselton summarizes the issue quite well:

> This passage [1 Cor. 11:3–16] is not merely relative to a dated context in the ancient world, as if it had no further relevance. Throughout history the choice of attire and dress codes has carried a symbolic as well as a literal significance. In Roman society the wearing of hoods (or veils, or some parallel symbolic

expression) marked a married woman as both "respectable" and deserving of respect. In this passage, moreover, Paul addresses *both* man *and* woman, not simply woman alone, in terms of a mutual and reciprocal respect each for the other gender, for the self (self-respect), and also for God, the focus of public worship. . . . It is a travesty of this serious passage to reduce it to a matter of "wearing hats," or to construe Paul's evenhanded theology of mutuality into supposed misogyny or patriarchalism.[23]

Authority can be and sometimes *is* abused, including abuses along gender lines. We should protect the dignity, strength, beauty, honor, intelligence, and gifts of our sisters inside and outside the church. The uniqueness of femininity must be extolled and promoted in order that women of God might flourish as God intends.

However, full feminine flourishing requires exercising gifts and abilities *within the bounds and limits that God establishes.* For all God's ways are right and good, even the ways He chooses to limit us. An earthly parent imperfectly sets bounds for the protection of their children. We recognize such boundary-setting as a necessary aspect of parental love. Our heavenly Father perfectly sets bounds for the protection of His children. We should recognize those boundaries as the expression of a perfect love that guards and blesses His church.

Women should use their gifts widely in the church and on the mission field. The range of teaching opportunities and evangelistic opportunities are actually quite plentiful. The Great Commission or Missionary Mandate of Matthew 28:18–20 applies equally to women. And the call to make disciples finds a particular application that only women can fulfill in Titus 2:3–5. When the church erects fences to protect authority, it should be careful not to build the fence in its neighbor's yard, taking away freedoms that Christ gives. But, the church must recognize that its health and vitality depend on such fences, which ought to be respected for the blessing of all.

Conclusion

We live in an age that stubbornly questions authority. We suspect power. The world knows its fair share of dictators and power mongers. Truth be told, we know of horror stories in the church as well. When the church abuses or misuses authority, it resembles the leaders and rulers of this world who do not know God. The church's witness is hurt and the world loses the much-needed display of human flourishing that results from joining healthy authority with love for the benefit of others.

So, the realignment of authority in the Black Church is an urgent issue. We need to see authority assigned to the correct office (elders), distributed to the correct men (a plurality of qualified elders), exercised within the bounds of Scripture (the ultimate authority), and used to serve the women of our churches rather than usurped by a few. When that happens, not only will our churches thrive but they'll model the beautiful intra-Trinitarian dynamic of love, headship, submission, equality, and purpose. Lord, hasten the day when all Your churches fully embrace Your vision of love and authority!

CHAPTER 8

Remove Ungodly Leaders

Do not entertain an accusation against an elder unless it is brought by
two or three witnesses. Those who sin are to be rebuked publicly, so that
others may take warning.
—1 TIMOTHY 5:19–20 (NIV)

Introduction

For decades now, news of Catholic priests abusing young boys
has sent the Roman Catholic Church and Catholic parishes across the
United States reeling. Early responses from bishops and Catholic Church
officials were case studies in denial, political spin, blaming the victim,
and enabling the accused. As time went on more families came forward,
more priests were implicated, and more lawsuits filed. Meanwhile many
victims and their families continued to be dissatisfied with Catholic
Church responses and perpetrators escaped censure. The country watched
in horror, then fumbled for explanations and remedies focused on celibacy
requirements, reporting systems, and clergy training.

The abuse appeared systemic, with cases emerging in Germany, the
Netherlands, Austria, Belgium, and Ireland.[1] The scandal thus far has
cost Roman Catholic parishes in the U.S. an estimated two billion dollars
in settlements alone,[2] not including legal fees and property closings. Costs

to the Catholic Church in public worldwide reputation and personal relationships cannot be calculated.

But what would be the cost of clergy scandal if we also included denominations and communions other than the Roman Catholic Church? What toll would be paid if we included adultery, misappropriation, and embezzlement of funds to the list of infractions? The damage to the cause of Christ defies the power of imagination.

As quiet as it's kept, the Black Church has suffered its share of abuses and scandals. In fact, one of the major impediments to the Black Church's mission in the community is the perception—sometimes based on actual events—that pastors only want money or sleep around with the women of the church. Many in the black community would rather reject or avoid the church rather than submit to predatory leaders. If staying away or acquiescing were the only alternatives, then staying away would certainly be the correct choice.

However, there's another option, a way to simultaneously revive the Black Church's reputation and improve its effectiveness. Remove ungodly leaders.

As Quiet as It Used to Be Kept

Black congregations tend to love their pastors—sometimes to a fault. The congregation's love and appreciation can be most misguided when challenged by a beloved leader's failure to keep the biblical requirements of the pastoral office. During the ordeal and in its aftermath, a range of emotions—from stunned silence, to frustration, confusion, and anger—keep a local church in disbelief and limbo. Overwhelmed by the furor ignited by scandal, most churches and members seem unable to cope apart from a commitment to silence.

The conspiracy of silence has existed for a long time. Veteran pastor Dr. Jeremiah A. Wright Jr. shares a telling anecdote regarding pastoral immorality during his teen years.

> I was eighteen years old; I was a college freshman and sophomore. This was my first time away from home. This was during the period of my life when I was exposed (for the first time) to the underside (or the seedy side) of the Black Church and hypocritical Black preachers.

My father was a Black preacher, but my father was "cut from the same cloth" as my maternal grandfather, uncle, John B. Henderson, and my mentor, Samuel DeWitt Proctor. My father did not drink. He did not smoke cigarettes. He did not chase women, and he was a seminary graduate.

I soon discovered that my dad and my mother's dad, my mother's brothers, and Dr. Proctor were the glowing "exceptions to the rule" when it came to Black preachers in America in the late 1950s and the early 1960s. That was a turbulent time for me![3]

Silence, hushed tones, and knowing nods historically shielded such immorality and scandal from public view and censure. This helps explain why someone with as rich a family and church legacy as Dr. Wright did not encounter "the seedy side" of the Black Church until he was away from home in his late teens and early twenties. Once, such scandals could go relatively unnoticed.

However, today's Internet and social media technologies make the most private acts very public. High-profile pastors can expect high-profile exposure of their misconduct. In the mercy of God, moral corruption and failure—what Jeremiah Wright called "the seedy side" of the Black Church—cannot be as easily hidden from public view. Examples abound.

In the late 1990s, Henry Lyons, then president of the National Baptist Convention (NBC) USA, the nation's largest historically black Christian denomination, came to public notice for an adulterous relationship and a lavish lifestyle financed with embezzled denomination funds. Rather than immediate resignation or removal, Lyons fought against the charges and fought for his position as denominational chief, even receiving at one point a vote of confidence from other denomination leaders.

For a while, it seemed no evidence would bring Lyons's church and the denomination to oppose him. As one journalist put it:

> It did not seem to matter that prosecutors had built a mountain of evidence against him, proving that Mr. Lyons, president of the National Baptist Convention, U.S.A., Inc., had even stolen money, about $250,000, donated to rebuild burned black churches.

It did not seem to matter that prosecutors had proved, with a paper trail of his own signatures, that he had sold out the good name of the convention, that he had made $4 million from peddling that influence and then used that money to live in a style that included luxury cars, waterfront property and mistresses.

Even as prosecutors presented their most incriminating evidence, his home church here seemed united behind him, the convention did not formally call for his resignation, and religious leaders, from as close as Tampa Bay and as far as Gary, Ind., filled the courthouse pews in support.[4]

Eventually Lyons was convicted on state charges of racketeering and grand theft, federal charges of fraud and tax evasion, and was divorced by his wife.[5] After serving nearly five years in prison, Lyons received a pastorate at New Salem Missionary Baptist Church in Tampa, Florida, and garnered the support of at least one hundred local churches in a failed bid to regain his position as leader of the National Baptist Convention USA. Supporters called attention to Lyons's organizational skills and dynamic leadership and evoked the theme of forgiveness and reconciliation.[6]

A decade after the Lyons scandal, Bishop Eddie L. Long, pastor of Atlanta-based megachurch New Birth Missionary Baptist Church, faced allegations of sexual misconduct with young boys. After months of denials and legal wrangling, Long settled lawsuits out of court for an undisclosed sum of money.[7] Following the legal actions and a brief hiatus from the pulpit, Long resumed his duties as pastor of New Birth. While some members left the church, many others remained and embraced Long's leadership. At one point following the settlement, Long was even "crowned" a "king" by Jewish Rabbi Ralph Messer. The apparently impromptu ceremony featured several men parading Long on their shoulders around the church "enthroned" in a high-back chair. The entire incident revealed a stunning lack of discernment and biblical knowledge on the congregation's behalf. Long later apologized for the crowning episode, but no such demonstrations of remorse or repentance have been given in the sex abuse scandal.

The pattern of silence, confusion, lack of discernment, and continued clergy failure gets repeated in smaller congregations with lesser known and unknown pastors. I recall the brokenness in my mother's voice when she told me that a pastor in my hometown had been accused of an adulterous relationship with my nephew's wife. My nephew, around twenty years old at the time, was understandably distraught at the betrayal of both his young wife and the man they called "pastor." My brother, not a Christian, was enraged by the devastation brought upon his son and daughter-in-law. Their tender marriage did not survive, but the pastor remains in the pulpit over a decade later. Their story and others like it get repeated on local television stations across the country. These tragedies span denominations, regions, and church size.

We may be grateful to God that most African-American pastors and churches are not embroiled in controversy and moral failure. That's easy to forget when the latest scandal is breaking news. But the many situations that do exist teach us that a few bad apples spoil the reputation of the Black Church. With congregations unaware and unprepared to fulfill their responsibilities wolves easily enter in and feed upon the sheep. We must be clear-eyed about the refusal of men like Lyons and Long to resign pastoral posts willingly and quietly. The church needs to remember that a person does not have to admit to transgressions in order to be disqualified for the ministry. The Bible lists failure to be "above reproach" and to "have a good reputation with outsiders" (1 Tim. 3:2, 7 NIV) as reason enough to warrant their removal.

One Bad Apple: The Effect of Leadership Misconduct on Members

While media attention zooms in on embattled pastors and their families, the most devastating effects of clergy misconduct are seen in the lives of church members. Clergy misconduct is not a victimless crime. Individuals and entire congregations suffer from the misdeeds of appointed leaders. The results of misconduct vary in scope and intensity. For instance, case studies and clinical interventions on clergy sexual misconduct "suggest that the results for the offended include self-blame; shame; loss of community and friends if forced to relocate either to escape the community's judgment or to escape an angry offender who has been discovered or reported; spiritual crisis and loss of faith; family crisis and divorce; psychological distress, including depression and post-traumatic stress disorder; physiological illness; and failed or successful suicide attempts."[8] In view of this litany of negative social and psychological effects, perhaps the best word to describe the aftermath of clergy misconduct would be "carnage."

In addition, clergy misconduct can negatively affect how church members understand and respond to past clergy offenses. First, the misconduct diminishes a congregation's expectations of pastors and leaders. Second, the misconduct paralyzes members between the competing biblical demands of accountability and forgiveness. Diminished expectations and paralysis, in turn, cripple the ability of members to rightly interpret and respond to the failures of its leaders.

Daphne C. Wiggins illustrates this problem by documenting the reaction of African-American women to clergy scandal in black churches.[9] Wiggins reports an interview she conducted with "Rosalind," whose response so well represents the reactions of many church members it's worth quoting Wiggins's summary at length.

> Rosalind, who joined the church aware of the past controversy surrounding the pastor, spoke of its impact on her as very slight, but she had not dismissed it altogether. "I wasn't there. I was aware of it, but I didn't get involved in it. I mean, [name of friend] is very close to Reverend King, so, uh, she kept me informed about what had happened and all that kind of stuff, but I don't get involved in politics in church." As I inquired as to whether she had been at all hesitant to join the church once she had this information, she quickly replied, "Nope, it was about the message, it was about what I felt at that church as a whole. So that never bothered me." She not only made her peace with these revelations; she had also reconciled knowledge of two other incidents of clergy misconduct. One concerned a pastor accused of mismanagement of funds and an extramarital relationship; the other concerned her encounter with a pastor during her teenage years. In this latter situation, she had fended off his sexual advances as he chased her around his office. The pastor was the individual who allocated the church's scholarship funds to high school students, and, in her estimation, she was later denied a scholarship because she had not given in to his sexual advances. Rosalind, who spoke matter-of-factly about these past incidents,

could be called a realist. She stated, "I don't get involved so much [in the politics of the church]. I'm not surprised at stuff that goes on in church, among human beings. We are still human beings." She never stopped going to church because of these incidents. She even spoke of extending forgiveness to those pastors.[10]

Rosalind's story reveals how church members can persist in attendance and support despite multiple experiences of clergy misconduct. Her response minimizes the scandals as "church politics" while marginalizing and disenfranchising herself as a bystander. Rosalind seems to allow the pastor's gifts in preaching and other strengths of the church to weaken her indignation and concern for the pastor's immoral behavior and character.

On the one hand, we must commend her persevering commitment to the Lord and His people despite the troubles of the church. But, on the other hand, *we ought never settle for moral failures and abuses outlawed by both the Bible and the state.* We ought to seek the revitalization of churches in order to benefit and bless the many "Rosalinds" who might be tempted to "settle" for less-than-biblical leadership and care. It is simply unacceptable for a teenage girl to be chased around her pastor's office and sexually blackmailed in exchange for a small scholarship. While we commend Rosalind's strength to resist and to push forward spiritually, she should not have to face such wickedness in the first place. The church's ineffectiveness at dealing with ungodly leaders turns the church into a hen house for predators rather than a haven for the weary.

Of course, women are not the only members of the community scandalized by ungodly Christian leaders. We need to seek healthier churches for the benefit of African-American boys and men as well. Some African-American pastors and observers of the church see a connection between the prevalence of clergy scandals and the absence of black men in church life.[11] Wiggins speculated that unaddressed misconduct hinders the participation of African-American men in the Black Church. She writes:

> Most religious communities expect a more stringent code of moral behavior from the clergy than from the membership. In reality, however, it seems that a lower standard of behavior for clergy is all too easily accepted. This has been particularly frustrating for men who are concerned that the clergy are forgiven for behaviors that are unacceptable for other men inside

or outside the church. Men are disconcerted by what appears to be a double standard that allows male pastors to violate the norms by carousing, womanizing, drinking, or gambling. They also believe the shortcomings of male ministers are forgiven by a largely female audience, while other men's indiscretions and "failures" are not and are not taken in equal stride. The church stands under indictment by some black men for its reluctance to admonish, correct, and restore those within its own ranks. Consequently, the folklore of clergy misconduct quietly undermines and diminishes the church's symbolic role as a haven, a locus of spiritual sustenance, and standard bearer for those outside (and inside) its walls.[12]

Unaddressed clergy sin affects everyone involved—members and nonmembers, adults and children, women and men, sheep and shepherds. Black churches should indeed have a double standard for its leaders—but it should be a *higher* expectation for godliness, maturity, and loving protection. Anything less cannot be legitimately called "Christian" and the effects of undisciplined indiscretion remains nothing short of devastating.

Removing Unqualified and Ungodly Leaders

Wherever misconduct goes unaddressed, it eventually hinders the work of Christ in that place. Serious steps need to be taken to protect the church from unscrupulous and unqualified men. But how might a congregation seeking revived health and effectiveness remove an ungodly leader? Three suggestions could frame congregational responses—prevention, removal, and restoration.[13]

An Ounce of Prevention: Never Place Unqualified or Ungodly Men in the Office

The best way to "remove" ungodly leaders is to never call or ordain them in the first place. An ounce of bad leadership prevention is worth a pound of scandal cure. Avoiding poor leadership selection requires understanding ministerial calling, leader selection, and a lot of patient discernment.

The phone call I received from my mother telling me of the conflict between my nephew and his pastor came just a few short months after a previous call. I remember her excitement in that first call. She wanted to let me know the family was about to have another preacher in its ranks. My then eighteen-year-old nephew would be preaching his trial sermon in a few Sundays. I choked back my surprise and sheepishly joined her in the celebration. Though I didn't know the church intending to license my nephew, I did know my nephew and wondered to myself whether they'd carefully examined his spiritual qualification and gifting.

A couple weeks later I had my answer. My family nestled into a wooden pew and joined the vibrant service already in progress. After several joyful songs, a few words of welcome, obligatory announcements, and a couple more songs, my nephew took the pulpit. He began in a rather official tone and cadence, typical to many black sermons but oddly formal for the young man that played video games in my apartment during summer breaks. A few minutes later he warmed to his topic, which I can't remember now, and a few minutes more he was ablaze with whoopin' and studied gesticulations. It was over in about twenty minutes. He took his seat. I smiled as I recalled one of my mother's encouragements to preachers: "Make 'em happy when you get up and happy when you sit down." We were happy he'd sat down.

Later that evening my nephew visited my mother's house, still wearing his new suit from that afternoon and carrying a large hardbound Bible. He began to ask me questions about the Scripture and to seek my feedback on his preaching. I wish I'd had more courage during that conversation. I would have told him, despite his eagerness, that I didn't think he was prepared for life as a licensed minister and that he lacked spiritual maturity for the charge. That would have been the loving thing to do. I might even have questioned the wisdom of a pastor that would license a boy preacher with barely any knowledge of the Bible's content. Had I been more courageous then, it might have saved him the pain he would suffer just a few months later.

It's not uncommon to meet a lot of persons in the ministry or aspiring to the ministry with little more qualification than their claim to be "called." They insist that they should serve because of an irresistible, inward, subjective burden to preach and lead. Sometimes these individuals elevate their sense of "calling" well above the perspectives and considerations of others. Their feelings—not the Scripture or the church—become the sole mandate for thrusting themselves into pastoral roles. Many of these persons reveal by their insistence that they either don't understand a calling or that they don't really possess one.

Samuel DeWitt Proctor and Gardner C. Taylor summarize well the problem with jealously grasping after the reins of leadership. "To undertake such a vocation for light and transient reasons, *to use it as a quick leap to prominence or as gratification for a boundless and pathological egocentricity is to profane it.* Persons who are pursuing answers to life's most imponderable questions, who are sorting out alternate lifestyles and competing paths to fulfillment, who are yearning for fellowship and conciliation with God, who are seeking strength sufficient to follow Jesus deserve to find something better than an impostor masquerading as God's servant."[14]

Historically, Christians have understood that a calling consists of two parts—the individual's personal, subjective desire *along with* the external congregational confirmation. Where one or the other was missing, no calling could be assumed.[15] The external congregational ordination acts as a check and balance against lone rangers usurping leadership authority without meeting biblical qualifications or youthful upstarts thrusting themselves into ministry. Confirming a person's qualifications, gifts, and calling is, therefore, one of the congregation's most important responsibilities. This is why the Bible demands that churches "not be hasty in the laying on of hands" (1 Tim. 5:22). Patience and prudence must prevail over pushiness and personal persuasion. Fulfilling this responsibility protects the church and the cause of Christ from the disrepute and reproach of ungodly men.

The best way to "remove" an unqualified or ungodly leader continues to be to never appoint them to the office in the first place.[16]

In the Presence of Two or Three Witnesses: Removing Disqualified Leaders Once in Office

Of course, perfect prevention of immorality and sin cannot be achieved on this side of glory. Even churches that faithfully carry out their responsibility in calling leaders may later discover that they missed something or that solid leaders sometimes fail miserably. "The sins of some men are obvious, reaching the place of judgment ahead of them; the sins of others trail behind them" (1 Tim. 5:24 NIV). In such cases, action needs to be taken to remove leaders who disqualify themselves.

Leading the church is not a right. Giftedness does not indicate fitness. Even swelling crowds is no indication that God approves of a man and his ministry. Some of the world's most notorious cult leaders have been surrounded by throngs of fawning followers. As Daphne Wiggins observes:

> To a significant degree, African American clergy still attract followers by the power of their charismatic leadership. In contrast to mainline denominations, which embed ecclesiastical authority in the office and the hierarchy of the church, a unique effervescence, effective leadership, and charisma are the attributes that maintain clerics in African American pulpits. The independent organizational structures of many black denominations mean that there is no formal process or extra-congregational authority to appeal to when one encounters accusations against a pastor. This leaves the responsibility for investigation and adjudication to the laity.[17]

If Wiggins is correct, then church offices must be protected from too high a valuation of a leader's gifts, personality, and following. No matter the gifts, popularity, leadership charisma, and apparent success, the Black Church must remove unqualified, ungodly, and fallen leaders from her offices.

Some churches and members will find it very difficult to remove disqualified leaders when situations require. But we must do this if our ultimate concern is the glory of Jesus Christ in the life of our local church and if we're concerned to obey God's Word. As Dr. John MacArthur puts it, "Gross sin among Christian leaders is a signal that something is seriously wrong with the church. But an even greater problem is lowering the standards to accommodate a leader's sin."[18]

The apostle Paul provides the biblical basis for removing leaders in 1 Timothy 5:19–20. He writes: "Do not admit a charge against an elder except on the evidence of two or three witnesses. As for those who persist in sin, rebuke them in the presence of all, so that the rest may stand in fear." Paul's instruction provides a brief procedural outline for establishing a man's sin and possible disqualification. First, fellow elders must not listen to charges leveled without evidence. Paul harkens to the Old Testament requirement that two or three witnesses corroborate an accusation. These "witnesses" must stand as co-accusers in the situation. The other elders act as a church court, weighing the evidence and rendering a judgment of the fellow elder's conduct and fitness for ministry.

Requiring charges to be established by multiple witnesses helps protect church leaders from unfair and unfounded accusation. However, leaders found guilty through corroborated accusations are to be rebuked "in the presence of all." Because a leader has a public role, their persistent sin must be publicly censored. Here, I think Paul has in mind the kinds of sins that would disqualify a man from Christian leadership (1 Tim. 3:1–13). Having been appointed as a public example of godly character, a man who fails to live such an example must be publicly rebuked and removed from office. The erring pastor's removal positively benefits the congregation, who learns to "stand in fear" of our holy God. Sin has consequences and hypocrisy is damnable. We should tolerate unrepentant sin and hypocrisy least of all in Christian leaders.

Some Practical Considerations When Removing a Fallen Leader

The process for actually effecting the removal is as important as the decision to remove a fallen or disqualified pastor. A few procedural principles can help make the difficult task of removal more effective and healthier for the congregation and the fallen.

First, congregations and denominations should establish very clear and strict policies for defining and sanctioning clergy misconduct. Some denominations have general policies but fail to specify sanctions or procedures. Many others, especially traditions that prize the autonomy of local congregations, have very little in the way of policies or guidance for churches to use. If a church makes hiring and firing decisions independent of denominational hierarchy, then conscientious pastors and informed church members should ensure their local churches stipulate in their bylaws, handbooks, personnel manuals, and employment contracts the biblical grounds for disqualifying and removing pastors. Not only should the policies and procedures be established, but they must also be dutifully followed in order to protect the church. The Catholic Church maintained policies and procedures during the entire period of the pedophile scandal. Those documents did little to protect children and families because they were not enforced.

Second, during and after reports of clergy misconduct, congregations should look to the plurality of leaders overseeing the church instead of looking solely to a senior pastor. One important benefit of plural leadership is its ability to keep a flock shepherded and tended during crisis. Multiple gifted and qualified elders at the helm, exercising and enjoying mutual responsibility for one another and the church as a whole, greatly improve the chances of properly correcting an erring leader and pursuing just biblical responses. Their role should be clearly defined in policies and procedures for correcting and removing erring leaders. Because they function as peers, they're able to engage other leaders from a position of authority. Because they're multiple in number, they're also able to outweigh and overturn a charismatic leader's actions through their collective strength. So, it's imperative that churches adopt the biblical model of plural leadership (see chapter 7), learn to support each man's ministry and authority during times of peace, and welcome their oversight in times of scandal and distress. Trusting a leadership team of multiple elders sharing authority can mean the difference between stunned silence and confusion or following the voice of the Chief Shepherd during a trying period of clergy failure.

Third, church leaders and congregations should resist the temptation to have accused or convicted pastors speak publicly to the congregation. Scandalized pastors often appear before their congregations shedding tears, vowing to fight the "slanderous charges" being brought against them, or pleading for forgiveness for their transgressions. Who can forget the weeping Jim Bakkers and Jimmy Swaggarts crooning out confessions to television cameras and large audiences? In the same way, Eddie Long stood before the members of New Birth vowing to fight the "slander" of his accusers and in the process waged a public campaign to sway the church's opinion and support. Because of the pastor's ability to manipulate and the congregation's vulnerability to division, public statements before or during an investigation are highly inappropriate. Some will feel such a measure is unfair to the pastor charged. But, in fact, victims are most often the persons who experience unfairness, stigma, and retaliation while misbehaving leaders receive lenient responses. Keep in mind that the fallen pastor has already proven himself to be morally disqualified; congregations cannot expect him to suddenly behave uprightly during the height of his scandal. Keeping the pastor from the microphone protects victims, congregations, and pastors from inflammatory and misleading public comments.

Restore Very Carefully and Slowly[19]

When a congregation successfully removes a fallen leader from leadership, their work is still not complete. One remaining question congregations and denominational officials must answer is, "Can a fallen pastor be returned to pastoral leadership?" Answering the question is not as easy a task as one might imagine. Sometimes competing biblical values collide in efforts to think through the restoration of scandalized pastors and deacons.

John H. Armstrong organizes congregational responses into three typical approaches: *immediate restoration* (within twelve months of sexual misconduct); *possible future restoration* after counseling and an extended period of repentance; and *personal restoration with no restoration to church leadership*.[20] Advocates of immediate restoration emphasize God's complete forgiveness and grace. Advocates of personal restoration without resuming church leadership emphasize the high standards of the pastoral office and the public witness of church leadership. While Armstrong argues from church history and Scripture for the third approach, most churches seem to fall into either the first or the second categories. Perhaps it's best to recognize that denominations and autonomous local churches will continue to take differing positions. Instead of repeating those discussions here, the best service might be to simply raise some issues that will need to be addressed in whatever position a group takes.

First, it seems prudent for church leaders and congregations to ask and answer the questions, "Who needs to be restored?" and "What do they need to be restored to?" United Methodist Church bishop William Willimon makes this a first principle in cases of restoration. "What are we after when we talk about restoration? Is it simply restoration to a position, or is it restoration in spirit and in the Christian life? The ultimate goal of any restoration process should be restoration to life in Christ, not just to a position."[21] These are vital questions because different audiences have different needs in any given restoration process. Churches instinctively think of the fallen pastor or deacon. But we must also remember any offended spouse and hurting children. Victims have been harmed, their trust and lives broken by the pastor's sin. Also, we must not forget that the entire church hurts deeply when a beloved leader's transgressions are exposed. So, "who needs to be restored?" and "what do they need to be restored to?" actually turn out to be big questions with multiple answers. At bottom, we can safely assume that everyone—pastor, family, victim, and church family—needs to be restored in their walk with Jesus Christ. That's primary—whether or not someone returns to public ministry. So churches need a plan for pursuing each party with the hope of reconciliation with Christ.

Second, leaders should also take care to preserve the unity and well-being of the church as a whole. Too often congregations receive too little counseling or opportunity to process the mix of feelings that inevitably flare up. The church body often "responds like a wife betrayed by her husband" while "the malignancy eats at laypeople's worship, daily use of time, and devotional life." The church risks deep splits, loss of members, and a decline in ministry activity. Elders should lead the congregation through a congregation-focused restoration process that emphasizes long-term, full disclosure instead of cover-ups or "putting it all behind" the church. Members will need an opportunity to talk safely with leaders in order to work through hurts, disappointment, anger, and resentment. If done well, this process can be an opportunity for members to grow spiritually and to examine their own lives for moral fault lines.[22]

Third, church leaders and congregations must develop a framework for deciding which offenses permanently disqualify a person from church office. Some infractions require lifelong suspension from church leadership. Whenever a leader's sin results in never being able to again satisfy the requirements of 1 Timothy 3:1–13, that leader should be restored to Christ but *not* to the offices of the church. Moreover, if a leader's sin requires church discipline for scandalous public sin (1 Cor. 5:1–11), continued failure to demonstrate repentance in personal sins (Matt. 18:15–17), or continued doctrinal errors (Titus 3:10), that leader should not be reinstated to church leadership. The best framework is simply to rely on the Scripture to define which offenses permanently disqualify.

But other sins and transgressions might fall short of church discipline and excommunication and short of repeated failure to meet the qualifications of 1 Timothy 3. For example, a teenage son or daughter might enter a period of rebelliousness requiring a break from ministry in order to ensure that relationships are repaired and the leader's children obey him with proper respect. Or perhaps a church leader experiences marriage difficulties short of adultery and pornography that nevertheless require a season of counseling and healing. Perhaps he has neglected his wife and children in a way that does not break the marriage covenant but needs correction and attention. In such cases, we're likely dealing with weakness rather than wickedness and, *depending upon particular circumstances weighed and judged by the elders,* men in this category *might* be restored to public leadership in the church. The point is that the denomination or elders of a local church must think through these definitional questions with Bible in hand so that when issues arise a framework for action exists.

Fourth, churches and elders must delineate the process by which someone may be restored to office. Eric Reed offers several questions for working through this issue, including:

1. Which offences require absence from ministry?
2. Is use of pornography an equally serious offense as an actual sexual affair?
3. How long is the pastor to be out of ministry?
4. What are the requirements for counseling and who will oversee it?
5. Will there be any financial support for the pastor and the family?
6. Will the pastor's spouse be included in counseling and in meetings with the denomination or restoration officials?
7. After the restoration process, how will the pastor find a new position, if deemed qualified?
8. And what will the new congregation be told about his indiscretion and period of removal from ministry?[23]

These are vital questions not only for the congregation experiencing the turmoil of leadership failure but also for any future congregations that might take interest in a pastor's leadership. For too long men have been able to simply pick up where they left off by applying to another church or starting a new congregation.

Churches and denominations electing to restore fallen pastors will typically need to provide extensive counseling and ongoing oversight for the leader and their family. Steps should be taken to look for evidence of genuine repentance and reformation of the leader's life. Men should not be rushed back into the fray of public ministry and responsibility. Those who manage the process have the difficult task of prayerfully discerning contrition, brokenness, and sufficient healing before the fallen pastor is able to care for others again.

Conclusion

In a very real sense, churches can only be as healthy as their leaders. The Black Church has long valued charismatic leaders capable of organizing and inspiring the faithful. From time to time, we've found that some men capable of inspiring congregations lack sufficient character to hold office. Whenever a black church must choose between character and gifts, she must choose character. As Samuel Proctor and Gardner Taylor remind us:

> All in all, a summons to the ministry is no light calling. Those of us who have heard the call and have discerned within it the voice of God live daily with its profound impact. The work of communicating the gospel requires us to be more than what we are—to exceed who we are. Then by the grace of God we will be delivered of the gospel to a world which is perishing without it.[24]

Indeed, the vitality and flourishing of the Black Church depends upon the presence of leaders who "exceed who we are" by living above reproach, keeping an excellent reputation inside and outside the church. Sometimes we have to remove some bad apples to keep the entire bunch from spoiling. May the Lord give us grace to do so and revive His churches in the process!

CHAPTER 9

Rethink Pastor Training

"And you shall love the Lord your God with all your heart and with all your soul and with all your mind and with all your strength."
—MARK 12:30

Unfortunately, the Black church is not known for promoting the intellectual side of the Christian ministry. We love God with our hearts and souls, but we often forget that we were also called to love God with our minds. The Black church suffers from a lack of intellectually accomplished and spiritually committed scholars who feel as deeply the need to understand the faith as preachers do to proclaim it.[1]
—JAMES H. CONE

Introduction

"So you're going to the 'cemetery.'"
"Seminary is where faith goes to die."

If you've spent any time in the Black Church, you've no doubt encountered such expressions. Negative attitudes toward theological education can be commonplace. While this is by no means a universal perspective, some African-Americans do view the seminary classroom as the enemy of vibrant faith and worship.

I recall a fellow high school classmate, Todd, who felt the call to ministry in his early twenties. A capable student and hardworking young man, Todd felt a longing to gain further education and training for the ministry. His father had served several churches without advanced training but supported his son's desire.

However, both father and son were surprised by the strong opposition they received from the church family and many area churches. Most men in the denomination lacked theological training, and it seemed they had spread an anti-intellectual, anti-training attitude in their networks. Todd found it difficult to get preaching opportunities during summer breaks and after his graduation. In time, he and his father grew apart as they discovered differences in their theological and ministry outlooks. Eventually Todd left his family, home church, denomination, and city to pursue pastoral leadership elsewhere.

Todd's story highlights a long-standing tension regarding pastoral training. How are men best prepared for a life of Bible preaching, shepherding, counseling, and leadership? Is it the local church or the seminary that trains men for ministry? Or, is it both? And, if both, how should seminaries be related to churches in the preparation of aspiring clergy?

How the Earliest African-Americans Were Trained (1700–1800s)

The first black Christians came to faith in the Lord Jesus Christ during the holocaust of the Trans-Atlantic slave trade. Chattel slavery forged a faith and resilience not often witnessed in the annals of Christian history. But if American chattel slavery forged faith, it also smelted a molten hot antagonism toward the development of African-American church leadership. Antebellum laws regulating slavery and postbellum Black Codes forced illiteracy on Africans and significantly limited mobility and opportunity. Governments essentially regarded the education of enslaved Africans as an act of sedition. Fearing revolts and insurrections, governments and plantation owners restricted the ability of enslaved Africans to assemble or meet in groups numbering more than a couple of persons without white supervision.

Joining the state in its repression of slaves, churches and denominations began to take theological steps to ensure that converted slaves did not interpret baptism or Christian freedom as grounds for temporal and physical freedom.[2] Moreover, the high literacy demands of most white denominations effectively barred illiterate African-Americans from formal ministry preparation. The conditions created by slavery and the mounting prejudice of Christian churches presented nearly overwhelming circumstances for any aspiring black pastor.

But despite the odds, some African-Americans were able to prepare for and conduct effective ministry. A range of activities provided their training. In the late 1700s, some began to preach immediately following their conversion. Their preaching labors became a kind of on-the-job training. For example, Richard Allen (1760–1831) began to preach immediately following his conversion at age seventeen. For nearly ten years Allen preached to anyone who would listen—his family, his master, and to blacks and whites throughout Delaware. He ventured to Philadelphia at age twenty-six, where he was later ordained a deacon by Francis Asbury (1745–1816), the first bishop of the Methodist Church. In 1816, Allen became the first bishop of the African Methodist Episcopal Church, the first of the historically black and independent African-American denominations.[3]

Other African-American preachers in the late 1700s and early 1800s received training through apprenticeships to white clergy. Such apprenticeships might have involved travel with itinerant ministers, rudimentary instruction in the Bible—sometimes limited to passages requiring slaves to obey their masters—preaching or "exhorting" to other slaves, and occasionally preaching to whites as well. One of the most famous black apprentices and itinerant ministers was Rev. Harry Hoosier. Also known as "Black Harry," Hoosier traveled as a servant and apprentice with Bishop Asbury. He preached from 1784 until his death in 1810 and was known to draw large black and white crowds.[4]

Young black aspirants also apprenticed with more seasoned African-American pastors. With the rise of independent black churches, black pastors were able to mold succeeding generations of black preachers. Henry Mitchell writes of one such effort in perhaps the earliest independent black congregation in the United States. "A history of the pastors of the First African Baptist Church of Savannah provides a typical example of the resourcefulness of many black pastors who sought training. Andrew C. Marshall served this church from 1812–1856, having no academic training. He did serve, however, what might be called an apprenticeship under his predecessor uncle."[5]

Still other African-Americans pursuing the ministry combined some level of education or apprenticeship with continuing self-education. Indentured to deacon Rose and his family at age five, Lemuel Haynes received some education in a small school along with the Rose children and participated in the family's regular spiritual exercises. As a young man, Haynes dedicated himself to studying the Bible, the Psalter, a spelling book, and *Young's Night Thoughts*. He poured over the works of Jonathan Edwards (1703–1758), George Whitefield (1714–1770), and Philip Doddridge (1702–1751). In addition to his early education and efforts at independent study, Haynes apprenticed with two influential Connecticut clergymen, Daniel Farrand (1722–1803) and William Bradford. With Farrand and Bradford, Haynes studied theology and classics. In 1780 he was licensed to preach and five years later became the first African-American ordained by any religious body in America. In 1804 Middlebury College awarded Haynes an honorary master's degree, making him the first African-American to receive that honor as well.[6]

Daniel Alexander Payne (1811–1893) provides another example of a largely self-educated pioneer in African-American Christian ministry. Born to free parents in Charleston, South Carolina, during the height of slavery, from infancy Payne's parents dedicated their son to the work of the Lord. "Between the ages of eight and fifteen, young Daniel received educational instruction from the Minor's Moralist Society and a popular Charleston schoolmaster named Thomas S. Bonneau. While employed as an apprentice to local shoe and carpentry merchants, Daniel taught himself Greek, Latin, and Hebrew. By age nineteen, Daniel Alexander Payne opened and operated a school for both slave and free Africans in South Carolina until the South Carolina General Assembly forced the closure of the school in 1835."[7] Following the school's closure, Payne moved north and received further education and training at the Lutheran Theological Seminary in Gettysburg, Pennsylvania. Though he initially resisted any call into full-time Christian ministry, the Lutheran Church licensed Payne to the ministry, and about two years later the Synod at Fordsboro, New York, fully ordained him.[8] As a pastor and later a bishop, Payne's most significant contribution was his successful bid to raise educational requirements for pastoral ministry in the AME Church.

Men like Payne stood at the head of a small but growing stream of formally educated African-American ministers in the late 1800s. For example, the AME Church included Bishop William Fuller Dickerson (Lincoln University) and Bishop J. M. Brown (Oberlin College). Dr. E. K. Love served as pastor of First African Baptist Church from 1895–1900 and completed his studies at Morehouse.[9] With the rise of African-American seminaries like Clark College in 1869 (later Gammon Theological Seminary), Atlanta Baptist Seminary in 1867 (later Morehouse School of Religion), Howard University School of Divinity in 1871, and Turner Theological Seminary, and Morris Brown College in 1885, more young men would have the promise of theological education opened to them.

Opening the Doors: Formal Education and Seminary Training from the 1950s to Present

For the first half of the twentieth century, pastoral training in the Black Church continued much as it had in the 1800s. Men prepared largely by some combination of serving with another pastor, self-study, on-the-job training, and more formal education for a few.

Some of the earliest studies of black clergy education revealed that by the mid-1900s, most rural clergy had little general education and very little formal theological training. Scholars of religion, C. Eric Lincoln and Lawrence H. Mamiya, briefly summarized two studies of educational attainment among rural clergy published in 1947 and 1950:

> In 1947 Richardson's survey of eighty rural ministers showed that 46.2 percent had eighth-grade schooling or less, and only 10 percent were professionally prepared with some seminary education. Felton's 1950 study yielded similar results, with 43.3 percent of the ministers who had less than an eighth-grade education and 58.2 percent who had never gone beyond high school.[10]

The situation in urban settings was not much better. Lincoln and Mamiya cited Benjamin E. Mays and Joseph Nicholson's report that 80 percent of urban pastors were not college trained and that 86.6 percent did not have a bachelor of divinity degree.[11]

To be sure, segregation and poverty contributed directly to such poor educational attainment figures. The systematic denial of opportunity along racial lines not only hindered the general advancement of African-Americans but also limited the abilities of the Black Church's leaders.

Getting Organized for Change: The Seabury Consultation

A decade after these studies, several prominent African-American and white church leaders convened to discuss the state of pastoral training and education. Sponsored by the National Council of the Churches of Christ in the USA, Inc., the Seabury Consultation gathered sixty-five church leaders from nineteen denominations for a "national consultation on the Negro in Christian ministry." Two-thirds of the attendees were African-Americans, including luminaries like Benjamin Elijah Mays, then president of Morehouse College; Harry V. Richardson, then president of the newly formed Interdenominational Theological Center in Atlanta; and John M. Ellison, chancellor of Virginia Union University.

At the Seabury Consultation, Harry Richardson reported "that for the 1200–1500 new pastors called by or appointed to African American congregations each year, there would be only 120–130 graduates of accredited seminaries available."[12] Moreover, the 66 schools affiliated with the American Association of Theological Schools during the 1958–59 academic year enrolled only 387 African American candidates for a professional theological degree. The majority (210) of those students attended one of the seven historically African-American seminaries.[13] The data would seem to suggest that not much had changed since Richardson's and Felton's studies in 1947 and 1950, respectively.

Participants in the Seabury Consultation suspected that the relatively unchanging number of African-American students pursuing theological studies might be owing to a number of problematic attitudes about the ministry itself. Chancellor John M. Ellison of Virginia Union shared with the meeting ten factors inhibiting African-American enrollment and pursuit of ministry. Ellison maintained:

1. The ministry has a poor image in the minds of educated youth.
2. The large body of untrained but ordained "unplaced" ministers among African-American Baptist churches are not inclined to increase their own competition by enlisting young people for the ministry; their unemployed status is no stimulus to young people to think about the vocation.

3. The poor social and economic milieu from which so many African-American youth come discourages them from attending college.

4. The status of religion in the minds of African-American college students is generally low.

5. The ministry is basically a "segregated" vocation.

6. Inadequate or virtually nonexistent denominational youth programs deny African-American youth necessary aid in interpreting church vocations.

7. High school guidance programs in schools attended by large numbers of African-Americans neglect church vocations.

8. More and more African-American youth are enrolling in public colleges and universities instead of church-related colleges, as was done in earlier days.

9. There are inadequate religious programs, both academic and extracurricular, at many colleges and universities attended by African-Americans.

10. Most African-American ministers receive low salaries.[14]

With this statistical background and these challenges before it, the Seabury Consultation ended with the group putting forward a number of recommendations for increasing student enrollment. A year later, partly in response to the Seabury Consultation and other discussions like it, the Fund for Theological Education received a significant boost.

One Effort to Increase Education: Fund for Theological Education (1960-1975)

The Fund for Theological Education (FTE) was created in 1954 "to strengthen Protestant churches by competing better for the most talented and able college graduates available in each generation."[15] To meet this objective, the FTE used funding from the Rockefeller Brothers Fund and the Seatlantic Fund, Inc., to launch the "Trial Year in Seminary" program, the Rockefeller Doctoral Program, and the Protestant Fellowship Program. Collectively, the programs allowed prospective students to "try out" graduate theological education as a prospective career in ministry (Trial Year in Seminary Program) and supported other students through their graduate education in preparation for service in the local church (Protestant Fellowship Program and the Doctoral Program).

The Trial Year in Seminary Program paid all expenses for one full year to a graduate theological school for sixty to seventy outstanding undergraduates each year. The scholarship and year of study allowed students to consider whether graduate education and a life of ministry were right for them. Students were not required to commit to pastoral ministry or a particular "call."

The Protestant Fellowship Program aimed to annually support thirty-five to forty persons fully committed to Christian ministry— hopefully in local churches—to engage in research about the Black Church and to organize activities that would strengthen local churches. While the Trial Year Program piqued interest for some students, the Protestant Fellowship Program provided the needed resources to finish a course of study and created a pipeline of theologically trained candidates for local congregations.[16]

Charles Shelby Rooks's firsthand account of the activities of the Fund for Theological Education highlights some of the historical and present-day challenges of increasing theological training among African-American pastors. Rooks, a past officer at the Fund for Theological Education, encountered four major hurdles in his effort to recruit and support black seminarians. First, he found that higher education officials and faculty were not very interested in African-American students in general or in promoting religious scholarship particularly. Rooks recalls, "Another dean of one of the most highly regarded African-American colleges, a college still receiving support from a Christian denomination, told me quite openly, 'I don't see why you're looking for such outstanding boys for the ministry. The average fellow can do quite well in the field.'" Rooks wrote, "I found that attitude to be the predominant one among college administrators and faculty."

Second, Rooks discovered that the attitudes of students toward the ministry were not much better:

> Many applicants that first year were openly rebellious against the image of the ministry they saw in their pastors and other clergy with whom they were acquainted. Over and over again, in both the written papers that were part of their applications and in their interviews, they told how much they had been repelled by the lack of training their pastors had, by dull and uninteresting sermons, by the seeming unconcern of their churches with

the problems of this life, and by what they regarded as open exploitation of the church by the pastors they knew. They were also largely uninspired by their college chaplains, many of whom were uninteresting teachers and uninspiring preachers.[17]

One wonders if much has changed in student perceptions of the ministry since Rooks's days at the Fund for Theological Education.

Third, Rooks and colleagues confronted a college education system with no discernible process for recruitment or enlistment. He writes:

> When I joined Walter Wagoner at the FTE a year after the Seabury meeting, no denomination—including the African American churches—had staff working even part-time at the problem of enlistment. There were no enlistment programs sponsored by seminaries either. Gammon Seminary, which was part of the new Interdenominational Theological Center in Atlanta, had begun to develop budget and strategies, but this effort was new in 1960. No specific faculty or administrators were assigned to give it consistent and significant staff time and energy.[18]

Fourth, Rooks and colleagues were challenged by anti-education attitudes among some African-American churches. Rooks quotes one African-American chaplain at a historically black university who summed up the attitude by saying, "Many of our people have been oriented around the idea that if the minister is called, then all this education we're getting isn't necessary. God will give you what you need. And with this education you get over our heads. You come with an educated sermon, and nobody can understand you."[19] Dr. Robert M. Franklin, former President of Morehouse College, recounted his pastor's confrontation of similar attitudes in the church of his youth.

> Although we were part of a Pentecostal tradition that did not think very highly of formal education, I was fortunate to have a pastor who supported academic excellence and a family that rewarded performance. I recall visiting preachers who would declare that studying was a waste of time for people who knew the Lord and could read the Bible. Depending on the age and status of the preacher, Pastor Ford would either keep silent or

refute the remarks. One day after a preacher had held forth on how he had never gone to school beyond fifth grade yet had been successful as a pastor, Pastor Ford simply asked the congregation whether they would seek a trained physician or any well-intentioned Christian if they needed brain surgery. The point registered.[20]

Such attitudes had to be addressed in an effort to turn young men's attention to theological education and help churches support them in their studies. As it turns out, my friend Todd was not alone in facing anti-education attitudes.

Where Are We Now? Trends in Pastoral Education

The impact of the Fund for Theological Education and other efforts like it can be seen in the dramatic rise in African-American participants in graduate theological education since the Seabury Consultation. Four observable trends stand out.

Increased Enrollment and Degree Completion

First, enrollment at graduate theological institutions has increased since 1970, when the Fund for Theological Education was in full swing. The Association for Theological Schools provides data on racial/ethnic enrollment by decade. African-American enrollment in member schools has grown from 2.7 percent of total enrollment in 1969 to 9.7 percent in 1999 (see Table 1 on the next page).

Moreover, the absolute number of African-American clergy and aspiring pastors completing training has increased. In their national survey of 1,895 urban and rural pastors between 1978–1983, Lincoln and Mamiya report significant improvements since 1950 in educational achievement among rural and urban clergy. They found that 58.3 percent of rural pastors had at least some college compared to the 46.2 percent who had less than an eighth-grade education in 1947. Twenty-eight percent achieved some seminary education compared to the 10 percent in 1947.[21] Among the 1,531 pastors from fifteen urban areas across the country, 70.2 percent of all clergy had some level of college training. Some 35.9 percent of all African-American clergy, urban and rural, reported

Table 1. Racial/Ethnic Enrollment by Decade (1969-1999)[22]

	1969	1979	1989	1999
Total Number of Institutions	170	193	202	237
Total Enrollment	29,815	48,433	56,171	70,432
Black/African Descent Total Enrollment	825	2,043	3,961	6,854
	(2.7%)	(4.2%)	(7.3%)	(9.7%)

having at least "some seminary or Bible school training beyond the college level."[23]

Nearly two decades after Lincoln and Mamiya's research, another study of historically black denominations revealed similarly positive results. The Interdenominational Theological Center/Faith Factor Project 2000 interviewed 1,863 pastors, assistant pastors, and lay leaders. Seventy-seven percent of respondents (1,482) were senior pastors. Researchers found that 30 percent of respondents had post-master of divinity work or degree, 26 percent had Bible college or some seminary, 24 percent had a seminary degree, and 9 percent reported having no degree. Only 4 percent of interviewees reported an apprenticeship and 3 percent a certificate or correspondence course.[24]

Increased Prominence and Numbers of African-American Scholars of Religion

In the 1960s and 1970s very few African-Americans held posts in religion or theology in higher education institutions. One aim of the Fund for Theological Education was to develop a scholarly community of African-Americans studying the Black Church and black religion. In 1980, the number of full-time faculty of African descent in ATS institutions totaled 101 persons—four percent of total faculty. In 1991, the number climbed slightly to 127 or 4.6 percent of all faculty. In 2001 more rapid progress had been made with 200 full-time faculty of African descent serving in ATS member schools. That 200 faculty accounted for

6.1 percent of all faculty, not quite commensurate with the 9.7 percent of African descent students enrolled in member institutions in 1999–2000, but an improvement nonetheless. Despite the growth, however, a full 40 percent of ATS member schools had no one from non-white ethnic groups on their faculties.[25]

Along with the increase in numbers has come an increase in prominence of some scholars in the black church community. Charles Shelby Rooks provides an appendix of the scholars and fellows supported by FTE programs. The list of past scholarship recipients reads like a "Who's Who" of black religious scholarship and ministry: Calvin O. Butts, Katie G. Canon, Cain Hope Felder, James A. Forbes Jr., Robert M. Franklin, Peter J. Gomes, H. Beecher Hicks Jr., Jesse L. Jackson, Marvin A. McMickle, James C. Perkins, James M. Washington, Vincent L. Wimbush, Randall C. Bailey, Brian K. Blounte, Kelly Brown, Allan D. Callahan, Benjamin E. Chavis, Michael E. Dyson, James H. Evans Jr., Jacqueline Grant, Dwight N. Hopkins, Willie J. Jennings, Marcia Y. Riggs, Cheryl J. Sanders, Renita J. Weems, and Jeremiah A. Wright Jr.[26] Anyone familiar with black church scholarship and leadership will recognize many of these names, a very small sample of the total number of men and women who benefitted from FTE's investment in their academic training. Their collective work and energy helped shape two generations of black church scholarship and theology.

Shifted the Locus of Training to White Seminaries

Though substantial progress in the formal education of black ministers has been made, not all the results have been happy. One unintended consequence of the push for seminary education was the shift of African-American students away from the major historically black institutions to predominantly white schools. In the 1958–59 school year, 54 percent of the 387 African-American candidates for the Bachelor of Divinity degree were enrolled at the seven historically African-American seminaries. The 1971–72 school year saw the percentage of African-Americans enrolled at predominantly white institutions rise to 71 percent.[27] By 1999, predominantly white seminaries accounted for two-thirds of all African-American students pursuing a Master of Divinity degree. The percentage of African-Americans studying at predominantly black ATS schools had dropped to 31 percent (1,156 of the 3,698 students).[28]

The move of black students to predominantly white schools indicated the growing effectiveness of integration and the removal of racial barriers. The dark night of segregation was over. In that sense, these statistics tell a positive story of progress in the country.

But on the other hand, that progress was mixed with the unintended decline of predominantly black educational institutions. The role once played almost exclusively by southern black colleges now belonged to an increasing number of schools around the country. With this shift, some of the training for pastoral ministry moved from the historical and cultural context of the Black Church to environments largely unfamiliar, indifferent, or hostile to the African-American context. While greater educational resources were available, questions began to arise about the appropriateness of that education to the needs of black people.

Moved the Pulpit to the Theological Left

It needs to be stated that the rise of seminary education among African-American clergy came largely in the wake of the black community's fight to end segregation and to integrate public facilities. It's not surprising, then, that seminaries supporting racial segregation were most likely to resist African-American enrollment. Those seminaries most often were also theologically "conservative." Conversely, the seminaries and divinity schools that supported and eventually pursued African-American enrollment tended to be not only socially but also theologically "progressive" or "liberal."

For example, eighteen of the forty African-American PhD graduates completing their studies between 1953–1968 attended the Boston University School of Theology. Institutions like the University of Chicago Divinity School, Harvard Divinity School, Princeton Theological Seminary, Union Theological Seminary in New York, and Yale Divinity School, Drew and Garrett joined Boston University in moving some future leaders of the Black Church away from the generally conservative and evangelical theology of their upbringing to German higher criticism, neo-evangelical, and classically liberal points of view.

Perhaps this helps to explain why so many Black Church leaders hold theological views out of step with the average black Christian. It also goes some distance in explaining why some African-Americans look skeptically at seminary education as a means of preparing for the ministry. Indeed, for some people seminary has been "cemetery," the place where well-meaning young men had their evangelical faith buried.

The Local Church and Ministry Preparation

The mixed results of seminary education remind us why the Black Church needs to rethink pastoral training. What's needed is an approach to preparing future ministers that centers on the priority of the Scriptures and the local church while using accountable theological institutions in a strategic way.

First, we're reminded that the Bible teaches us that pastors and churches are responsible for training future leaders. We see this in the straightforward vision of 2 Timothy 2:2 (NIV). "And the things you have heard me say in the presence of many witnesses entrust to reliable men who will also be qualified to teach others." Preparation for ministry most naturally and effectively occurs as one qualified and seasoned man entrusts his experience and learning to subsequent generations. Pastors are meant to replicate themselves in others. Consequently, we are better off if we recover a healthy apprenticeship model of pastor training. That model has always been a part of the Black Church's effort at clergy training, but it perhaps needs updating and fresh energy.

Indeed, there are encouraging trends in this direction. Local congregations and networks of local churches are establishing well-organized internship programs to expose young men to the joys and demands of pastoral ministry and to equip them for future service. Often these initiatives work intentionally toward planting new churches in urban areas—thus avoiding the placement problems encountered by Rooks and others working in traditional black churches, where leaders sometimes feel threatened by gifted young men.

One such effort is the Rebuild Network.[29] The Rebuild Network aims to plant and re-plant multiethnic churches in urban areas. Leaders of the network help young men assess their calling and gifts, build leadership teams for their churches, and raise financial support to sustain the church. One of the leaders of the Rebuild Initiative, Dhati Lewis, pastors Blueprint Church in Atlanta, Georgia, where he also operates a full-time internship program to train aspiring pastors. Similarly, David Helm leads Chicago's Holy Trinity Church's ministry leadership program.

The training combines classroom instruction at the church, ministry experience, and mentoring. These are but two of a number of promising efforts to rethink pastoral training by returning the training responsibility to the local church. More churches should follow suit.

Second, we're reminded that seminaries have a limited role and scope. There are some things schools of theology can do quite well. And some of these things are not easily replicated in the local church. For example, teaching biblical languages or advanced courses in systematic theology might best be achieved in the classroom. They can be taught in the local church, but concentrated study in a classroom setting might be more efficient. Where we find these efficiencies we should seize them. But on the whole, we should rethink whether universities and seminaries should be given the entire responsibility for pastoral training.

I remember the stunned look on my assistant pastor's face when he walked into my office a few weeks into his service at the church. He wearily slouched down into a chair and looked at me overwhelmed. He shared with me the anxiety he felt. Having recently returned from Bible college, he was keenly aware of how much people thought he now knew and could help them with. But just weeks into the job he recognized that most of what he was experiencing he had never studied in college. I smiled as he talked. When he finished I repeated something my mentor taught me, "It is the church that trains pastors." A lightbulb went off for my assistant. It dawned on him that while school had given him a few tools and some good experiences, his pastoral education was just beginning. A few years later, I heard him telling young men, "It's the local church that trains pastors."

We should not automatically conclude that a person desiring to pursue the ministry should attend college or seminary. Instead, we should think strategically about whether seminary can be *an added training or specialization* for the person. What does this person need to know that they cannot gain in the local church? Does the person's personal circumstances or family demands permit or hinder formal academic study? What subjects are best suited for study in the classroom environment? What schools will provide this education in a biblically sound, rigorous, and faithful way? Or, can this particular person be best encouraged, equipped, and sent with a more organized training approach in the local church?

Third, we're reminded that seminary education and institutions must be accountable to the local church. Some congregations and church leaders have rightly been frustrated when they've sent a promising young man off for training only to have them return denying the integrity and authority of the Scripture, proffering alternative gospels which are really no gospel at all and denying any accountability to the church that nourished and supported them. Most divinity schools and seminaries were established to train pastors and to serve the local church. Originally, seminaries were para-church organizations that understood themselves to be handmaids to the church. But in time, many broke away from their denominations and justified their existence with appeals to "academic freedom" and "critical scholarship" for its own sake. Consequently, great institutions like Harvard and Yale now contradict the very principles and goals of their founding.

The Black Church should not throw the baby of seminary training out with the wash. But it should take steps to make sure the education being provided and supported strengthens the local church and remains accountable to it. This may mean refusal to financially support or send students to some institutions. Increasing accountability will mean pastors taking an active role in grounding the life of the institutions and students in the local church. One excellent example of this is the African American Leadership Initiative (AALI) at Reformed Theological Seminary in Jackson, Mississippi.[30] The AALI partners the seminary with the denomination (Presbyterian Church in America) and the local church to offer students four things: mentoring by seasoned African-American pastors and leaders, modeling in applied settings, meeting formally and informally for fellowship with other students and church leaders, and money (a 50 percent scholarship) to make the seminary education affordable.

Conclusion

The revival of black churches, humanly speaking, will be aided by a growing cadre of biblically qualified and thoroughly trained leaders. Producing such leaders will require dusting off old methods of training, like apprenticeships, and rethinking the place of current methods, like seminary education. The church will likely need a combination of resources, but the priority and responsibility must be restored to the local church, the community of saints who truly know the potential and pitfalls of a young man's life.

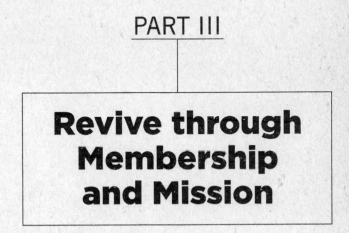

PART III

Revive through Membership and Mission

CHAPTER 10

Rekindle Personal Piety and Discipleship

Then Jesus came to them and said, "All authority in heaven and on earth has been given to me. Therefore go and make disciples of all nations, baptizing them in the name of the Father and of the Son and of the Holy Spirit, and teaching them to obey everything I have commanded you. And surely I am with you always, to the very end of the age."
—MATTHEW 28:18–20 (NIV)

Introduction

I had not been a Christian for very long myself. Perhaps two years. But the Lord had already begun to burden me with a longing to see my family growing in the Lord. I had listened to a sermon series by Pastor John Cherry called "The Family Man" and was being challenged to be a man of God in my own immediate and extended family.

My wife and I prayed about the possibility of driving to my hometown each Saturday to lead a Bible study with my family. The drive was about an hour and a half each way, but we figured the investment would be worth it. But there was one problem: I was too nervous to broach the subject with my family. Would they be offended? Would they be interested? Would they think me proud or overbearing? For a couple of months the fear of man seized my heart.

As providence would have it, I had to travel through my hometown on the way to a meeting for work. I took the opportunity to stop by my mama's house and then to visit one of my sisters. The visits were brief but good, and I had forgotten about leading a family Bible study. As I wrapped up my visit with my sister, she walked me to the car and asked if she could tell me a funny story. I said, "Sure."

It was a short story that went something like this:

> Mama and me were in church on Sunday when Rev. Cade announced his text. We didn't quite hear what he said but we did hear something about Paul. So we started looking for the Book of Paul in our Bibles. We were all over our Bibles and couldn't find it! Then we got the Bibles from the pew and started looking in them! After the service, we told Rev. Cade we couldn't find no Book of Paul in the Bible. And that's when he told us, "Because there ain't one." We laughed 'til we cried.

My sister is a very humble and gracious woman. She loves to laugh those deep, belly-holding shoulder-jiggling laughs. That early evening as the summer crickets chirped, she laughed at herself all the way through the short story.

I laughed along with her. And as I chuckled at the story, I knew I had to ask: "Would you be interested in having a family Bible study to get to know the Scripture better?" Without hesitation and still laughing, she said, "Oh, yes! We'd all love that. When can we start?"

If revival of the Black Church depends upon the life-giving Word of God being central to the life of the church, churches must ensure the saints actually know and understand their Bibles. The Bible can no longer be "revered but not read" if the church is to thrive and succeed in her mission. Revival depends on cultivating a warm devotional life among active disciples.

Discipleship in the Black Church

I certainly don't want to project my sister's biblical illiteracy onto the entire Black Church. That would be unfair and misrepresentative.

But the data does indicate that we live in an age of widespread biblical illiteracy across the church world. For example, "*Time* magazine observed in a 2007 cover story that only half of U.S. adults could name one of the four Gospels. Fewer than half could identify Genesis as the Bible's first book."[1] Nearly every major survey of American evangelicals reveals similar findings. By and large, American Christians do not know their Bibles very well—which at least suggests that something has gone wrong with Christian devotion and discipleship.

The African-American church, like churches of other ethnic composition, offers an array of discipleship activities for its members. In a survey of more than 1,800 black churches, researchers found that 71 percent of black church leaders feel they assimilate new persons either "very well" or "quite well."[2] This same research revealed that most congregations offered a wide range of religious and social programming designed to help people understand the faith and follow the Lord in obedience. "More than nine in ten congregations participated in Bible study, prayer or meditation groups, community services, and youth programs. Large majorities participated in the other activities examined: spiritual retreats, parenting and marriage enrichment, theological study, and young adult and singles programs."[3]

All of this poses a critical question: If black churches assimilate new persons so effectively and offer a range of discipleship opportunities, why are significant numbers of persons remaining biblically illiterate?

Why Some of Our Efforts to Make Disciples Are Proving Unfruitful

Despite the plethora of activities aimed at disciple-making, fruitfulness sometimes remains elusive. Many traditional black churches face at least three challenges to effectively making disciples and helping people closely follow the Lord.

Poor Content and Methodology

Roland G. Hardy Jr. provides a vivid sketch of what happens in most traditional Sunday school gatherings in African-American churches. He helpfully illustrates the method often used and the content challenges that can result:

On any Sunday morning in the African-American church community, just as in any other church community in America, you will find the ritual of Sunday school being conducted. Men, women, and children gather before the worship hour to learn about their faith by "going through Sunday school lesson." Traditionally, this lesson time is limited to an hour and includes the mandatory opening hymn, prayer, and remarks by the Sunday school superintendent before the students assemble in their respective classes. Prior to dismissal, the offering is taken and the treasurer's report and student lesson summaries given. The actual time devoted to teaching the lesson ends up being approximately twenty-five to thirty minutes, about enough time to read the lesson and review the memory verses. If by the time the superintendent rings the bell signaling time to take up the offering, a class has not completed the lesson, the teacher rushes through the balance of the lesson for completion's sake.

What is communicated when lessons are presented as described above? I suggest little more than disconnected Bible information in the name of content. Although Sunday school literature publishers make a valiant attempt to organize and design user-friendly, Bible-based curricula, the constraints of the traditional Sunday school format, coupled with the disconnected information, prevent students from gaining an understanding of the full counsel of God. Students experience difficulty connecting the historical significance of Bible stories and personalities to the advent of Jesus Christ and then to their present circumstances and individual journeys. This sense of disconnectedness is exaggerated by the "rush through" format.[4]

While Sunday school ministries have a rich history of blessing and equipping the saints, and while such ministries continue to be useful in making disciples, care must be taken to ensure that we don't inadvertently reduce the Great Commission to one hour on Sunday morning. Teaching people to obey *everything* Jesus has commanded cannot be effectively achieved in one crammed hour per week. Much more needs to be done in more varied settings with an eye toward passing on a comprehensive understanding and application of the entire Bible. As Hardy rightly points out, Christians cannot embrace "the full counsel of God" by rushing through materials that can sometimes be disconnected, moralistic, and ahistorical. *What* we teach and *how* we teach significantly impacts whether our people learn to follow Jesus.

Competing with "Foreign" Teachers

Easy access to bad teaching poses another challenge to faithful disciple-making in local congregations. Sometimes spiritual weakness results from poor spiritual diet. The problem may not be with the local church's efforts, but with the tendency of many Christians to seek their primary spiritual food from teachers who are not accountable to their local congregations. These "foreign" teachers may with immunity confuse and mislead many people.

The messages our members hear from their favorite Christian personalities can be quite contrary to the message we attempt to teach in our local assemblies. I have sometimes been astounded at the ability of some congregants to one day listen to preachers I have *publicly named* as heretical and the next day listen to me teach *the opposite message*. They take in both messages with equal delight, failing to discern the vital differences and implications. This lack of discernment has real-life consequences for the person's discipleship. They may listen to a television preacher tell them that their sickness stems from a lack of faith and that they should not rely on doctors. When they hear me tell them that medicine is a gift of God's common grace, and they should definitely see a doctor about that growth or pain, they feel stuck and confused. Competing questions plague them: Is seeing a doctor a lack of faith? Or, is seeing a doctor wise stewardship of my body? This confusion comes almost entirely from not knowing their Bibles well enough to apply its teaching to all of life while listening to teachers offering messages sometimes at odds with the Scripture and their spiritual leaders. The result is stunted discipleship.

Poor Definition of Growth

Some church leaders focus too much on numerical growth and too little on spiritual growth. When that happens, insufficient attention may be paid to the quality of people's lives. A living church is a spiritually maturing church (Eph. 4:16). The most essential growth is growth in godliness. Dr. William C. Turner Jr., senior pastor of Mount Level Missionary Baptist Church in Durham, North Carolina, and homiletics professor at Duke University Divinity School, summarizes this issue well when he writes:

> Of all the ways a church can grow, to grow in knowledge and holiness stands first in line. A church may grow numerically. But it matters little if the church is not growing in its knowledge of God, its understanding of grace, and its holiness. Increase the size of a church facility without an understanding of what God has called the church to be, and members won't know what to do with their building. And so, first and foremost, we strive for greater knowledge of God.[5]

If church leaders aim merely at increasing figures for attendance and giving, they will likely miss the harder-earned yet more meaningful and lasting growth of righteousness, peace, justice, knowledge, and love. Where Christian virtue ebbs at low tide, we might rightly question whether the "growth" we're witnessing in our churches is true spiritual life.

A Vision for Discipleship in Black Churches Seeking Revival

In one sense, the entire purpose of the church is to make disciples (Matt. 28:18–20). When Jesus commands the church to go into the world baptizing and teaching, He suggests that disciple-making ought to consume us. The local church ought to be driven and animated by a vision for the worldwide worship of Jesus—starting at home and reaching the farthest people and place. Lloyd C. Blue frames the challenge well. "As pastor-teacher, you must get beyond merely talking about evangelism and discipleship and dedicate yourself to making it the central focus of the church."[6]

What might such a dedication and central focus on disciple-making entail? How can we cultivate such a consuming and compelling vision? Of course, no one answer will fit every context or situation. People and places vary in their needs and resources. But, in principle, a few things seem biblical and necessary for moving the Black Church forward in the care and nurture of our people into more complete Christlikeness.

Be Clear and Careful with Conversions

Many African-Americans have been socialized into the Black Church. Belonging to the church was almost a community right and an early rite of passage. Children who were "old enough to join the church" were customarily pressured by parents to be baptized and seek membership. Many times young people are coerced to respond to an altar call or to talk with the pastor. A great many young people responding to such socialization later drift away from the church—sometimes for years.

What are we to think of such experiences? Should we regard such people as genuine Christian disciples?

We need to be careful here. A person cannot be *socialized* into the true spiritual Church of Jesus Christ. She may learn all of the Christian lingo and how to negotiate life in the culture of the church, but unless she is truly born again she is neither a Christian nor a true member of the church. The fact that significant numbers of persons have had this experience indicates that pastors and church leaders need to be careful with a person's conversion.

First, a pastor or leader should make sure the person has a good basic understanding of the gospel. They don't need to be theologians to be Christians, but they should be able to confess belief in God, belief in God's Son—Jesus Christ, belief in Jesus' sinless life and sacrificial death on the cross for our sin, belief in His resurrection and His Second Coming. We might call this the basic doctrinal tests for conversion.

Second, a new convert should be able to confess repentance from sin and personal faith in Jesus as their righteousness and their Savior. We might call this a basic experiential test of conversion. Here, it's vital to help new converts or nominal Christians understand the difference between repentance and remorse or regret. Repentance is not simply feeling guilty or sorrowful, though people often do feel these things. Genuine repentance involves a change of mind, a turning away from the old life of sin with abhorrence and a turning to God with a new heart of love and trust.

In the same way, we must be careful to distinguish genuine saving faith from its counterfeits. Biblical faith is not merely agreeing with gospel facts or a vague and general belief in God. According to the Bible, faith rests specifically on the Person of Jesus Christ and includes a holistic trust in and surrender to Jesus as Lord and God. Faith lays hold to the promises of God to forgive, justify, and save *solely* through His Son. Because so many counterfeits abound, the most loving thing a pastor can do is take his time to be sure people understand and have experienced genuine conversion.

Of course, this has implications for soul care in the Black Church. At the least a pastoral concern for conversion means explaining the gospel clearly in sermons and at altar calls if you have one. It also means not assuring people they are "saved" simply because they "walked the aisle" in tears, but patiently counseling them with effective follow-up. Careful pastors might also ask persons who wish to join the church to share their testimony of conversion as part of a membership interview and at their baptism. We must be careful with a person's conversion because their eternal future and the church's spiritual vitality depend on possessing genuine spiritual life.

Teach the Place of Obedience in the Christian Life

The term *disciple* means student or follower. The four Gospels show Jesus' disciples literally doing both—following Jesus from place to place and learning from Him. When Jesus gives us the Great Commission, He does not merely say, "Teach them everything I have commanded you." That's close, but it's not entirely accurate. The Master says, "Teach them to *obey* everything I have commanded you." True discipleship requires transferring learning into obedience.

But many churches and Christians treat "obedience" like it's a dirty word. They recoil from any emphasis on actual obedience as if such an emphasis alone amounts to legalism. Point some people to the commands of Scripture and you're likely to hear, "We're under grace, not law." Or, "Who are you to tell me what to do?" Such persons do not have a good grasp on what discipleship means.

On the other hand, there really are legalists and moralists in the world. There are men who teach the Bible as if the main message were, "Earn God's approval by keeping His commands." These Christians—if they are genuine Christians—are unclear on obedience and discipleship, too. Some men want to be teachers of the law, but they do not know what they are talking about or what they so confidently affirm (1 Tim. 1:6–7). They do not understand the proper relationship between grace and obedience.

The Bible repeatedly joins faith, grace, and obedience in the Christian life. Paul writes of "bring[ing] about the obedience of faith" (Rom. 1:5). He also insists that God's saving grace teaches or trains us to "renounce ungodliness and worldly passions, and to live self-controlled, upright, and godly lives in the present age" (Titus 2:12). Faith and grace insist upon change. Faith and grace give power for change (2 Pet. 1:3–11). The person who claims to know God but disobeys Him lies (1 John 1:6, 8). Worse, such a person proves by their disobedience that they do not love Jesus (John 14:15, 21, 23).

So discipleship efforts in the Black Church must stress faith-powered and grace-motivated obedience to all Jesus requires. Otherwise, the church will only transfer interesting Bible data and continue to see pockets of stagnation and moribund spiritual "living."

All-of-Life Discipleship

When Protestant churches were born in the 1500s through a recovery of the Scripture and the gospel, a significant revolution happened in prevailing views of the Christian life. Prior to the Protestant Reformation, Roman Catholics were taught that only the priests and hierarchy glorified God. The priestly vocation stood as the only or best means of honoring the Lord. But with the Protestant Reformation came a new view. The Reformers taught that *all* of life should be lived *Coram Deo*—before the face of God. Not only were priest and ministry sacred vocation, but every Christian and every vocation—baker, cobbler, and so on—was a calling to glorify God. Every Christian consequently needed to learn how to honor God in their "ordinary" pursuits. That revolution in views gave rise to an entire worldview that produced the "Protestant work ethic" and helped bring Europe out of the Dark Ages and into Industrialization and literacy.

Black churches are descendants of the Protestant Reformation. But we need a Copernican revolution in the church's view of discipleship and disciple-making. Men, women, boys, and girls must be helped to bring their entire lives under the lordship of Jesus Christ. Too often people divide Sunday from Monday through Saturday. Christianity becomes a once-weekly event rather than a controlling life and worldview. In principle, we want to teach people to yield their family, work, financial, dating, sex, political, and cultural selves to the rule of Jesus through His Word.

What would such a disciple look like?

Let's call her "Sonia." Sonia works at a local government office. Despite the mediocre performance and listless attitudes of some of her coworkers, Sonia approaches work as worship. She doesn't necessarily talk about Jesus all the time or keep a large reference Bible on her desk. She might. But more frequently she does her job as if the Lord were her supervisor. Because her reward comes from her Savior, she strives for excellence in her work (Col. 3:23–24).

While Sonia approaches work as worship, she does not worship her work. She sets appropriate biblical priorities in order to manage her life. God comes first, then family. Work trails in third place. Sonia has turned down promotions that would have paid significantly more but also taken her away from her family and interfered with her ability to meet with God's people. Despite significant pressure, she works to keep balance by keeping priorities.

Sonia had her first child before marriage. At the time she was a professing Christian. The pregnancy left her feeling both joy and guilt—joy that God had blessed her with a child and guilt over the sexual sin. With counsel from her elders, she submitted to the church's loving correction, repented of her sin, and learned to walk in God's grace sexually pure. She ended the relationship with the father of her child, a relationship she knew was inappropriate since he was not a Christian (1 Cor. 7:39; 2 Cor. 6:14). While singleness and purity were tough, she persevered through friendship with older sisters in the church, prayer, and a continuing joy in serving God.

After seven years of remaining devoted to the Lord as a single woman, she later met and married a young man in her church. Years of independence makes submission to her husband's leadership difficult for Sonia, but she works prayerfully to honor Christ in this area (Eph. 5:22–24). Finances place the biggest strain on their relationship. But together they're working to use their resources to honor God by giving more, spending less frivolously, saving for the children's future, and meeting their basic needs. They've had to learn entirely new values and attitudes toward money, but they do so because they see the wisdom and righteousness of God's Word on the matter.

In many respects life looks very "normal" for Sonia. She worships with her church, cares for her family, and faithfully goes to work each day. But the thing that is extraordinary is her commitment to do all these things in submission to Jesus' rule in every area of her life.

What Strategies Help Create All-of-Life Disciples?

All-of-life discipleship has implications for a local church's disciple-making strategy. We won't see many people like "Sonia" in our congregations if we are not intentional about helping people grow into this perspective.

An "As You Go" Strategy

The Great Commission more literally begins with, "Going into all the world . . ." "Going"—along with baptizing and teaching—helps define how we "make disciples." One implication, then, is that our disciple-making should be done "on the go." Indeed, teaching on the go is precisely what God demands of Israel as they teach their young:

> Hear, O Israel: The LORD our God, the LORD is one. You shall love the LORD your God with all your heart and with all your soul and with all your might. And these words that I command you today shall be on your heart. *You shall teach them diligently to your children, and shall talk of them when you sit in your house, and when you walk by the way, and when you lie down, and when you rise. You shall bind them as a sign on your hand, and they shall be as frontlets between your eyes. You shall write them on the doorposts of your house and on your gates.* (Deut. 6:4–9, emphasis added)

People need to *see* obedience, not simply hear a call to obedience. Such instruction by example was a major part of apostolic practice (2 Cor. 4:15–17; 2 Thess. 3:6–10; 1 Tim. 4:12). Sunday school, mid-week Bible study, and other organized teaching sessions should not be abandoned. Rather, they should be complemented with some form of going and modeling. It's as we take teaching into the walk-around work-a-day world of church members that discipleship becomes increasingly an all-of-life reality.

Renovation Church in Atlanta, Georgia, provides a helpful example of approaching disciple-making in an "on-the-go" way. A major emphasis of the church is helping disciples see the necessity of making other disciples as they go. They facilitate this in part with their "city groups," small groups of members who meet in a group leader's home. The group alternates their meetings between typical small group Bible study and community projects. One week they study together, the next meeting they serve in the community as part of their mission to the community. Group leaders must feel a specific call to people in a neighborhood in the city. This embeds mission in the group and gives it focus. The church provides a budget to each city group in order to help facilitate community projects and outreach. The approach gets members moving and people learning as they go.

A Replication Strategy: Disciples Making Disciples

Sometimes Christians think of the faith in largely individualistic terms. A Christian's "personal relationship with Jesus" can become his or her only spiritual relationship. Faith gets privatized. Fellowship gets marginalized. When that happens the church is pushed to the periphery of their spiritual lives. If a person only cares about their own spiritual well-being, they will not help others mature in Christian obedience. The entire church and its effort to fulfill the Great Commission suffer.

But Matthew 28:18–20 strongly implies that a true disciple makes other disciples. To be a Christ follower is to make and help other Christ followers. Each one must teach one. That's how spiritual replication happens in a living, vibrant church. Colin Marshall and Tony Payne capture the heart of New Testament discipleship when they write:

> [T]he goal of Christian ministry is quite simple, and in a sense measurable: Are we making and nurturing genuine disciples of Christ? The church always tends toward institutionalism and secularization. The focus shifts to preserving traditional programs and structures, and the goal of discipleship is lost. The mandate of disciple-making provides the touchstone for whether our church is engaging in Christ's mission. Are we making genuine disciples of Jesus Christ? *Our goal is not to make church members or members of our institution, but genuine disciples of Jesus.*[7]

Eric Russ serves as senior pastor at Mack Avenue Community Church in inner-city Detroit, Michigan. The church emphasizes personal discipleship in a number of ways. First, they equate "disciple" with church membership. To be a member of the church is to be a disciple of Jesus Christ. To be a disciple shows itself in active commitment to the entire body of Christ. That's a helpful corrective to spiritual individualism and a tendency of some to think they can live the Christian life without the local church.

Second, every disciple/member is asked to commit to serving in a community group and personally helping one to two others grow in the Lord. With this requirement the church joins together personal faith with personal accountability for other individual Christians. As a consequence, no one remains unattached in the life of the church. Everyone has at least one meaningful spiritual relationship, a small group, and connection to the entire body of Christ. Mack Avenue Christian Church roots all of this in the church's understanding that disciples make other disciples.

A "Get in Where You Fit in" Strategy: Many Avenues into Discipleship

If it's true that black communities and black people vary greatly (and it is true!), then a one-size-fits-all approach to discipleship won't likely work for everyone. If our churches include a range of people from seniors, educated professionals, high schoolers, drop-outs, former convicts, intact families, hurting families, and everything in between, then we will need different ways of teaching these different people how to obey everything Jesus commanded in their particular life situations.

Eric Mason, lead pastor of Epiphany Fellowship in Philadelphia, recognized the challenge this diversity poses for disciple-making. When the church first began, a number of people recommended Mason start small group Bible studies right away. Mason hesitated because he understood that some members had never attended churches with small groups, others were suspicious of having people in their homes, and still others balked at practicing hospitality because they knew the unflattering backgrounds or past habits of some persons.

So rather than kick against the goads of people's experiences and fears, Epiphany attempted implementing a variety of disciple-making strategies. Structured small groups fit the schedules of some working professionals. Opening the church for discussions during the week eased the concerns of members uncomfortable with having people in their homes. A lot of time was invested in serving the community and helping people work through deep struggles with poverty, addiction, crime, and sexuality. Along the way, leaders challenged individualistic and sometimes selfish attitudes that worked against a culture of making disciples. The idea was to foster many ways of "going" and many ways of involving members with each other and the community. Members could join the work wherever and whenever they fit.

A Multigenerational Gender-Based Strategy

Intentional disciple-making will also require a strategy sensitive to the differing needs of men and women. Sometimes churches make the mistake of gearing the feel and teaching of their churches to one gender or the other. They then assume that a one-size-fits-all approach will meet the needs of all their attendees and members. But men and women have discipleship challenges unique to their particular status as men and women.

The Bible makes it clear that church leaders should give attention to both the generational and gender needs of the congregation. Consider the approach the apostle Paul requires of Titus as he organizes the church in Crete.

> You must teach what is in accord with sound doctrine. Teach the *older men* to be temperate, worthy of respect, self-controlled, and sound in faith, in love and in endurance. Likewise, teach the *older women* to be reverent in the way they live, not to be slanderers or addicted to much wine, but to teach what is good. Then they can train the *younger women* to love their husbands and children, to be self-controlled and pure, to be busy at home, to be kind, and to be subject to their husbands, so that no one will malign the word of God. Similarly, encourage the *young men* to be self-controlled. In everything set them an example by doing what is good. In your teaching show integrity, seriousness and soundness of speech that cannot be condemned, so that those who oppose you may be ashamed because they have nothing bad to say about us. (Titus 2:1–8 NIV, emphasis added)

Paul's multigenerational approach ensures that no segment of the congregation gets left out. In too many churches older members are pushed to the side in favor of younger, "dynamic" forms of worship and ministry. Churches who do this—sometimes unintentionally—rob themselves of the seasoned wisdom God intends to use in the discipleship of younger persons. That's why Paul insists that Titus include a focus on older men and older women in his teaching.

In turn, the older men and women become part of the disciple-making ministry. When mature older saints disciple, they help shoulder the ministry load often faced by pastors. Older women train younger women in areas of women's discipleship that most men would be poorly equipped to teach (vv. 4–5). Men know little about how difficult it is to care for a husband—even a good one! And most have little knowledge of effectively managing the competing demands of marriage, childrearing, and work outside the home. But older Christian ladies do and should be engaged in a gender-related approach to discipleship.

Similarly, older men must teach younger men one essential feature of mature manhood: self-control (v. 6). Men make men. Women have valiantly stood in the gap in many cases. But it takes spiritually mature older men to help younger men plumb the depths and challenges of manhood. Such a multigenerational gender-based strategy gets the entire church involved in the mission of making disciples.

A Church-Centered Strategy

Finally, black churches need a disciple-making strategy that centers on the local church as the hub of spiritual life. This is a new idea to many Christians. In our new members' class I like to ask attendees, "How would you define spiritual maturity?" Most attendees list things like: faithful Bible reading and prayer, sharing the faith with others, making good decisions, and so on.

None of those answers are wrong. They're just incomplete. They focus almost exclusively on the individual Christian and the activities they do in isolation from the church. This kind of individualism is endemic to Western culture, including the Black Church. Consequently, many people have no idea that their spiritual lives are connected to the entire congregation and that the congregation's spiritual vitality depends upon their walk with the Lord. It's in the fellowship of the local church that we're constantly reminded of what Jesus has done for us (2 Tim. 2:11–14). It's in assembling with other believers that we are stirred up in love and good deeds (Heb. 10:24–25). When we meet with other

Christians, we give and receive God's love in word and truth and receive assurance of our salvation through our love for one another (1 John 3:17–18; John 13:34–35).

Yet most Christians build their lives around their individual pursuits rather than their local church family. Christians move to new cities for a new job without ever stopping to ask, "Is there a solid gospel-preaching, disciple-making, life-giving local church there that I can join?" Many Christian college students choose a major and a university without ever asking, "Is there a church nearby where my soul gets fed and where I can help others grow as disciples?" Many times these Christians go years without active involvement in a local church—their souls and the church paying the price. Rather than build our lives around our own interests, we should build our lives around the collective interests and agenda of our local church.

Fellowship with God's people is not something that can be safely pushed to the margins of life, fit in when convenient. It ought to be something made central to our lives, with recreation, career, and other pursuits built around the church. Even the family routine should place the life and rhythm of the local church before little league games, school concerts, and other extra-curricular activities. Putting this kind of energy into our churches revives our church.

Conclusion

If the Lord gives me that grace, I will never forget that family Bible study He allowed my wife and me to lead. My mom, sisters, brothers, nieces, and nephews all gathered to learn and apply the Scripture. We studied Romans and the Gospel of John. In the first several weeks, a number of my family members made professions of faith in the Lord Jesus Christ. They were subsequently baptized, joined the local church, and continue in the obedience of faith today. What a joyful privilege it is to see God's work in the lives of His people. He means for us to be conformed to the image of His Son (Rom. 8:29). He accomplishes this goal through the fellowship of the local church (Eph. 4:11–16). The revival of black congregations will happen as the Spirit of God rekindles the hearts and minds of black Christians in discipleship.

CHAPTER 11

Redraw the Lines of Membership and Discipline

In the beginning was the black church, and the black church was with the black community, and the black church was the black community. The black church was in the beginning with the black people; all things were made through the black church, and without the black church was not anything made that was made. In the black church was life; and the life was the light of the black people.[1]
—JOSEPH WASHINGTON

Introduction

Fifty years ago most people took church membership for granted as a sign of "respectable" adulthood. No one questioned the virtue of belonging to a church. In fact, you faced a fair amount of social sanction if you failed to regularly attend services.[2]

Joining the church became a rite of passage. Sensing a child was "old enough to be baptized" and taken into the communion of the church, parents often applied pressure to ensure it happened. Both child and pastor felt cornered by parents eager to guarantee their children had a proper relationship to the church. Membership signaled maturity, morality, and mutual belonging.

We understand why belonging to a local church held such importance. For much of African-American history, the fortunes of black people rose and fell with the fortunes of the Black Church. The status of individual African-Americans depended in part on whether a wider hostile society viewed them as upstanding and respectable. The church and the people shared one concern for survival and one hope for justice. As Joseph Washington put it, "The black church was with the black community, and the black church was the black community." Community and church were coterminous.

And coterminous with the community is how we've come to think of the church in our day and age. Most African-Americans regard the church as existing with and for the broader African-American community, in some cases without respect to whether people in the broader community share the church's faith. Since we see ourselves sharing the same *fate*, we sometimes overlook whether we share the same *faith*.

But it's not always been that way. There was a time when the Black Church—though actively concerned for the black community's future— maintained a healthy distinction between the church and the world. That distinction gave vitality and focus to its spiritual mission. Over the long course of its history, though, the line between church and community has been blurred. That blurring of the line has affected the church's witness and holiness.

It may seem counterintuitive, but the path to the church's revival *and* the community's vitality involves redrawing a dividing line between the church and the world.

Redrawing the Borders of Church Membership

Today it's not uncommon to hear professing Christians ask whether church membership is even a biblical concept. Some reject the notion as an old command-and-control approach to the Christian life. They emphasize the importance of *spiritual* membership in the body of Christ over local visible membership in congregations. But is that the best way to define what it means to be "the church" or Christian discipleship?

A Biblical Theology of Church Membership

In both the Old and New Testaments God calls His people to come out from all the other nations in order to form an identifiable community that embodies His character. We see this from Genesis to Revelation.

Membership in the Old Testament. The call to membership in the covenant community begins as early as God's call to Abram in Genesis 12. Abram, a pagan man when we meet him at the end of Genesis 11, is separated from his father and his homeland in order to become a "great nation" in the land God promised to show him (Gen. 11:27–12:3). Abram's descendants will bear the mark of their covenant relationship with God: circumcision. That ritual cutting of foreskin symbolized their belonging to God. The ritual of circumcision was in a sense the first "church membership class." Anyone without the symbol of the covenant was to be "cut off" from the people (Gen. 17:12–14). From the onset of His redemptive work, God established an "in" and an "out" for His people. Either there was the cutting off of the foreskin for those who were in or there was the cutting off of membership in God's covenant community for those who were out.

God's people would not only have an "in" and "out" to clarify membership, they were to also maintain a distinct *identity* from all other people groups. They were to be "God's people." In the Exodus, God repeatedly declares His intention to distinguish Israel from Egypt and all the other nations. The Lord proclaimed to Pharaoh through Moses, "On that day I will deal differently with the land of Goshen, where my people live; no swarms of flies will be there, so that you will know that I, the LORD, am in this land. *I will make a distinction between my people and your people*" (Exod. 8:22–23 NIV, emphasis added). The distinction God made between Israel and the nations served to make it clear that Israel belonged to God as His covenant people. Moses reminds Israel that "as for you, the LORD took you and brought you out of the iron-smelting furnace, out of Egypt, *to be the people of his inheritance, as you now are*" (Deut. 4:20 NIV, emphasis added).

They were distinct and special for no other reason than God chose them and loved them.

For you are a people holy to the LORD your God. The LORD your God has chosen you out of all the peoples on the face of the earth to be his people, his treasured possession. *The LORD did not set His affection on you and choose you because you were more numerous than other peoples,* for you were the fewest of all peoples. *But it was because the* LORD *loved you and kept the oath he swore to your forefathers* that he brought you out with a mighty hand and redeemed you from the land of slavery, from the power of Pharaoh king of Egypt. Know therefore that the LORD your God is God; he is the faithful God, keeping his covenant of love to a thousand generations of those who love him and keep his commands. (Deut. 7:6–9 NIV, emphasis added)

Unlike other nations, Israel's blessedness did not come from great numbers, swelling armies, or even historical happenstance. They were small in number. They had no army to speak of in the Exodus. Rather, God chose and loved them. Because He loved them, He fought for them. Their future was guaranteed because God was sure to keep His promises. Providence guided them, not happenstance. God's electing love made Israel different—nothing else.

Moreover, God made Israel distinct and special by living among them. His presence set them apart. Moses recognized this. That's why he asked God, "How will anyone know that you are pleased with me and with your people unless you go with us? *What else will distinguish me and your people from all the other people on the face of the earth?*" (Exod. 33:16 NIV, emphasis added). God's covenant people were a community in which God Himself dwelled. Because God dwelled among them, the Israelites were to share in God's character. In the dramatic scene on Mt. Sinai, God gave to Israel His holy Law, which embodied His character and was to define the community's character. Being near to God, they were to be like God. The Lord spoke to them, saying, "Now if you obey me fully and keep my covenant, then out of all nations you will be my treasured possession. Although the whole earth is mine, you will be for me a kingdom of priests and a holy nation" (Exod. 19:5–6 NIV).

God's intent throughout the Old Testament was that Israel should be a visible, distinct, holy community in which He lived with His people. They were to be treasured by God because He loved them, chose them, and taught them His statutes. There was to be a clear demarcation between being *in* covenant with God and being *outside* the covenant of God's people. Israel was to be unlike any other nation on earth. An Israelite's entire identity and sense of purpose depended upon their membership in the community. To be "cut off" was the worst possible fate; to be included was for the Israelite to be established "in praise, fame and honor high above all the nations [God] has made" (Deut. 26:19).

Membership in the New Testament. Most people will admit that God's covenant with Israel created a distinct religious and even ethnic community with clearly marked membership. But many people fail to recognize the same pattern in the New Testament. They rightly understand that the coming of Jesus Christ opened the way of a new covenant not just with Israel but with all the nations of the earth. But some mistakenly think this broadening of God's redemptive purposes erases the borders of membership. On the contrary, the New Testament takes the foundation laid with Israel in the Old Testament and extends it to all those brought into new covenant relationship with God through faith in Jesus Christ.

For instance, the New Testament's view of church membership includes a very clear "in" and "out," but that "in" and "out" depends neither on sociology nor ethnicity. Membership is not a matter of joining a club or of being born into the correct ethnic group. New Testament church membership relies upon a distinctively Christological idea—our union with Christ through faith. The word "member" or "part" comes from the unique "body of Christ" metaphor used to describe the Christian church. For example, Paul writes, "You are the body of Christ, and each one of you is a part [or member] of it" (1 Cor. 12:27 NIV). Bear in mind Paul writes this to a *visible local congregation*, not to the invisible, universal church. Persons are either "in Christ" or they are "separated from Christ, alienated from the commonwealth of Israel and strangers to the covenants of promise, having no hope and without God in the world" (Eph. 2:12). So the "in" and "out" comes from whether or not we are united to Christ through faith and our status is reflected in our membership in visible, local churches.

Moreover, God expresses great care in designing the body of Christ. Each Person in the Trinity plays a part in assembling the members of the local congregation. "The body is a unit, though it is made up of many parts; and though all its parts are many, they form one body. So it is with Christ. For we were all baptized by one Spirit into one body—whether Jews or Greeks, slave or free—and we were all given the one Spirit to drink. . . . In fact God has arranged the parts in the body, every one of them, just as he wanted them to be" (1 Cor. 12:12–13, 18 NIV). Christ incorporates us into His body. The Spirit baptizes us into Christ. The Father arranges us just as He wants. From this divine activity we get the uniquely Christian notion of church membership.

Nearly all the membership motifs describing Israel in the Old Testament—they're distinct from the unbelieving peoples, God's dwelling among them, their specialness to God, and separation from the unholy— in the New Testament get applied to the local church. The apostle Paul captures the New Testament imperative to be a distinct and holy people in his letter to the Corinthian church:

> Do not be yoked together with unbelievers. For what do righteousness and wickedness have in common? Or what fellowship can light have with darkness? What harmony is there between Christ and Belial? What does a believer have in common with an unbeliever? What agreement is there between the temple of God and idols? For we are the temple of the living God. As God has said: "I will live with them and walk among them, and I will be their God, and they will be my people." Therefore come out from them and be separate, says the Lord. Touch no unclean thing, and I will receive you." And "I will be a Father to you, and you will be my sons and daughters, says the Lord Almighty." (2 Cor. 6:14–18 NIV)

Further, the promise of God to dwell among His people in the Old Testament finds greater fulfillment through Jesus' indwelling in the New Testament. Consider the Savior's promise to the disciples in John 14:

> "If you love me, you will obey what I command. And I will ask the Father, and *he will give you another Counselor to be with you forever*—the Spirit of truth. The world cannot accept him, because it neither sees him nor knows him. But you know him, for *he lives with you and will be in you.* I will not leave you as orphans; *I will come to you.* . . . On that day you will realize that *I am in my Father, and you are in me, and I am in you.* Whoever has my commands and obeys them, he is the one who loves me. He who loves me will be loved by my Father, and *I too will love him and show myself to him.* . . . If anyone loves me, he will obey my teaching. My Father will love him, and *we will come to him*

and make our home with him." (John 14:15–18, 20–21, 23 NIV, emphasis added)

Jesus' words harken back to God's promise in Exodus 19:5–6. But where God promised to dwell in the tabernacle in the midst of Israel, Jesus now promises that the Spirit will be in the disciples. The Father and the Son will come to the disciples and make their home with them, even *in* them just as the Son is in the Father. The New Testament people of God are a people *in* whom God dwells as a temple (1 Cor. 3:16; 6:19).

In the new covenant the church becomes what Israel failed to be. The apostle Peter writes to "God's elect, strangers in the world, scattered throughout Pontus, Galatia, Cappadocia, Asia and Bithynia" (1 Pet. 1:1 NIV). Peter clearly assigns to the local church the characteristics and roles once attributed to Israel. He declares, "You are a chosen people, a royal priesthood, a holy nation, a people belonging to God, that you may declare the praises of him who called you out of darkness into his wonderful light" (1 Pet. 2:9 NIV; compare with Exod. 19:5–6).

And just like Israel in the old covenant, the new covenant church also received a sign of membership to its ranks: water baptism. From the days of John the Baptist, those who repented gave testimony to that fact and declared their faith in Jesus the Messiah through baptism (Matt. 3:6; Acts 2:38). But unlike the old covenant, a person is not eligible for this sign by being naturally born into the covenant community. He or she must be born again (John 3:3).[3] Baptism marks the repentant and regenerate believer as an initiate in the family of the faithful. Acts 2:41 records the typical pattern: "Those who accepted his message were baptized, and about three thousand were added to their number that day" (NIV).

Finally, we see New Testament church membership in action in the various "one another" passages that require Christians to live together in empathy and sympathy. For example, Paul exhorts the Corinthian church with the words, "But God has combined the members of the body and has given greater honor to the parts that lacked it, so that there should be no division in the body, but that its parts should have equal concern for each other. If one part suffers, every part suffers with it; if one part is honored, every part rejoices with it" (1 Cor. 12:24–26 NIV). Because we are united to one another in the body of Christ, formed into one new man or spiritual ethnicity in Christ (Eph. 2:15), we're called to love one another, serve one another, honor one another, forgive one another, bear with one another, and many other things befitting the people of God.

The local church, then, is to "come out from among" the unbelieving community. It must be identifiable for its unity, holiness, love, and fidelity to the apostolic gospel of Christ.

Why Does Church Membership Matter?

To some people, discussions of church membership seem to be an exercise in elitist exclusion, an out-of-date administrative formality, or a case of supercilious theological snobbery. Drawing a line between the church and the world can feel unloving, like forsaking those in need. In the Black Church context it can even feel like a betrayal of the church's mission to and in the community.

But a sound biblical understanding and practice of membership expresses love for *both* the church *and* the community. Church membership represents a way of being *for* the community by being different *from* the community. A healthy practice of church membership yields at least four benefits.

First, an identifiable church membership helps clarify the gospel. When God's people assemble into distinctive communities and live in accord with the grace that is in Jesus Christ, the unbelieving world gets to see the gospel in action. Recall the distinction God made between Israel and Egypt in the Exodus. God delivered Israel in the Exodus "so that [Egypt] will know that I, the LORD, am in this land" (Exod. 8:22–23 NIV). Likewise, in the New Testament, God calls the church to live in loving community so that "all men will know you are my disciples" (John 13:35 NIV) and to live sanctified by the word in oneness "so that the world may believe that [the Father has] sent [Jesus]" (John 17:17, 21). Such a community is formed by the gospel. For the world to see our love and heed our message, it needs to see an identifiable church membership obeying Jesus.

Second, an identifiable church membership strengthens the church's reputation. If the church becomes indistinct from the world by being in it *and* of it, the church loses its saltiness and its light. Its deeds are no longer visible and no longer bring praise to God the Father in heaven (Matt. 5:13–16). When we fail to practice church membership effectively, we are like hundreds of individuals lost in a vast, dark wilderness with small flashlights. From the dim torches, we see here and there a faint glow. But when we assemble the hundreds of Christians together, all with their flashlights beaming, we magnify the light in that vast darkness. Clarifying church membership concentrates and magnifies the witnessing light of Jesus Christ in the local church and it strengthens the church's reputation.

Third, an identifiable membership promotes the spiritual and practical transformation Jesus brings into the world. Churches are made up of renewed and rehabilitated sinners. This means local churches should be filled with transformation stories. The church becomes a commercial for radical new life. Churches should be communities of people who all testify that we were sexually immoral, idolaters, adulterers, prostitutes, homosexuals, thieves, greedy, drunks, slanderers, and swindlers "but [we] were washed, [we] were sanctified, [we] were justified in the name of the Lord Jesus Christ and by the Spirit of our God" (1 Cor. 6:11). We're a community where the old things have passed away and all things have become new (2 Cor. 5:17). That transformation gives powerful hope to those in need of newness of life. Clarifying the membership of the church helps those looking for hope know how powerful God is in the life of the repentant and trusting.

Fourth, a healthy practice of church membership creates an alternative community and culture to the world. The world longs for joy, peace, love, and hope. Yet, the world does not and cannot find what Dr. King called "the beloved community" as long as it continues under the rule of darkness. Lawlessness increases and love grows cold (Matt. 24:12). The world watches in horror as "evil people and impostors . . . go on from bad to worse, deceiving and being deceived" (2 Tim. 3:13). Each community outside the church turns out to be like all other communities. Only one group promises an alternative culture built on love, joy, peace, patience, kindness, goodness, gentleness, and self-control—the local church. But if its members are dispersed among and unrecognizable from the world, then the alluring hope of an alternative community evaporates. When congregations identify their membership and live out the faith in new covenant commitment, then the church becomes a "city on a hill," the city of God beckoning wayfarers into its gates of peace.

Maintaining the Borders of the Church through Church Discipline

But such a community cannot long exist without some caretaking of its borders. All communities need a mechanism for preserving their character and integrity. The local church is no different. How can a healthy church full of love, unity, and holiness maintain these qualities?

Critics often charge the church with hypocrisy. The watching world takes note of our shortcomings and spares no time in pointing them out. And let's be honest: Far too often they're correct. Churches *do* suffer from inconsistency and hypocrisy—especially when they condemn the sinful practices of the world while failing to correct those of the church.

But the Scripture calls us to get the logs out of our own eyes before we bother the specks in the eyes of a watching world. Moreover, in both Testaments of Scripture God calls His people to the loving practice of correction and discipline as the process for ensuring integrity and removing hypocrisy. That's how the Black Church protects its borders while renewing life inside the community.

A Biblical Theology of Church Discipline

Discipline in the Old Testament. Just as the Old Testament records the assembling of Israel into a new community set apart as God's people, it also records for us God's insistence that Israel practice discipline among its members. Old Testament discipline practices appear harsh and unloving to many in our day. And there are many horror stories of discipline gone wrong. There's reason to approach this topic with caution. Poor practices hurt people. But rightly understood, what the Bible says about correcting others is a means of restoration and love in difficult situations.[4]

The practice begins right at the onset of God's deliverance of Israel from bondage so they can worship Him. Celebrating the Passover was required of all Israelites. Those who failed to observe the commemoration were disciplined. "If a man who is ceremonially clean and not on a journey fails to celebrate the Passover, that person must be cut off from his people because he did not present the LORD's offering at the appointed time" (Num. 9:13 NIV). To be "cut off" from the community was to be removed from all the redemptive work of God among His people. It was to be shut out of fellowship, separated from the presence of God in the midst of the people, and to be barred from the life-giving Word of God. No more serious sanction existed.

Other infractions also required being "cut off." Misuse of the anointing oil and incense set apart exclusively for worship resulted in dismembering the guilty (Exod. 30:33, 38). Profaning the Sabbath earned the community's discipline (Exod. 31:14), as did killing animals without offering sacrifices (Lev. 17:3–4, 8–9) and eating the blood of animals (Lev. 17:10).

The practice of discipline helped to remove "detestable things" (NIV) from God's holy community (Lev. 18:29 NIV) and correct people who "desecrated what is holy to the LORD" (Lev. 19:8 NIV). The Law required stoning to death when the "disgraceful thing" of "being promiscuous" was done. Israel was to "purge the evil from among" them (Deut. 22:18–21 NIV). The very language of "detestable," "desecrated," "disgraceful," and "purge the evil" reminds us that, in practicing discipline, the covenant community assumed God's perspective against sin and sinners rather than the sinner's perspective against God and holiness. In discipline God "set his face against" the guilty party. In like fashion, the community was to set its face against the sin and sinner. We find a clear example of this in Leviticus 20:1–5, when the Lord requires capital punishment for those Israelites who sacrificed their children to the idol Molech:

> The LORD spoke to Moses, saying, "Say to the people of Israel, Any one of the people of Israel or of the strangers who sojourn in Israel who gives any of his children to Molech shall surely be put to death. The people of the land shall stone him with stones. I myself will set my face against that man and will cut him off from among his people, because he has given one of his children to Molech, to make my sanctuary unclean and to profane my holy name. And if the people of the land do at all close their eyes to that man when he gives one of his children to Molech, and do not put him to death, then I will set my face against that man and against his clan and will cut them off from among their people, him and all who follow him in whoring after Molech."

The human heart tends to identify with man in his sin over God in His holiness. As a consequence, we tend to "close our eyes" to sins that we ought to address. God's gift of discipline helps the covenant community avoid that fallen tendency and remember their highest allegiance is to God's holy name. That's why the Lord requires the entire community to enact these sanctions. "The hands of the witnesses must be the first in putting [a sinner] to death, and then the hands of all the people" (Deut. 17:7 NIV). In this fashion the entire nation witnessed against and punished the sin of Achan in Joshua 7. The group's participation in the discipline illustrates their partaking of God's holiness as their own and acceptance of responsibility for executing God's charge against the wrongdoer.

Consider, for example, the Lord's instruction in the case of blasphemy:

> Then the LORD spoke to Moses, saying, "Bring out of the camp the one who cursed, and *let all who heard him lay their hands on his head, and let all the congregation stone him.* And speak to the people of Israel, saying, Whoever curses his God shall bear his sin. Whoever blasphemes the name of the LORD shall surely be put to death. *All the congregation shall stone him.* The sojourner as well as the native, when he blasphemes the Name, shall be put to death." (Lev. 24:13–16, emphasis added)

If upholding the sanctity of God's name is the goal for the entire community, then the entire community must join in the solemn duty of ridding itself of sin and evil. There is no way for the correction to have the desired effect unless everyone plays their part.

Though the old covenant sanctions for unrepentant sin were stiff, the correction had redemptive purposes as well. God required strict discipline in order to arouse reverence for His holy Law. Consider how God instructs Israel to discipline rebellious sons.

> "If a man has a stubborn and rebellious son who will not obey the voice of his father or the voice of his mother, and, though they discipline him, will not listen to them, then *his father and his mother shall take hold of him and bring him out to the elders of his city at the gate* of the place where he lives, and they shall say to the elders of his city, 'This our son is stubborn and rebellious; he will not obey our voice; he is a glutton and a drunkard.' Then *all the men of the city shall stone him to death with stones.* So you shall purge the evil from your midst, and *all Israel shall hear, and fear.*" (Deut. 21:18–21, emphasis added)

Upholding discipline was a responsibility that fell to every Israelite, from fathers and mothers, to elders of the city, to the entire nation. The goal was fear or holy reverence for God. That's why anyone showing contempt toward the Word of God or the teachers of God's Word were to be put to death. When the sentence was executed, "All the people will hear and be afraid, and will not be contemptuous again" (Deut. 17:12–13 NIV). The Lord's correction was meant to bring repentance and restoration to greater Israel (see, for example, Lev. 26:21–24).

We should note one final aspect of Old Testament discipline. The Old Testament repeatedly links discipline to God's Word. At bottom, sin is breaking the law. It is disregarding God's commands. The Word of the Lord must be honored by all His people. God does not negotiate for obedience any more than the American government negotiates with terrorists. Defying His Word amounts to blaspheming His Person. "Anyone who sins defiantly, whether native-born or alien, *blasphemes the LORD*, and that person must be cut off from his people. Because *he has despised the LORD's word and broken his commands*, that person must surely be cut off; his guilt remains on him" (Num. 15:30–31 NIV, emphasis added). The community maintains its integrity, protects its borders, and exalts the name of the Lord by heeding the Word of the Lord. As the community keeps God's Word in its heart, God keeps the community in His heart.

Discipline in the New Testament. The New Testament continues the Old Testament's concern for the holiness of God's people. The Lord Jesus Himself insists that the new covenant community "must be perfect, as your heavenly Father is perfect" (Matt. 5:48). The apostle Peter transfers God's call on Israel to the church scattered throughout Asia when he writes, "just as he who called you is holy, so be holy in all you do; for it is written: 'Be holy, because I am holy'" (1 Pet. 1:15–16 NIV). Paul reminds the Thessalonians that "God did not call us to be impure, but to live a holy life" (1 Thess. 4:7 NIV). And John the beloved disciple expresses the call to holiness with the words, "If we claim to have fellowship with him yet walk in the darkness, we lie and do not live by the truth" (1 John 1:6 NIV).

As with the old covenant, new covenant discipline concerns itself with personal relationships, doctrinal fidelity, and moral purity. In the case of *personal relationships*, the Lord Jesus gives the disciples clear instruction in Matthew 18:15–17. An offended brother has the responsibility of going to his brother to reveal and discuss the offense that has taken place. The aim of the conversation is to "win your brother" to reconciliation. If the private discussion fails to achieve the goal, then the offended brother must take two or three witnesses along also. Involving a small group of witnesses to exhort the offender to repentance communicates the seriousness of the personal offense and the necessity of repentance and reconciliation. If the sinning brother will not listen to the witnesses, then the matter must be brought to the entire church who acts as the final court of appeals. Just as in the old covenant, discipline continues to be a community responsibility. If the church cannot persuade a brother or sister to repent and be reconciled, then they are to remove the person from their fellowship and "treat him like a pagan or tax collector." That is, they are to "cut off" the sinner from the life of the community and from the ordinances, regarding the unrepentant as they would an unbeliever until such time as repentance takes place.

The congregation must also take action in cases of *moral transgression*. Discipline can take place in the case of any observable and unrepentant sin, but the New Testament gives particular attention to sexual immorality. We're told "There must not be even a hint of sexual immorality" among "God's holy people" (Eph. 5:3 NIV). We're warned that "No immoral, impure or greedy person—such a man is an idolater—has any inheritance in the kingdom of Christ and of God" and "because of such things God's wrath comes on those who are disobedient" (Eph. 5:5–6 NIV). Likewise, Paul urgently commands the church at Thessalonica to pursue God's will in sanctification, avoiding God's avenging judgment against the sexually immoral (1 Thess. 4:3–8).

Paul instructed the Ephesian church not to be "partners" with such people. To use the words of the Old Testament, they were to be "cut off." The apostle exhorted the church at Corinth not to "associate with anyone who calls himself a brother but is sexually immoral or greedy, an idolater or a slanderer, a drunkard or a swindler" (1 Cor. 5:11 NIV). The Corinthian Christians were not to even eat with such a person. Instead, the congregation was "with grief" to "put the man out of [their] fellowship" (1 Cor. 5:2 NIV), which was synonymous with "handing him over to Satan" (1 Cor. 5:5 NIV). Far worse than the punishment of immediate stoning required by the old covenant, the new covenant envisions a living chastisement at the hands of the Adversary outside the safety of the church.

The New Testament also calls the church community to exercise discipline in the case of *doctrinal error*. Departures from God's Word bring division in the body of Christ and lead to a host of other moral problems and sins. So, Paul teaches Titus, "Warn a divisive person once, and then warn him a second time. After that, have nothing to do with him. You may be sure such a man is warped and sinful; he is self-condemned" (Titus 3:10–11 NIV). Paul calls the church in Rome to "watch out for those who cause divisions and put obstacles in your way contrary to the teaching you have learned. Keep away from them. For such people are not serving our Lord Christ, but their own appetites. By smooth talk and flattery they deceive the minds of naive people" (Rom. 16:17–18 NIV). And the apostle insists that the church in Galatia pronounce an anathema on anyone who "preach[ed] a gospel other than the one [the apostles] preached to [them]" (Gal. 1:8 NIV). Paul's charge to the Galatian congregations rather than the elders or another body of leaders makes it clear that the responsibility of protecting the church belonged to the Christian community as a whole, just as it did with Israel as a whole.

With all this talk of discipline, we need to be careful to also observe the *spirit* of these instructions. Though the Lord calls His church to exercise correction, He never calls the church to do so in anger or self-righteousness. Rather, as in the case with Corinth, He calls the church to grieve over sin and to be gentle with the brethren caught in sin (Gal. 6:1–2). The Lord calls the church to excommunicate unrepentant sinning members so they might, by His grace, be restored to fellowship with Christ and with the church. So, "hand this man over to Satan" has a purpose—"so that the sinful nature may be destroyed and his spirit saved on the day of the Lord" (1 Cor. 5:5 NIV). With gentleness we warn the divisive opponent once and a second time "in the hope that God will grant them repentance leading them to a knowledge of the truth, and that they will come to their senses and escape from the trap of the devil, who has taken them captive to do his will" (2 Tim. 2:25–26 NIV). The goal of new covenant discipline most emphatically is *not punishment*. The goal of biblical correction is restoration and recovery of erring saints.

The faithful practice of discipline helps protect the name of Christ, sanctify the church, and recover the erring. Discipline communicates the truth and power of the gospel in the midst of a world certain of the church's hypocrisy.

The Black Church's History of Practicing Discipline

The idea of church discipline may be new to many of our churches and to many Christians. Often when things appear new to us we reject them as "alien" or "foreign" to our community and culture. But in truth, church discipline is not new to the African-American church.

The practice of discipline was one of the early strengths of black churches. Greg Wills, church history professor at The Southern Baptist Theological Seminary, describes the practice among African-American Baptist churches in the late 1800s:

> The picture that emerged is clear: African-American Baptists filled the dockets of their ecclesiastical tribunals well into the twentieth century. In the antebellum period, the sample churches prosecuted 4 percent of their members annually, a rate 39 percent higher than white-controlled churches attained. They excommunicated members at a rate 65 percent higher than whites, nearly 2.5 percent of members each year. Between 1861 and 1900, when the white churches were relaxing their discipline, the African-American churches maintained most of their rigor. They still prosecuted 3.5 percent and excluded 2.3 percent of their membership annually. Defendants in the black churches received excommunication more frequently than in the white churches. Both before and after the Civil War, black churches excluded more than 60 percent of those accused.[5]

From the early days of her founding into the early twentieth century, African-American churches excelled at this command of the Lord. As stated in many of their covenants, they endeavored to "walk together in brotherly love, as becomes the members of a Christian Church, exercise an affectionate care and watchfulness over each other and faithfully admonish and entreat one another as occasion may require." They were faithful to the name of Christ and faithful to love the sinning brethren by admonishment and even excommunication. Loving correction made the church strong and contributed to its growth. They were convinced that the key to the church's power is not found in numbers but in holiness. So they pursued a biblical vision of life as the community of God's people in the midst of a world estranged from God. The Lord blessed them for their faithfulness.

Does Church Discipline Have a Future in Black Churches?

Today, many leaders could hardly imagine growing the church by reducing her membership. They want to woo members at all costs, hardly addressing how they live out the faith. But the abandonment of discipline blurs the lines between the church and the world, sapping the bride of Christ of her beauty and power. Revival of the African-American church depends upon the recovery of healthy discipline practices.

But do our churches' leaders have the biblical integrity and the courage of faith to slowly and wisely reestablish a practice that's so commonly out of favor with professing Christians? Few things will make us less popular with some members than returning to biblical correction of unrepentant sinners. Few things will likely lead to more misunderstanding in the wider community than "putting people out of the church."

Yet, few things could be more clear than the Lord's demand that His churches be holy as He is holy and remove the yeast of sin from their midst.

If we're going to right the ship and recover what has been lost, we will need to commit ourselves to a few important principles. *First, we'll need to commit ourselves to constantly preaching and applying the gospel until our people thoroughly understand what kind of life is consistent with the gospel.* Every Christian constantly needs their mind renewed (Rom. 12:1–2). We need to be squeezed into a new gospel mold so that our lives are worthy of the calling we've received in Christ (Eph. 4:1; Col. 1:10; 1 Thess. 2:12). But we cannot drift into a gospel lifestyle; we must "work out [our] salvation in fear and trembling" (Phil. 2:12). We must "put off [our] old self" and "put on the new self, created to be like God in true righteousness and holiness" (Eph. 4:22, 24 NIV). This requires thoughtfulness and effort in applying the transforming power of the gospel to our lives and to the culture of our churches.

Second, we'll need to commit ourselves to teaching God's people about membership and discipline. If we have been born again, then we have been born into a new family. It seems many have forgotten the Bible's teaching about these topics or never received instruction in the first place. We'll need to lead with patient, thorough, and repeated teaching on the subjects of membership and discipline. Existing and prospective members will need to take individual and collective responsibility for one another's welfare. Anonymity and sinful independence must be replaced with familiarity and healthy interdependence.

Third, we'll need to commit ourselves to creating a culture and community where membership means something and is highly prized. If our "community" only gathers on Sunday and people have very little connection with one another, we won't have the relational context needed for making or correcting disciples. Our efforts at inclusion and correction will look like intrusion and cultic control. Moreover, if membership means next-to-nothing, then excommunication will mean next-to-nothing. Belonging should be so valued among the people of God that just the thought of being removed would work reverence and repentance. After all, the local church is supposed to be a family—the family of God. Either losing our place in the family or losing a sibling from the family ought to break our hearts. Membership should mean that much to us.

From *the Community,* for *the Community, while* in *the Community*

We might summarize the Bible's teaching on church membership with three prepositions: *from, for,* and *in.* A local church wishing to maintain spiritual dynamism and relevance must first be distinguishable *from* the community. She must be called out from the world and set apart unto Christ. Having a clear membership practice and obeying the call to loving church discipline help distinguish the church from the world. Second, the local church discovers its vitality and power as she works *for* the community's redemption. She separates from the world so that she might model *for* the world the transforming grace of God. The community benefits as the congregation's life reflects the truth and reality of the gospel. But such benefits will only be accessible if the church operates *in* the community. Her witness cannot be seen from a distance. It must be observed up close, right in the midst of the wider community's daily life and struggles.

The importance of being distinct *from* the community, *for* the community, while *in* the community comes into focus when we consider the plight of large numbers of African-Americans in major cities. Many African-American churches today find it difficult to reach people in our country's inner cities, especially young people from the hip-hop generation. Ralph Basui Watkins, associate professor of evangelism and church growth at Columbia Theological Seminary, attributes the church's difficulty in reaching this generation of city dwellers to the political and economic success that made it possible for the church to leave major cities for the suburbs. Contrasting the influence of hip-hop with the Black Church, Watkins writes:

> The black church is now . . . finding it difficult to reach inner-city, working-class, working-poor, and nonworking-poor African Americans. But the communities that are difficult for the African American church to reach are the very places hip-hop culture lives. It reaches out, touches, affirms, and communicates with the pain, struggles, and realities of these communities. The face of the black church has changed; its membership does not consist of many in the hip-hop generation. . . . The class divide within the African American community is partially responsible for hip-hop being the first major cultural movement rooted in African American culture that wasn't nurtured by the African American institutionalized church. Hip-hop was nurtured by the very streets from which the African American church retreated and now finds difficult to reach. The institutionalized church didn't nurture and lead the hip-hop prophetic movement. As the class divide within African American community widened, the black church continued to become a middle-class bastion.[6]

In Watkins's view, success made the church irrelevant to the community in part by moving the church outside the community. With the rise of megachurches and satellite campuses, the "local" in "local churches" is fast disappearing. Where the body of Christ ceases to be local, it ceases to be visible and transformative. Salt must season the dish; light must shine in dark places. There's no effective way to be a preserving or enlightening agent if the church does not operate in decaying and dark places. If Watkins's analysis is correct, then the flight of the Black Church to suburban America represents a materialistic monasticism, an upscale Amish retreat from the very places where being different *from* is most likely to result in benefits *for* the community.

Conclusion

Biblical approaches to membership and discipline can be recovered. Their recovery will mean a revitalization of the church. Moreover, by redrawing the lines between the church and the world, the world will have a visible alternative to the brokenness and sin that afflicts it. But this will only happen if the lines that are redrawn are in local communities of need.

CHAPTER 12

Reclaim Black Men and the Black Family

There is something strange and even demonic about the case against the black male. Maybe the origin of this strange, demonic behavior is as ancient as the story of the birth of Jesus in an oppressed Jewish family. The Jewish mother, Mary, has been venerated. But the Jewish father, Joseph, has been virtually ignored. . . . He, a poor and persecuted Jewish man, responded according to the requirements of grace. And for so doing, Joseph has become invisible and virtually ignored when the story of the birth of Jesus is celebrated annually. Black men, and especially poor black men, exist in the tradition of Joseph—invisible, ignored, and denied. Nevertheless, their way of life is something of value—essential and significant in social organization. The lessons they can teach we ignore at our peril.[1]
—CHARLES V. WILLIE AND RICHARD J. REDDICK

Introduction

I was a college student the first time I heard someone refer to black men as "an endangered species." A professor made the remark at an orientation for incoming African-American freshmen.

I'm not sure I processed all the implications of the remark when it was made. But I did sense two things. First, I realized I was being watched in a new way. I felt as if I was living in a story not of my making, a kind of alienness to what I thought was my own life. I felt like a spectator watching others watching me. Second, I felt vulnerable and dangerous, slightly cornered and threatened. Something wild stirred. I was "endangered," like a sperm whale or bald eagle. I wondered how such animals felt—perhaps alone, chronic low-level fear, uncertain.

Various speakers and writers bandied about the "endangered species" label and supporting statistics until they became ubiquitous in the 1980s. They gave us a dire projection: "One in four black men will be in jail or prison or dead by the year 2000" or "by the age of twenty-one." Before long, speakers restated the projection as a *fact*. "One in four *is* . . ." Some drew the comparison with college students more sharply. They told us, "There are more black men in jail or in prison than in college." Such statements became unquestioned orthodoxy regarding black men. Little else needed to be stated or interpreted. There it was in a statistic—black men are in danger of extinction.

I left for college a promising young man. I arrived a statistic.

I think our administrators and leaders were simply trying to challenge us to make the most of college. We were to finish our education and, once graduated, contribute to changing the statistic. But how?

No one explained how a statistic could change another statistic, how the collectively "endangered" could change their status. We simply were supposed to. I felt stuck somewhere between *Menace to Society* and *Do the Right Thing*, trying to find a way to be angry and righteous, all while untutored and confused about true manhood.

One campus staff worker, Dr. Thomas Conway, helped me escape the "School Daze." One day he said in passing, "You know . . . the difference between you and the young brother shot or in jail is the five seconds you stop and think before acting." Having already been arrested as a young teen, I immediately knew the truth of what Dr. Conway said. He was right. My life was as precarious and precious as all the lives of other black men marked "endangered." I knew the turns in my life could happen as rapidly as five seconds of thought—even less. I knew also that too many young men like me did not have a Dr. Conway telling them this truth.

Too many still don't.

Dr. Conway, a rare African-American faculty member at a predominantly white university, was awakening my young conscience. He was raising my awareness of a challenging reality. The continuance of black communities and the revival of black churches depend upon the reclamation of black men and boys.

Biblically Define Manhood

African-American churches must define and teach biblical expectations for manhood. As Dr. Eric Mason points out, "Young men are forced to wing it when it comes to manhood." As a consequence, "what we're finding now . . . is that 'childhood' is growing longer and longer. Boys are not only failing to become responsible and godly men; they aren't becoming men at all."[2]

Defining manhood itself may be the greatest challenge facing men today. Confusion about the concept of manhood gives rise to many other challenges men face. Not until we're clear on what a man *is* can we be certain about what a man *does*.

The book of Genesis gives us some of the most foundational teaching on what it means to be a man. There we find manhood illustrated with three critical relationships. The church has to continue to teach this basic theology of manhood and help the men of the community embrace and apply it.

First, a man is someone who stands in submissive relationship to God in worship. Any man living apart from God is not, in the higher sense, a "man." He lives beneath his calling and purpose because he is not properly oriented to his Maker. A man, to put it simply, is a worshipper. The entire creation account of Genesis 1–2 intimates worship. First, we see that man is created "in the image and likeness of God." This characteristic allows man to commune with his Creator. Second, we see hints of worship in the different names used for God in Genesis 1 and 2. In Genesis 1, the writer primarily uses the name *Elohim*. But in Genesis 2, he switches to God's covenant name, Lord God or *YHWH Elohim*. It's a name implying a relationship, a bond, or intimacy. The use of God's covenant name foreshadows God's intention that man be oriented to Him in worship. Third, the Sabbath rest represents a call for men to worship. The Sabbath is the first thing God makes holy. One theologian describes the Sabbath as a "temporal shrine" designed for man's communion with his Lord. The apex of manhood is worship. This is true of women too, but the point needs to be stressed for men because men tend to view worship as weak and feminine.

Second, a man is someone who stands in ruling relationship to creation in work. After creating Adam, God places him in the garden of Eden (Gen. 2:8–17). There, God gives man work to do. He is to "work and take care of" the garden. For the remainder of Scripture, the phrase "work and take care of" is only used of the temple priests. Perhaps that continuing usage illustrates how sacred a relationship man has to creation in the call to work. In effect, Adam is to be the priest of the garden. Adam's work is part of his worship. Moreover, Adam's work extends God's dominion and glory from this central place of paradise to the ends of the earth. Adam's rulership over all things—while real—merely reflects an image, a shining forth of God's ultimate dominion. The garden becomes a place for God-worship, not self-worship. A biblical man works as a form of worship, but he does not worship his work.

Third, a man is someone who stands in intimate relationship to a woman as his wife. The Lord God completed all of creation in its vast array, surveyed it all, and concluded, "It's all good." Then in Genesis 2:18 (NIV), the Lord takes a look at Adam and says, "It is *not* good for the man to be alone. I will make a helper suitable for him." It's not that Adam had some creative defect, as though God goofed on the basic design. But, in light of the work mandate Adam received and God's design to reveal something of His love in human marriage (Eph. 5), Adam was incompetent. Alone Adam could not do all the work God desired in creation. Adam needed a helper. So, God in His wisdom and grace created woman out of Adam's side as a suitable helper for him (Gen. 2:18–24). As a helper she is to "honor his vocation, to share his enjoyment, and to respect the prohibition."[3] As a "suitable" helper, she is equal and adequate. Her contribution is essential. It is not good for him to be alone. So he must stand with his wife in the structured relationship of marriage—he leads, she helps. Marriage and leadership are inextricably connected to being a man.

Marriage is also the proper context for the expression of sexual intimacy. Too many boys and professing men separate sex from marriage. They make sex the supreme sign of manhood and in so doing actually diminish it. We need the church to strengthen its effort to teach a healthy biblical sexuality and its proper relationship to manhood and marriage. As Eric Mason puts it:

Right now young men learn about sex from the streets, friends, or pop culture; it must instead begin to be the regular practice of the covenant community to make sure the sexual education of the young begins in our homes and churches. It will be a witness to their bodies as well as their souls. Gathering as a group of responsible men and taking the time to be responsible with the hearts and minds of our sons is imperative. If we do, they will forever remember who pointed them to the King of kings as the author of sex and sexuality.[4]

Marriage is to be celebrated and embraced by men. Adam himself celebrates God's gift of a wife with a poem in Genesis 2:23. And like other things in the garden, marriage is to be worked and cared for, nurtured and protected. It's obviously an institution for a man and a woman based on complementarity. The woman is made uniquely and suitably to complement a man for the glory of God. This is why a male's *avoidance* of marriage (except in cases of a gift of singleness) generally signals immaturity and a questionable understanding of what it means to be a man. It's also why a male's *abuse* of a woman is glory-stealing wickedness and rebellion against God. Both *avoidance* and *abuse* distort the biblical picture of man's relationship to woman. The biblical truth lies in an exquisite middle where a true man commits himself for life to one woman and enjoys communion (not conquest!) with her alone, forsaking all others. A "real man" grows up, settles down, and remains in marriage with his wife for life.

What's Going on with Black Men and the Black Family?

To understand what's happening with black men and families, we need to get our minds around the big picture. Renowned African-American sociologist William Julius Wilson has spent a career studying the African-American family and black men in the urban context. Wilson summarized and synthesized his work in the book *More than Just Race: Being Black and Poor in the Inner City*.[5] Wilson tells a complex story of a community besieged by racial inequality, concentrated poverty, and family struggles.

The Economic and Political Situations Black Men Face

Wilson begins the story with a description of large-scale economic and political decisions adversely impacting African-Americans. For example, he recounts how demand for low-skilled labor has sharply declined since the 1960s. That decline disproportionately affects African-Americans who—due to the social legacies of Jim Crow segregation, job discrimination, and failing segregated schools—begin with a larger percentage of low-skilled workers than most other ethnic groups.

Not only have low-skilled labor opportunities decreased, the low-skill jobs that remain have moved out of city centers where so many African-Americans live. Growing suburbanization results in "job spatial mismatch—the notion that work and people are in two different places."[6] Wilson illustrates this mismatch with research from large cities.

> Boston welfare recipients found that only 14 percent of the entry-level jobs in the fast-growth areas of the Boston metropolitan region could be accessed via public transit in less than an hour. And in the Atlanta metropolitan area, fewer than half the entry-level jobs are located within a quarter mile of a public transit system. To make matters worse, many inner-city residents lack information about suburban job opportunities. In Detroit, Philadelphia, and Baltimore, for example, less than 20 percent of the jobs are now located within three miles of the city center.[7]

So, if you're an African-American living in a major city without private transportation, chances are good you're stuck in a community with few job opportunities and no way to reach the communities that do have them.

In addition to major economic factors, a string of major political actions have worked to concentrate poverty in African-American neighborhoods. The policies themselves may not be race-based in any explicit sense, but they do have disparate and disproportional effects on poor ethnic groups. Wilson discusses redlining, freeway planning and construction, housing market incentives, suburbanization, public housing, minimum wage, and conservative fiscal practices as examples of policy decisions that historically have negative impacts on the well-being and futures of African-Americans.[8]

Any effort to describe the condition of African-American men and the black family must consider these major macroeconomic and political factors. When we do, we understand why Wilson states the bottom line so bluntly: "The economic predicament of low-skilled black men in the inner city has reached catastrophic proportions."[9]

The Cultural and Personal Factors Black Men Face

Critics of Wilson's earlier work charged him with paying too little attention to cultural factors in explaining the condition of African-Americans. In response, *More than Just Race* argues that the situation black men find themselves facing cannot be chalked up to large-scale societal forces like economic trends and public policy alone. Cultural factors play a role as well.

Cultural Attitudes toward Poverty. Take, for example, cultural attitudes toward the poor. Most Americans believe individualistic factors are the biggest explanations for poverty and poor life outcomes. Citing a 2007 Pew Research Center study, Wilson reports that a "full two-thirds of Americans believe personal factors, rather than discrimination, explain why African-Americans have difficulty getting ahead in life." That figure includes 71 percent of whites, 59 percent of Hispanics, and 53 percent of African-Americans.[10] With most Americans believing that individual factors more likely determine poverty, it's not surprising that so many poor people find themselves isolated from social supports and informal networks that can provide much-needed opportunities. And it's not surprising that so much despair results from the combination of social isolation and self-blame.

Cultural Attitudes toward Crime. Cultural attitudes toward crime also impact black men in significant ways. Major cities during the 1970s–80s saw a simultaneous rise in violent crime, in crack cocaine usage, and in "tough on crime" attitudes. Incarceration of black men and women soared as a result. Even during periods when the overall rate of crime *decreased*, incarceration rates for African-Americans rapidly *increased*. Consequently, as much as 30 percent of all young black males between the ages of 16 and 34 have a criminal record of some sort. With criminal records come diminished prospects for employment and the diminished ability to support families.[11] If a man doesn't work or can't find work, he can't eat. Neither can his children.

Cultural Attitudes toward Family. Cultural attitudes also shape the very notion of manhood and family itself. As Wilson summarizes, "cool-pose culture blatantly promotes the most anomalous models of behavior in urban, lower-class neighborhoods, featuring gangsta rap, predatory sexuality, and irresponsible fathering."[12] Such attitudes weaken community norms against premarital sex, out-of-wedlock pregnancy, and nonmarital parenthood. Relationships between men and women become "fractious and antagonistic."[13] As one writer put it, "Some men become vigilantes of lost manhood by conquering women sexually."[14] Cool-pose cultural attitudes and predatory sexuality lead inevitably to high levels of distrust between men and women and lower chances for forming healthy marriages. When that happens, children and families suffer tremendously.

Family Well-Being

Wilson contends that the factors most significantly affecting black men and black families are the large structural forces. Culture plays a role. However, from a research perspective, culture's role does not sufficiently explain what we see happening with black men and families in African America. According to Wilson, "cultural arrangements reflect structural realities."[15] Both structure and culture contribute to family outcomes, but structure (or large-scale social and political forces) plays the larger, more determinative role.

Many scholars debate Wilson's conclusions about precisely how structure and culture relate. That debate has raged at least since publication of the Moynihan report in 1965. But what cannot be debated is that African-American families have taken a beating in almost every area over the last fifty years. To see evidence of this struggle we need only consider what has happened to African-American rates of marriage and family formation since the 1960s. In 1965, one in four African-American children was born to unmarried women. By 2005, that number had climbed to seven out of ten! In 1965, 25 percent of families were headed by single women. In 2006 the percentage had risen to 45 percent.[16]

Why do decreasing marriage rates and increasing out-of-wedlock birth rates pose a problem? Aren't single mothers just as capable of raising children as families headed by men and women? Well, despite the fact that many women like my mother have done heroic jobs without the aid of a husband—a situation that most of them did not want—the research has for decades repeatedly told the same story. Everybody does better when men assume responsibility as husbands and fathers. Wilson summarizes the research:

> In addition to the strong connection linking single parenthood with poverty and welfare receipt, the available research indicates that children from low-income households without fathers present are more likely to be school dropouts, become teenage parents, receive lower earnings in young adulthood, be welfare recipients, and experience cognitive, emotional, and social problems. Moreover, daughters who grow up in single-parent households are more likely to establish single-parent households themselves than are those raised in married-couple households. And finally, single-parent households tend to exert less control over the behavior of their adolescent children.[17]

These findings are not the opinions of people with a "conservative agenda" or people who "don't understand the black community." These are the research findings of African-American scholars who care deeply about and have worked tirelessly in these very communities. We tend to not talk about unflattering realities for fear of outsiders attaching racist stigmas, misrepresenting the facts, or blaming the weak. Speaking publicly about black family formation breaks the community code that forbids discussing the problems of the black community outside the black community. We all remember the swift and sometimes harsh response Bill Cosby received following his remarks about black family responsibility at a NAACP gathering.

But if we're going to see our young men rescued from harmful economic, political, cultural, and family forces, we're going to have to talk very openly and work very aggressively for it. We will have to take these discussions out of the realm of opinion and political posturing so we can deal with real information and make real choices. We will have to ignore the "white gaze" in order to embrace the healing truth. That's why the research is so important. And the research paints a clear picture: When African-American men do well economically and marry, the entire family does well also. When men vanish from the picture, the family—women and children—suffer in nearly every category. As two other African-American scholars summarized it, "Living arrangements are now more important than race when it comes to child poverty—black children in two-parent families have a much lower poverty rate than white children living in mother-only families."[18]

Men are more than paychecks. When they're healthy and present, they provide stability, resources, leadership, and intimacy to families. The challenge and opportunity, then, is how to strengthen black men on the way to strengthening black families, churches, and communities.

Strategies for Reclaiming Black Men and Families

At least four broad strategies need to be implemented by black churches who want to turn the tide with men in their communities. These are not quick fixes, nor do they cover everything that needs to be done. These strategies define the *basic* actions that *churches* can and must pursue.

Change the Perspective of Black Men on the Church

Before black churches can impact the lives of black men and families, they must first gain access to the lives of black men. Women make up as much as 60 percent of the membership in most black churches, while black men are nearly twice as likely (16 percent vs. 9 percent) to be unaffiliated with any religious tradition.[19]

Dr. Robert M. Franklin, a graduate and later president of Morehouse College, reflected on the church affiliation of his fellow students when he attended Morehouse. He writes:

> At Morehouse College, I was one of a small group of students who attended church regularly. On Sunday mornings the dormitories were deathly silent compared to the frivolity of the previous evening. Sunday morning provided time for party animals to recover from the weekend rituals. On arriving at church, I noticed that women usually outnumbered men by a significant margin. Then I thought about all of those talented young brothers asleep in the dorm.[20]

Franklin's Morehouse experience stuck with him. Following his student days at Morehouse, Franklin went on to graduate studies at

Harvard Divinity School. There he completed his master's thesis on gender difference in church attendance. Conducting interviews with black men, Franklin found both institutional and personal factors affected their participation in and view of the church.

Institutional Factors. Franklin found that black men sometimes avoid the Black Church because they object to certain qualities they perceive to be true about the church. College-educated men said they did not attend church because (1) the church encouraged a meekness and passivity incompatible with and dangerous in the community; (2) Christian character did not fit with a "macho persona"; (3) most churches did not engage in social action; (4) churches were not radical or prophetic enough; and (5) the aesthetics and symbols of churches were too Eurocentric. In short, Franklin found that African-American men considered the church incompatible with their view of manhood.

In addition to interviews conducted with college graduates, Franklin also led interviews in a local barbershop, a proxy for working class and non-college-educated black men. These men cited three other institutional factors for not attending church: (1) services were unnecessarily long; (2) churches are too concerned with raising money and insensitive to the poor; and (3) churches seem to tolerate hypocrisy in its leaders, especially when it comes to personal morality.[21]

We might boil down these criticisms of the institution to two broad things: some African-American men find that the church is neither "manly" enough nor faithful enough to the community. If the church wants to be effective in the lives of men, it will have to engage and change this perspective.

Personal Factors. Franklin also discovered a number of personal factors that prevented men from attending churches regularly. Some did not attend because they were not ready to reform their lives. Others were generally disinterested in organized religions. Some others felt their spiritual needs were met in fraternal orders.[22] On the one hand, no one should be surprised that men who are not yet Christians express disinterest in being a part of a church community. On the other hand, this disinterest suggests that black churches will have to do more than simply hold church services if they want to have an impact on the lives of men in the community.

Reverend Norman Freeman of St. Paul Missionary Baptist Church in Homestead, Florida, speculated along similar lines. "The church is sometimes more geared toward the female than the male. Sometimes because of our ways of preaching, the way that we do ministries and even in our decor, men don't feel masculine enough. Especially when we're talking about brothers that we want to take out of the streets. If a brother does not see his reflection in the church, then he has nobody to connect with."[23]

Churches will have to figure out another entry point for significant numbers of men. Moreover, church leaders and black Christian men will have to establish a greater degree of integrity, trust, accessibility, and interest if genuine relationships and opportunities for gospel proclamation and healing are to be developed.

Change the Black Church's Perspective on Black Men

Of course, black churches have a lot to say about black men too. Anyone who has ever attended a special women's day or Mother's Day celebration in a black church has likely heard comments that disparage African-American men. Sometimes the comments seem designed to attract an "Amen!" or get a quick laugh from the women in attendance. Other times anger or hurt seep through the speaker as they denounce black men for their failings and sins.

We underestimate the deep spiritual harm that can be done to African-American men by the negative judgments of a church community. Duke University professor of law and literature Dr. Karla F. C. Holloway, captures this potential to unintentionally harm in her poignant remembrance of her church's reaction to the Atlanta child killings.

> Early in 1981, I joined the members of my AME church in our small Michigan community as we wrapped black armbands around our children's slender arms and solemnly marched from Sunday school to the church service—expressing our collective grief over the murders and disappearances of black youths in Atlanta. Their tiny figures were dwarfed as they entered the massive sanctuary, and their procession on that winter Sunday morning echoed for me, back to the decades-old anti-war and civil rights marches through our nation's capital and our community's streets.

Holloway continued:

> Flimsy black cloth tied over their Sunday school wear marked
> them as kin to the victims in Atlanta, branding them with our
> understanding of the lesson we knew they would learn despite
> our intervention—that being black was a necessary danger in
> the United States. The event was well-intentioned. However, *our
> activism had a consequence we had not anticipated. It collected our
> children into a community of victims.*[24]

I'm sure that many of the comments and actions directed at black
men by the church are as well-intentioned as this quiet march and
protest held by Dr. Holloway's AME church. But it's also quite likely
that many of our attitudes, comments, and actions have had deep and
lasting negative impact—unintended but real. Holloway describes the
unintended negative result in more detail:

> We did not anticipate that our political and communal solidarity,
> and the way in which we marked our children, could work other
> than to make them feel wanted. Our purpose had been to help
> them understand their membership in a national community of
> African Americans who cared about our common dangers. To
> display their kinship to the Atlanta children. To indicate to an
> urban community far removed from Atlanta that we too were
> vigilant, and wary. We wanted our children to know of our activ-
> ist history and their legacy and to feel secure in the presence of
> their parents and community elders. *We could not guess, nor did
> we anticipate that some of them could feel dangerously vulnerable
> and could come to associate that vulnerability with the color of their
> skin.*[25]

Despite their best intentions, the members of the church were branding
black children as victims and locking them in a prison of skin-associated
vulnerability and negative attitude.

The mistake Holloway recounts gets repeated with alarming fre-
quency. As I write this chapter, a Florida jury has returned a "not guilty"
verdict in the trial of George Zimmerman. Zimmerman, a "white
Hispanic" resident and volunteer for his neighborhood's community
watch program, shot and killed seventeen-year-old African-American

Trayvon Martin. In protest, one pastor preached his Sunday sermon while wearing a hoodie like the one Martin wore when killed. President Obama identified with the slain Martin by saying if he had a son he would look like Trayvon. Over one hundred protests across the country took place with untold numbers of people declaring, "I am Trayvon Martin." All these respondents are attempting to express collective solidarity and grief over the loss of another young black male—the same kind of identification Holloway warns may associate skin color (and gender) with dangerous vulnerability.

Shortly following Trayvon Martin's death in 2012, Time.com published a short piece by noted African-American journalist, Touré. In "How to Talk to Young Black Boys about Trayvon Martin," Touré counseled a fictional teenager to understand that "Black maleness is a potentially fatal condition."[26] Following the "not guilty" verdict, another African-American television journalist, Bruce Johnson, interviewed three Howard University students in Washington, DC. The segment asked the question, "Are young black men an endangered species?" The black male students all responded, "Yes."

While watching the various responses to the Martin-Zimmerman tragedy, my mind wandered back to my incoming class of college freshmen hearing for the first time that we were "an endangered species." I wondered, *What are we doing to black men if we train them to think of themselves in such vulnerable and animal-like terms? Though well-intentioned, what damage do we cause a boy or a man who learns to associate the color of his skin and his maleness with vulnerability and near-extinction? Are we again making the tragic mistake of collecting our children and young black men "into a community of victims," as Karla Holloway put it? How can the Black Church help black men if we cripple them with our negative perception and fear?*

Dr. Holloway helps us to see our complicity:

> Although our cause was not malicious, I hold all of us responsible for those psyches we injured that winter—those who felt just a little bit more exposed, a little less strong. *Not all of our children come with the resilience it takes to survive color in America.* And *when our behavior helps them along in their adolescent and childhood fears rather than secures their stability and trust, we have*

enabled nothing more dangerous than their potential evolution as victims.

If we look back and wonder at how we have lost so many of our African American youth to violence and abandoned so many to the heartless justice of the streets or the careless justice of juvenile courtrooms, then we must at least consider our complicity. We seem amazed that their violent activities in our communities and their constant entanglements with judicial authorities could be so far removed from our safe and nurturing concern. And it is difficult for us to understand how effectively their behaviors have distanced us from them. It seems as if bureaucratic political, social, and judicial systems are more intimately involved in their lives than are our traditionally exemplary parental, church, and community behaviors.[27]

Without stopping to think, many churches and Christians have associated pathology with person, sin with skin. "Color and character have become linked in an abusive construction."[28] We have gone some ways in teaching many of our men and children—especially African-American boys—to think of themselves in this way when we should have been nurturing strong Christian identity and family resilience. We have, perhaps unwittingly, adopted a negative and fearful view of our own men—even in the redemptive spaces of the local church. With that outlook comes deeper alienation between black churches and black men.

To reclaim black men, the church will need to reform our thinking about them and begin to send redemptive signals and messages of loving inclusion. If the Black Church will be used to reclaim black men and families, we'll have to learn a new way of looking at ourselves and at black men. Our ministry to African-American men depends, in part, on our attitude toward them. If we don't reexamine our attitudes, we're likely to repeat those actions that distance and disenfranchise black men.

Use the Social Networks of the Church to Help Men Find and Keep Jobs

Black churches and communities have sometimes downplayed the importance of defining manhood as the ability to earn a living and care for one's family. Some have argued that a woman earning more than a man should not be all that important to men. Men should "get over it" and learn not to be threatened by a black woman's success.

I'm the first to admit we should challenge the kind of male pride that cannot joyfully accept a wife earning more than the husband. Men can and do sometimes make earnings an idol and a stumbling block for relationships.

Yet for most men, black men included, the ability to provide for their family is the *sine qua non* of masculinity. Even as economic prospects have shrunk for so many African-American men, many men have not abandoned providing as one measure of manhood. Instead, they've simply redefined the level of provision in keeping with their perceived ability. Where men once prided themselves on providing a nice home or a good education, many now build their esteem as men on picking up their children for the occasional weekend visit or giving the mother a little money for diapers. In other words, the work and financial provision aspects of manhood stubbornly resist elimination from the manhood equation, even when men face dire economic conditions. Nearly all men *want* to be the kind of men that provide for their own, even if they despair of ever doing so. Consequently, the church might do well to rethink our message. Are we inadvertently lowering the bar on manhood by lowering our emphasis on providing?

More practically, the work of the Black Church in impoverished communities must include addressing chronic unemployment and under-employment one black man at a time. A local church will never fix the macroeconomic environment—and is not called to do so in the Scripture. But churches can chip away at individual unemployment. Failure to help in this practical way amounts to a failure to love. "If anyone has material possessions and sees his brother in need but has no pity on him, how can the love of God be in him?" Instead, "let us not love with words or tongue but with actions and in truth" (1 John 3:17–18 NIV).

A church is nothing if it is not a network of social relationships. Those relationships represent social capital. Local congregations can at least leverage their social networks to help black men find jobs. Men with criminal records will likely need more of the Christian community's help in finding gainful employment. These are the men most isolated from the kinds of social relationships that often lead to job recommendations, a good word with employers, and a ride to work. Without the church meeting the challenge of helping men get on their feet with work and income, many of our men will not feel like—and in a real sense will not be—the men of God they are called to be.

Fostering Healthy Marriages and Father Involvement

Finally, the church must embrace the challenge of fostering and supporting healthy or "good enough" marriages. While it is a well-known fact that everyone does better when adults marry and raise their children together, research studies consistently reveal that male-female mistrust exists at alarmingly high rates in the African-American community. This relational turbulence makes marriage formation extremely difficult. If we want to see men, women, and children flourish in the community and the church, we will need to invest significant energy in helping men learn to love, protect, communicate with, and lead women as Christ leads and sacrifices for the church (Eph. 5:25–32). We will need to provide relationship and marriage preparedness opportunities, celebrate anniversaries and new marriages, fight for marriages in difficulty, support women fleeing abuse, and call rebellious and abusive men to account. We will need to restore community norms and values that esteem marriage highly, encourage men to "do the right thing" as an act of repentance and responsibility, and teach men and women to reserve intimacy until the commitment of marriage. No organization has greater moral authority and potential than the Black Church for addressing the values involved in black manhood.

As we disciple men, we will also find a significant number of men who already have children. Some of these men will have little to no contact with their children. In fact, the older the child becomes, the less contact they will have with their absentee fathers. Several challenges confront any effort to reengage fathers with their children. Child support payments and increasing arrears present an obstacle for some. Significant mother-father conflict makes it difficult for others. But where the church has opportunity to disciple a man as a follower of Jesus, they also have responsibility to help him work out his faith in the concrete situation of fatherhood. Faith in Christ means forgiveness of all our sins; it does not mean absolution of all our responsibilities.

Conclusion

Twenty-five years after my freshman orientation, many people still think of African-American men as an "endangered species." Most continue to take that status for granted.

But recently the "endangered" status has been revisited.[29] Ivory Toldson, associate professor of psychology at Howard University in Washington, DC, and editor-in-chief of *The Journal of Negro Education*, has taken a look at the figures used to conclude more black men are in prison than in college. He found that in 2009 there were *600,000 more black men in college than in prison*. Toldson found that nearly 1,700 colleges and universities failed to report African-American enrollment numbers when the original statistic was calculated. That meant nearly 100,000 black college students never made the count. We've been so accustomed to hearing the doomsday scenario for black men that we've never stopped to check the numbers. While African-American men continue to be incarcerated at disproportionate rates and given stiffer sentences for minor crimes, some things are not as bad as we've believed. There's opportunity. We have to ask ourselves how much more could be done if we stopped thinking of ourselves as "endangered" and amplified the slow, profitable work of reclaiming black men in the church.

CHAPTER 13

Re-engage Missions

And Jesus came and said to them, "All authority in heaven and on earth has been given to me. Go therefore and make disciples of all nations, baptizing them in the name of the Father and of the Son and of the Holy Spirit, teaching them to observe all that I have commanded you. And behold, I am with you always, to the end of the age."
—MATTHEW 28:18–20

And they sang a new song, saying,
"Worthy are you to take the scroll
*   and to open its seals,*
for you were slain, and by your blood you ransomed people for God
*   from every tribe and language and people and nation,*
and you have made them a kingdom and priests to our God,
*   and they shall reign on the earth."*
—REVELATION 5:9–10

There is no doubt in my mind that Africa is our field of operation and that [as] Moses was sent to deliver his brethren, and as the prophets were members of the race to whom they were sent, so I am convinced that God's purpose is to redeem Africa through us. This work is ours by appointment, by inheritance, and by choice.
—EMMANUEL K. LOVE, BLACK BAPTIST FOREIGN MISSION CONVENTION OF 1889

Introduction

My wife and I had been Christians for perhaps a couple of months. Like all fresh converts, everything seemed new to us. As the old song goes, "We looked at our hands and they looked new; we looked at our feet and they did, too!" Though we'd grown up in and around the church, the world glistened with freshness. As adult converts we were now privy to much more. We were starting to feel a sense of ownership for our new church family and we wanted to be more actively involved.

Pastor Anderson was preaching his way through the book of Acts on Sunday mornings. The worship and witness of the early church enthralled us. His expositions were giving us a larger vision of the local church and the possibilities of the Christian community. With this newfound enthusiasm we attended our first church business or members' meeting.

The meeting began like most business meetings. We were called to order. Pastor Anderson led us in prayer. Then we began to work our way through various reports. The deacons shared an update. Some church ministry or another filed their report. Then we heard the financial update. According to a church trustee or treasurer, we had approximately $80,000 in the church's account, an amount that had been growing from meeting to meeting. A brief discussion ensued and we were told there were no immediate plans for the money and that the church was without debt. Saints nodded and praised God for His provision.

Then we came to the missions section of the meeting. As I remember it, there was only one item of business. The missions committee, made up almost exclusively of older women and chaired by a deacon's wife, brought a recommendation that $600 be spent to purchase window-unit air conditioners for the local orphanage. She gave us a sense of living conditions at the orphanage and indicated that this modest investment would bring some basic comfort for the kids through the summer. It all seemed very reasonable to me.

What seemed completely unreasonable was the discussion that ensued. For twenty minutes, this dear woman endured what could only be compared to a McCarthy-era "investigation." Every question and comment seemed calculated to do one thing: keep the $600 in the church's coffers. I grew angry. Angry at the members' tone. Angry at the stinginess and greed on display. Angry at the deacon for sitting mute while this church-turned-mob attacked his wife over $600. What happened to that Acts-like community we thought we joined?

Finally I raised my hand to comment. The pastor sheepishly acknowledged me. Folks looked at me with curiosity, as if to wonder, what will this newcomer say? I made my comments in support of the motion. I pointed out that we held in our bank account over $80,000 for which we had no plans. I suggested that $600 was not a lot of money and that the benefit to the orphanage would be immediately measurable. I appealed to the congregation to approve the request. The deaconess nodded ever so slightly toward me to communicate her thanks and appreciation. She had not anticipated anyone speaking up for the motion and wore the look of a beaten woman. Not long after, the motion failed.

Sadly, scenes like this happen far too often in far too many churches. Sometimes things can become much more combative and destructive. There's much that could be said about the dysfunction of such meetings. But what I want to draw our attention to in this final chapter is the Black Church's sense of mission. What is the church's mission? What priority does that mission play in the life and work of the church? What does it say about a church's sense of mission if it struggles to invest $600 in air conditioners for orphans? And most important, how does reengaging a biblical view of missions bring life and dynamism to the local church?

What Is the Mission of the Church?

What is the mission of the Black Church? Is its mission any different from that of any other ethnic expression of the church? If so, what is that distinction and where does it come from? As Raphael G. Warnock, senior pastor of the historic Ebenezer Baptist Church in Atlanta, Georgia, points out, "Hardly any question is more vociferously argued in the black community, even among those who do not attend, than the meaning, message and mission of the black church."[1]

Warnock suggests that the Black Church has a "double mind" regarding its mission. That double mind stems from a "faith profoundly shaped by white evangelicalism's focus on individual salvation (piety) yet conscious of the contradictions of slavery and therefore focused also on sociopolitical freedom (protest)."[2] As Henry Mitchell puts it, "An accurate record would have to report early African American churches as striving both for people to be saved from sin and to be set free."[3] For nearly all of its history, the African-American church has maintained this two-fold view of its mission to respond to the material and political needs of the community and to spread the gospel of Jesus Christ around the globe.

The Early Mission to Plant Churches at Home

At its founding the Black Church focused on the spread of the gospel. We see that emphasis in the itinerant ministries of slaves and freedmen given opportunity to take the good news to fellow African-Americans on plantations and in some cases to white audiences across the developing nation. We also see this gospel impulse in the early emphasis on church planting once African-Americans began the independent church movement in the late 1700s.

Domestic Church Planting. For example, Andrew Bryan, a slave, organized a meeting of a small group for preaching and worship in Savannah, Georgia, in the early 1780s. From modest beginnings, this group became First African Church and in a matter of decades also became a force for the establishment of other churches.

By 1790 Bryan's congregation had grown to a membership of 225 communicants and about 350 converts not yet admitted to full membership. The congregation became the First African Baptist Church of Savannah. In 1803, a Second African Church was organized from members of the First, and a few years later a Third African Church was formed, both led by black pastors.[4]

Bryan's efforts at First African Church were typical to the early mission history of the Black Church. The early 1800s featured a remarkably industrious pursuit of church planting and the founding of denominations. Absalom Jones played an influential role in shaping St. Thomas African Episcopal in Philadelphia in 1794. Thomas Paul served African Baptist Church in Boston in 1804. Josiah Bishop organized and led the historic Abyssinian Baptist Church in New York City in 1808. And John Gloucester led the African Presbyterian Church in Philadelphia in 1807. Soon individual churches coalesced in independent black denominations. Bethel African Methodist Episcopal Church in Philadelphia, founded in 1794 by former slave and Methodist preacher, Richard Allen, launched the African Methodist Episcopal Church in Philadelphia in 1816 with

Allen as its first bishop. William Spencer founded a denomination known as Union Church in 1815 in Wilmington, Delaware. And in 1821 the African Methodist Episcopal Zion Church got its start in New York City. As historian Albert J. Raboteau observes, "These black churches formed the institutional structure for the development of free black communities. They also gave African Americans a platform to express publicly their own visions of Christianity and of the United States."[5]

The organization of denominations rapidly advanced the spread of black churches in the 1800s. A significant proportion of that growth came from withdrawing from predominantly white churches and denominations. Again, Raboteau summarizes this development quite well:

> As a result of their missions, Northern black denominations in effect became national churches as they increased in size and geographical extent. For example, between 1860 and 1870 the AME Zion Church increased in membership from 27,000 to 200,000, with the great bulk of its growth in the South. By 1880 the AME Church had grown to 400,000 members, most of them Southern blacks. But by far the largest institutional growth was achieved by the black Baptists, and it did not require missionaries from the North.
>
> Following the Union Army's victory, black Baptists swarmed out of Southern Baptist Churches. To take one example, *in 1858 the Southern Baptist Conference in South Carolina counted 29,211 black members; in 1874 there were 1,614.* Black Baptists simply withdrew and formed their own congregations. Gradually they formed state associations (North Carolina in 1866, followed by Alabama and Virginia in 1867). Eventually, a National Baptist Convention was formed in 1895. Meanwhile, former slaves who had belonged to the Southern Methodist Church withdrew into AME or AME Zion churches, or they joined a new black Methodist denomination, the Colored (later renamed Christian) Methodist Episcopal Church, which separated from the Methodist Episcopal Church in 1870. *In South Carolina, the black membership of the Southern Methodists fell from 42,469 in 1860 to 653 in 1873.*[6]

The skyrocketing growth of the Black Church changed the religious landscape of the country and made "Protestantism . . . one of the central frameworks of African American society."[7] Though African-Americans had participated in the country's earlier revivals and white churches where possible, now they embraced the opportunity to establish churches on their own terms. Black missionaries jealously guarded the South against encroachment from Northern white missionaries. "The arrival of Northern missionaries in the South occasionally created resentment and conflict. Black missionaries resented competition from their white rivals in adding freed people to the churches' rolls. *Black missionaries saw this field as their particular mission even before the Civil War ended.*"[8]

International Missions in the Eighteenth and Nineteenth Centuries

African-American zeal for spreading the gospel could not be contained to American shores and new church starts. Almost as soon as African-Americans began to plant domestic churches, they also invested in international gospel missions and church planting. As one historian of the Black Church puts it, "The black Baptist church was born a missionary movement" with a "missionary motivation . . . innate in the 'being' of the church movement. The foreign mission motif *predates* home mission in general among black Baptists."[9]

In fact, early African-American Christians felt a deep responsibility and unique privilege when it came to gospel missions in the African diaspora. Absalom Jones represented many African-American Christians when he interpreted slavery as a means of converting slaves "in order that they [enslaved Africans] might become . . . messengers of it, to the land of their fathers."[10] Many leading nineteenth-century thinkers in the Black Church took a similar view. They called for "the Redemption of Africa" and considered it "the Mission of the Darker Races" to proclaim the gospel among African peoples on the continent. Rev. T. L. Johnson sounded the rallying cry in 1886, saying at the first meeting of the American National Baptist Convention, "Knox lifted Scotland; Luther lifted Germany, and it remains for us to lift the heathen in the land of our fathers—Africa."[11] Baptist minister Emmanuel K. Love expressed the sentiment well before the Black Baptist Foreign Mission Convention in 1889:

There is no doubt in my mind that Africa is our field of operation and that [as] Moses was sent to deliver his brethren, and as the prophets were members of the race to whom they were sent, so I am convinced that God's purpose is to redeem Africa through us. This work is ours by appointment, by inheritance, and by choice.[12]

In a sense the views of Jones, Love, and Johnson represented one solution to the question of black identity and the meaning of black suffering. "African-American churches lacked the resources to sponsor large-scale missions to Africa, but the ideal of Christianizing Africa held great symbolic value for black Americans. The ideal provided them with a major role in the drama of world history and offered an explanation for African-American history: that God was drawing good out of the evil of slavery by using the American descendants of African slaves to take Christianity to the lands of their ancestors."[13] With this unique sense of its place in world evangelization, the Black Church took its place in international missions.

The earliest efforts at cross-cultural missions began with John Marrant (1755–1791) in the late 1700s. Marrant, a free black from New York, preached among Native Americans, including the Cherokee, Creek, Catawar, and Housaw. He later journeyed to Nova Scotia to serve as a missionary among African-Americans fleeing slavery.[14]

Around the same time Marrant worked in Nova Scotia, freed slave George Lisle (1750–1820) left for Jamaica. In 1783 Lisle became the first missionary to leave American soil. Lisle helped to establish Baptist churches in Jamaica and counseled British missionaries in their efforts to reach the island. Moses Baker, a convert of Lisle, went on to found the second Jamaican Baptist Church, one of three additional congregations Lisle helped start. George Vineyard and John Gilbert carried the gospel farther into the interior of Jamaica and its plantations thirty years before British missionaries would begin work on the island.[15]

Another former slave, Prince Williams, sailed for the Bahamas in 1789. Around 1791 Williams organized the Bethel Baptist Meeting House and the Society of Anabaptists. At age seventy, Williams founded another church, Saint John Baptist Church, where he served until his death thirty-four years later. Over 160 churches spawned from Williams's pioneering efforts in the Bahamas.

But African-American missionary endeavors reached farther than the Caribbean to the continent of Africa itself. Both independent and agency-sponsored efforts sent African-Americans to parts of Africa to advance the gospel and repatriate former slaves. Among the earliest independent efforts occurred in 1792, when David George (1743–1810) led a group of some 1,200 African-Americans to Freetown, Sierra Leone. In doing so, George became "the first black Baptist pastor in the United States and Canada, and the first Baptist pastor (white or black) in Africa; planter of the first black Baptist churches in the [Canada] Maritimes and the first Baptist church (white or black) in Africa."[16]

In most cases these eighteenth-century efforts were undertaken with no formal organizational support. But with the rise of denominations and the maturity of the early Black Church came more organized efforts at supporting missions.[17] The American Colonization Society (ACS), founded in 1816 with the mission of sending former slaves back to Africa, became one of the first agencies to sponsor missions work in Africa by African-Americans. It's through the ACS that the first free African-American clergyman of the AME Church led a missions effort to Africa.

On February 6, 1820, Daniel Coker, from Baltimore, MD, along with 90 others, left New York, NY, harbor, on the ship the *Elizabeth*, as the first party of emigrants sent by the ACS to what would become Liberia. Coker was sent to Africa, a year before Lott Carey, as a missionary with a subsidy from the Maryland Colonization Society. Daniel Coker was the first African American to leave for Africa with a clear missionary purpose, although he had not been appointed by any particular missionary board. Ten days after the ship left New York, Coker organized the first foreign branch of the AME Church on board the ship.[18]

Baptists were swept up in a flurry of organizational initiatives to reach Africa with the gospel. Lott Carey worked to form the Richmond African Baptist Missionary Society in 1815. In 1840, Baptists founded the American Baptist Missionary Convention. The year 1873 saw the development of the Baptist African Missionary Convention of the Western States and Territories. In 1880, along with 150 Baptist leaders, the Rev. William W. Colley organized the Baptist Foreign Mission Convention, involving Baptists from eleven states in the cooperative venture of foreign missions. In 1897 delegates at a meeting at Shiloh Baptist Church in Washington, D.C., organized the Lott Carey Baptist Home and Foreign Mission Convention. Several other state associations launched foreign missionary efforts as well.

Many of these early organizational efforts prompted the formation of the National Baptist Convention in 1895 with the primary aim of facilitating aggressive domestic and international missions programs. However, black Baptist missionary efforts were hampered by limited funding, divisions over whether to cooperate with white Baptists, changing conditions in colonial territories in Africa, and disputing over the priority of foreign missions itself. What began as an outwardly focused missions-minded church gradually "turned inward in an attempt to revitalize a decaying conventional movement."[19]

The Early Mission to Serve the Community

At the same time the Black Church committed itself to church planting and international missions, it also faithfully labored for the progress and uplift of African-Americans at home. This aspect of the church's work originated with the need to abolish slavery and resist systematic oppression.[20] Emancipation required the church to step up its community efforts since African-Americans were freed penniless into a moneyed economy with few other agencies to render assistance.

The Freedman's Bureau provided something of a prototype for the church's efforts at community relief and development. But Freedman Bureau efforts did not address the full range of needs and interests necessary for progress. So catastrophic was the devastation of slavery and the Civil War that social and economic progress required a full-time indigenous movement.

> The main issues that absorbed the attention of free blacks in the North were the social conditions of poverty and illiteracy that afflicted the majority of African-American communities, the legal and social discrimination that restricted the rights of free blacks, and coming to terms with the troubling existential question, what did the black experience in America mean? As the single institution that black communities controlled, churches played an active role in addressing these issues, as did their ministers through sermons, speeches, and deeds.

Black churches helped form self-help organizations, such as benevolent societies, that were designed to aid widows, to pay for burial of the poor, and to teach children to read and write. Moral reform societies also served to foster racial pride and community activism. Through these societies black people acted cooperatively to change the conditions in which they lived. Convinced that progress for the race and escape from poverty depended upon education, temperance (abstaining from the consumption of alcohol), thrift, and responsibility, black ministers emphasized the importance of moral behavior and self-respect.[21]

No one else had sufficient interest and motive for the complete rebuilding of black people following emancipation but black people themselves. The only institutional opportunity for reconstructing the people came from the Black Church. Consequently:

> In cities with large black populations, church-based freedman's aid societies sprang up, such as the Union Relief Association founded by the Israel Bethel Church of Washington, D.C., led by Henry McNeal Turner. Bethel Church in Philadelphia established the Contraband Committee to aid blacks who had escaped slavery by seeking refuge behind the Union Army's lines (these people were called "contrabands," or seized property of war). In New York City, the African Civilization Society, founded in 1858 by Henry Highland Garnet and others to promote missions to Africa, took on the activities of a freeman's aid society during and after the war.[22]

In time, the community-building efforts of the church gave rise to new institutions. For example, historically black colleges and universities received their start at the hands of white and black churches.

> From small, unimpressive beginnings, several of the freedman's schools grew over the years into major black educational institutions of long-standing importance. Some of the historically black colleges and universities originated in modest freedman's schools funded by white churches are Shaw University, Raleigh, North Carolina, opened in 1865 (Baptist); Morehouse College, Atlanta, Georgia, in 1867 (Baptist); Morgan, now Morgan State,

Baltimore, Maryland, in 1867 (Methodist); Fisk University, Nashville, Tennessee, in 1866 (AMA); Talladega, Talladega, Alabama, in 1867 (AMA); Hampton Institute, Hampton, Virginia, in 1868 (AMA); and Knoxville College, Knoxville, Tennessee, in 1875 (Presbyterian). Schools founded by black churches included Morris Brown, Atlanta, in 1885 (AME); and Livingstone College, Salisbury, North Carolina, in 1879 (AME Zion).[23]

The eighteenth and nineteenth centuries were a time of organizational development, growth, and missionary zeal at home and abroad.

The Uneasy Balance

However, the Black Church's dual focus on spreading the gospel and serving the community proved difficult to maintain. When colonial powers made African missions more difficult and internal tensions redirected energies to the needs of denominations, international missions and church planting receded to the background while community development came to the fore. Competing interests detracted from a focus on missions even at the founding of some missionary conventions. For example, "Many of the pastors and local churches became concerned over the apparent attempt of the convention's leaders to make missionaries of too many pastors. To be sure, the foreign mission motif was the dominant reason for the organization of the American Baptist Missionary Convention. Hence, some of the most ambitious pastors in the convention resisted what they believed to be an over-emphasis on missions, charging the leaders with 'demoting the elders.'"[24] By the mid-1900s with the rise of Jim Crow segregation, black mission work abroad was in serious decline.

Consequently, much of the church's rich gospel mission history was either forgotten or replaced with an emphasis on the early twentieth century's "social gospel." Moreover, the heroic rise of the Civil Rights Movement meant the church's attention shifted decidedly to the fight for full inclusion in America. The rank and file of the Black Church became foot soldiers in the march to end segregation and systemic racism. The latter half of the twentieth century witnessed the entry of the so-called "prosperity gospel," which turned the church toward individualism and further withdrawal from missions. The sad consequence is that—despite its rich mission history and several factors that make African-Americans ideal candidates for international church planting—much of the Black Church simply is not taking an active part in the Great Commission given by the Lord (Matt. 28:18–20; Acts 1:8).

Richard Coleman, a researcher who studies African-American missions, described the change well:

> When you look at the civil rights movement, everyone had to focus inward and everybody was needed to deal with this big issue at home. They had to suspend other ventures. And once we got the same rights and privileges as everybody else, human nature—and this is not a black thing or a white thing or any color thing—pursues security, comfort and equality. And so when the playing field became a lot more level, I think our pursuits changed toward building up the community and I don't think we've really begun to look outward.[25]

Based on available data, Coleman is surely correct. Of the 39 million African-Americans in the United States, only an estimated 300–1,100 serve full-time in international missions. The 2007 African American Missions Mobilization Manifesto reports that only one percent of the 118,600 total U.S. missionaries are African-American.[26] One retired missionary describes the situation as "the Great Omission of the Black Church."[27]

The picture remains bleak whether discussing predominantly African-American congregations in predominantly white denominations or local churches belonging to historically black communions. For example, though the number of predominantly black congregations cooperating with the Southern Baptist Convention grew by eighty percent to 3,400 from 2000–2010, African-American missionaries only accounted for 27 of the over 4,900 international missionaries supported by that body. That represents about one-half of one percent of missionaries in a denomination whose African-American membership is about 6.5 percent or one million persons.[28] The percentages in the SBC reflect the national story.

Historic African-American denominations suffer similar levels of inactivity. The AME Church reported more than eight thousand member congregations with a total membership of 3.5 million people. But their investment in overseas missions totaled only $253,000—less than the purchase price of your average church building and only $31 per church per year. The National Baptist Convention, USA's investment per church came to a paltry $1 per church per year. Officials for the AME Zion Church could not supply any missions-related investment data,[29] but it's not likely their investments differ much from the rest of the Black Church.

The story looks much the same way at the individual local church level. At one time one of the largest black churches in the country, New Birth Missionary Baptist Church near Atlanta, Georgia, boasted a membership of twenty-five thousand people. Yet the church only supported two or three missionaries working full-time on the mission field.[30] As one African-American missionary noted, "More money is spent on the men's breakfasts and women's auxiliaries in the typical black church than Is spent on the primary call of going into all of the world to win souls for the kingdom."[31]

The Connection Between International Gospel Missions and the Revival of Black Churches

The history of the church in every ethnic and social setting demonstrates that when churches shift their focus to social, political, and economic strategies as the means of church and community life, they end up losing biblical gospel focus, missionary zeal, and the true spiritual life that comes with it.

Professor Eddie S. Glaude argued that the Black Church is dead because she no longer effectively engages in a range of political, social, economic, and health-related activities. Dr. Glaude suggested that life for the church comes from such activities. But arguably the church has given its attention almost completely to Civil Rights and community development initiatives for the past sixty years—without revival!

Many in the Black Church object to international gospel missions by saying, "The Black community has too many significant needs to send people and resources across the world to people we don't know." They seem unaware that the Bible teaches it's more blessed to give than to receive and that God sends life and abundance to those who participate in His mission to save the lost from every tribe and nation. As sociologist Robert Woodberry found in his ten-year study of missions in Africa, it's actually an ardent focus on preaching the gospel and calling for conversions that impacts every other sphere of life. The influence of gospel missions on social development holds true in places as diverse as Africa, Asia, Latin America, and Oceania.[32] In other words, political action is not the *root* of spiritual life; rather, social progress is the *fruit* of genuine spiritual life.

Gospel preaching produces spiritual life. And that life gets amplified all the more when a local church crosses cultures to take the good news to the lost. Any church that fails to seriously embrace and engage the Great Commission signs their own DNR—do not resuscitate—order.

Getting on and Staying on the Battlefield of Our Lord

If you're reading this chapter and you're a leader or a member in a predominantly African-American church, the statistics say you're very likely to be in a church that does not actively engage in cross-cultural gospel missions. Perhaps you appreciate the rich African-American history of missions and, more important, you recognize that the Lord Jesus Christ's last command to the church—including the Black Church—was to go into all nations and make disciples (Matt. 28:18–20). If that's you, you may be asking, "What can I do? What are the next steps?"

It's not easy to turn an armada as large as the historical Black Church. Change takes a lot of prayer, patience, time, and grace. But there are a number of simple first steps you can consider in an effort to see the Black Church revived by participating in the Lord's mission to reach every nation.

Embrace the Missionary Purposes of God

From the beginning of the Bible to its end, God works to make for Himself a special people. He created Adam and Eve as vice-regents of creation with a mandate to not only subdue the earth but also to fill it with children (Gen. 1:26–28). In fact, God instituted marriage for the very purpose of gathering for Himself an offspring (Mal. 2:15). Of course, Adam and Eve through their sin and disobedience to God plunged the world into chaos, brokenness, and death (Gen. 3). But does this thwart God's plan to have a people that would be His very own? No. He preserves

Noah's family from the flood of His judgment (Gen. 6–9). Then the Lord God begins a special work of redemption by making Abraham the father of a new covenant people called Israel (Gen. 12–50).

But God's promise to Abraham foreshadowed God's concern for all nations. Indeed, in His promises to Abraham, God preached in advance that the Gentiles (all the nations outside of Israel) would be justified or made right with God through faith in God's Son, Jesus Christ (Gal. 3:8). Israel was a commercial for the creation of an even greater people to come—a people who were not His people (Rom. 1:16; 9:24–26) but who have become a new spiritual ethnic group through Christ (Eph. 2:11–22). In the end, this new spiritual ethnicity will surround the throne of the Lamb and raise their voices in eternal praise to Him (Rev. 5:9; 7:9–10). All of history points to this great climactic conclusion.

The Black Church needs to be excited about this missionary God and His mission. We need to learn to read our Bibles with this story line in mind and play our part in its fulfillment. We need preachers who will put the Bible and their sermons in this overarching context so that our churches will be constantly reminded of their great purpose in the world. Without a view to international missions, our aspirations will be limited to the growth of our local churches or the progress of our personal fortunes. Those ambitions are too small to give us real spiritual life.

Choose an Area of the World or a People Group

The world can seem a large place when first initiating a mission agenda in a local church. Where to start? One place might be identifying a specific location of interest. Even if your church has not had an active investment in cross-cultural mission, there may be leaders or members with ties to missionaries or churches in international settings. Those relationships provide a good starting point, a living connection with a part of the world that may benefit from your church's prayers and labors. Start where there are relationships or, if there are no relationships, where there are interests. Pick a few places in the world without a strong Christian witness and begin to pray for the people in those countries. Perhaps use bulletin inserts to begin educating the congregation about these areas of interest.

Or, choose a specific people group. Of the estimated 11,240 people groups in the world, evangelical Christians make up less than 2 percent of the group in approximately 6,538 of them. Missiologists call these groups "unreached." There are no known plans or coordinated efforts to reach over 3,000 of these groups, earning them the label "unengaged." An estimated 1.4 billion people live in groups with very little contact with the gospel of our Lord. If the gospel is to be preached to every creature, then these groups will need someone to develop intentional efforts to reach them. Several helpful resources could be used to introduce these groups to your church for prayer and as possible sites for mission investment.[33]

Connect with Established Missions Agencies

Both denominational and independent mission agencies would love the opportunity to engage our local churches. Most agency personnel feel disconnected from local churches and long for more support. Pastors, elders, deacons, and committees can find ready resources, expertise, and encouragement with a phone call to mission bodies. Moreover, those agencies can be helpful in training and educating members, connecting churches to missionaries on the field, and helping people discern their calling in missions.

Get Involved with Short-Term Mission Trips

God does not place everyone on the long-term mission field. He will call some to that great venture. But even if we don't yet sense a long-term call to serve in cross-cultural missions, we can still contribute to the work through short-term trips. Short-term trips are perfect for getting an introduction to another place, people, and culture. They provide an opportunity to both advance the gospel and to discern our ongoing role.

When Fred Luter, senior pastor of New Orleans' Franklin Avenue Baptist Church, became the first African-American president of the Southern Baptist Convention, he admitted that he'd never been on a mission trip. He accepted the challenge to take his first trips as Convention president and to encourage other black churches to do the same. Luter pursued three specific missions-related goals: to model a personal commitment to international missions, educate churches about the need, and instill a vision for the world in young people. Luter understood that "We need to reach the people in our neighborhoods and get African Americans out on the foreign field."[34]

Ask your pastor about the possibility of joining a short-term mission team. Pastor, begin praying with your leadership about opportunities to take small groups of people to another country to spread the gospel. Perhaps partnering with another local church provides encouragement, shared resources, and international connections that will make the initial efforts easier.

Make the Support of Missionaries a Financial Priority for the Church and the Family

When African-Americans do sense a call to the mission field, they're often met with discouragement and a lack of funding support. After getting a strong grip on how important missions is to God's purposes in the world, committing financial resources to support those who go is perhaps the most important commitment local churches need to make. Financial support literally makes the difference in whether persons can give their attention to the work of missions and whether the nations hear the soul-saving gospel of Jesus Christ.

One missionary's experience is all-too-common:

After I graduated from seminary, I went on the mission field for 11 years. In those 11 years only one African-American church supported me and my family and that was the church that I grew up in, Faith Community Church. The only reason that they did it was because my father was a deacon and he said he was going to make sure that we didn't starve on the mission field. When I went to African-American churches, they were very supportive of my going to the mission field, but they did not have the internal financial discipline or infrastructure to support my family on a long-term basis. They took up tremendous one-time offerings that definitely met a need, but our month-to-month support on the mission field wasn't there. It wasn't that the African-American churches were not sympathetic as supporters, but this was something new to them.[35]

In order to be effective contributors to the work of global missions, churches will need to make funding a high priority. Missions pastor Jack Gaines of Calvary Evangelical Baptist Church of Portsmouth, Virginia,

illustrates how making funding a priority makes a difference in a church's
growth and activity in cross-cultural missions:

> I think it is very important to lend our financial support to those
> serving overseas. When I became a missions director, there were
> some things in place already. One of the structures that my pas-
> tor established when he came to our congregation of about 60
> people, was that 10 percent of the morning offering would go
> towards missions. Also all of Wednesday-night Bible study offer-
> ing and all of Sunday evening service offering would go toward
> missions. Now that we are running about 900 members, that is
> a significant amount of resources for missions. As a result we are
> sending support to approximately 23 missionaries around the
> world. We praise God for that. . . .[36]

Much can be done if local churches would put missions funding in
their annual budgets. Churches should at least tithe in mission all they
receive in member giving. The Lord Jesus Christ taught that "where your
treasure is, there your heart will be also" (Matt. 6:21). That's as true of
congregations as it is individual Christians. We need to put our treasure
in the mission of God so that increasingly our hearts will be there as well.

Families can make the same commitment whether or not their local
churches fund mission efforts. Many observers point out that non-black
missionaries often have a network of personal and family support on
the mission field possible, while African-Americans lack such support.
Getting on the mission field depends on knowing people who will support you financially. Families can build potential missionaries' social and
economic capital by committing some portion of their family or individual income to support the African-American missionaries who visit
our churches or make financial appeals. The spiritual reward will be great
(2 Cor. 9:6–15).

Conclusion

As we look to revive the Black Church by reengaging the work of
cross-cultural gospel missions, we'll often be asked the question, "Why
should we give our money and go across the globe when so many needs
exist in our own communities?" We need to embrace this question and

answer in as biblical a manner as possible. We can no longer allow an exclusive focus on our own communities to blind us to the greater work the Lord has for the Black Church to do. So, in love and empathy, we must answer, "Because our Lord commands us to, because people will die and go to hell without the gospel, because others have needs too, and because it brings revival to us when we see the nations saved." Not everyone will immediately feel compelled by that answer. But some will. And the others, if they love what Jesus loves, will come along as they get a vision for the worldwide worship of Jesus Christ. In the end they will see what the apostle John saw:

> There before me was a great multitude that no one could count, from every nation, tribe, people and language, standing before the throne and in front of the Lamb. They were wearing white robes and were holding palm branches in their hands. And they cried out in a loud voice: "Salvation belongs to our God, who sits on the throne, and to the Lamb." (Rev. 7:9–10 NIV)

Afterword

The only force capable of reviving the Black Church in whatever area she needs revival is the Spirit of God animating the Word of God. Apart from a Spirit-enabled recovery and submission to the Word of God, there can be no hope of lasting revival among any of God's people. Programs may appear to "work." Special events may continue to inspire. Sermons may motivate—for a time. But all these things will fizzle and fade. The only thing that brings lasting life and vigor to a congregation is the Bible, rightly preached and taught, defining and guiding leadership, shaping and motivating the life of the body of Christ. That's because the Word itself is "living and active, sharper than any two-edged sword, piercing to the division of soul and of spirit, of joints and of marrow, and discerning the thoughts and intentions of the heart" (Heb. 4:12).

But the church finds herself divided and torn on precisely this point—the role of the Bible in giving the church its life. Some tell us that the Bible is not the Word of God, or that it merely *contains* the words of God, and that we need to loosen our grip on the Bible because it's culturally and socially bound, stuck in a first-century world with little relevance to our own. Others teach from an open Bible all the time and regularly call the people to believe what the Bible says and expect what the Bible promises. Yet, they seldom emphasize the Bible's priorities while turning the Bible's promises into a talisman, or a mantra that if chanted and repeated with enough fervor *causes* God to do what the worshipper wants. Neither of these approaches to the Bible actually gives the Word of God its central, life-giving place in the church.

Truthfully, a fierce battle rages for the imagination and heart of the Black Church. We see the battle fought in the pages of books, in the sermons of preachers, and in classrooms that train future servants of the church. Much of the Black Church remains unaware of the fight, assuming the best of all its leaders and teachers, thinking that the use of the same language and words means agreement among all. Like so many Trojan horses, men and women by day smuggle their armies into the camp of the church in order to release their forces at night while the normally alert soundly sleep. Unless we are willing to be overrun by midnight marauders, we need to heed the Bible's call to watch, to wake from our slumber, and do the works of our first love (Rev. 2:2–7). The church's life depends on it.

The question becomes who will say to the Lord, "Here am I, send me"? Who will enroll as the Lord's watchmen, hear the call to battle, and do the courageous with the hope of seeing the Lord once again stir the mighty giant called "the Black Church"?

Be assured that no revival comes easily or cheaply. No revival comes without sweat in prayer, diligence in study, earnestness in preaching, risks in leadership, striving in sanctification, waiting for glorification, seriousness about hell, or joy in the Lord's salvation.

We cannot fear man and hope for the Lord to send revival. We must fear God alone. We cannot expect revival while failing to love God's Word, love God's people, or love our neighbors and enemies. We cannot serve our traditions and hope that God will do a new thing in the church. We must stand on the Word of God and realize that the "new thing" is actually an old thing, the thing that was always true—God revives by His Spirit and His Word. We cannot hope to see God's glory while we put on shows for church attenders or seek the praise of men. His glory cannot be "performed," faked, programmed, bought, bartered, or scheduled. When it falls, all the earth will be silent and men will feel themselves to be the dust that we are, crying, "Holy, holy, holy is the Lord God Almighty!"

In all likelihood the revival we crave and need will come at a time we least expect through a means we too often neglect: the simple though diligent application of the Word of God to all of life. When revival comes, we will have our shoulders harnessed to the yoke of Christ's Word, plowing the straight furrow, looking ahead and not back. Despite all the bent-back labor, when revival comes we will feel a new life in our souls, a vigor springing from deep wells inside us, an ineffable holy joy compelling us onward in Christ. Our sufferings will feel momentary and light while His glory descends on us like a cloud. Every pebble we trod will become to us a holy mountain where we meet with God. The songs of the saints will sound angelic and the prayers of the people like the very language of that holy Zion, the New Jerusalem. The preaching of pastors and prophets will ring with the authority of Christ's own voice. Husbands will love their wives and lead their children as if Christ Himself dwelled in them. Wives will honor their husbands and care for their children as if Christ lived in them. Workplaces will be filled with the aroma of heaven and block-by-block communities will be transformed into outposts of another world. Without ever having marked it on a calendar, while doing the "ordinary" thing of seeking God in His Word . . . we will be revived!

In the final analysis, the question is not whether the Black Church is dead. The question is and always has been: Will we take God at His Word? Will the church remain faithful to the end, obeying all that Christ has commanded? If she does, then she just might see those new days of the Spirit's outpouring and refreshment we call revival. Make no mistake: It will only happen by the Word God has given us. When it happens by the Word of God, it will be revival indeed!

Notes

Introduction

1. Eddie S. Glaude Jr., "The Black Church Is Dead" (February 24, 2010). Downloaded on January 28, 2012 at http://www.huffingtonpost.com/eddie-glaude-jr-phd/the-black-church-is-dead_b_473815.html.

2. Ibid.

3. Ibid.

4. Ibid.

5. Audio of the panel discussion can be found at http://ircpl.org/2010/rethinking-religion/events/podcasts/is-the-black-church-dead-2/#more-1418.

6. Byron Williams, "Eddie Glaude, Jr. Is Right: The Black Church Is Indeed Dead" (April 20, 2010). Downloaded on January 28, 2012 at http://www.huffingtonpost.com/byron-williams/eddie-glaude-is-right_b_544756.html.

7. Ibid.

8. William H. Crouch and Joel C. Gregory, *What We Love about the Black Church: Can We Get a Witness?* (Valley Forge, PA: Judson Press, 2010).

9. Joel C. Gregory, "The Black Church: Alive and Well" (May 5, 2010). Downloaded on January 28, 2012 at http://www.huffingtonpost.com/joel-c-gregory-mdiv-phd/the-black-church-alive-an_b_565411.html.

10. I explore this theme more fully in *The Life of God in the Soul of the Church: The Root and Fruit of Spiritual Fellowship* (Scotland: Christian Focus Publications, 2012).

11. Raphael G. Warnock, *The Divided Mind of the Black Church: Theology, Piety, and Public Witness* (New York, NY: NYU Press, 2014), 1.

12. Glaude Jr., "The Black Church Is Dead."

Chapter 1

1. James Albert Ukawsaw Gronniosaw, *A Narrative of the Most Remarkable Particulars in the Life of James Albert Ukawsaw Gronniosaw, an African Prince, as Related by Himself* (1772), cited in Dwight Allan Callahan, *The Talking Book: African American and the Bible* (New Haven, CT: Yale, 2006), 13.

2. John Jea, *The Life, History, and Unparalleled Sufferings of John Jea, The African Preacher, Compiled and Written by Himself,* in *Pioneers of the Black Atlantic: Five Slave Narratives from the Enlightenment, 1772–1815,* ed. Henry Louise Gates Jr. and William L. Andrews (Washington, DC: Counterpoint, 1998), 379. Emphasis added.

3. Ibid.

4. Callahan, *The Talking Book,* 19.

5. Jupiter Hammon, *Address to the Negroes in the State of New York,* in Sondra O'Neale, *Jupiter Hammon and the Biblical Beginnings of African American Literature* (Metuchen, NJ: American Library Association, 1993), 237–38.

6. Daniel Alexander Payne, *Welcome to the Ransomed, or, Duties of the Colored Inhabitants of the District of Columbia* (Baltimore, MD: Bull & Tuttle, 1862), 7.

7. Payne, *Recollections of Seventy Years* (Nashville, TN: AME Sunday School Union, 1888), 233–34.

8. Jea, *The Life, History, and Unparalleled Sufferings of John Jea,* 369–70.

9. See Thabiti M. Anyabwile, *The Decline of African-American Theology: From Biblical Faith to Cultural Captivity* (Wheaton, IL: IVP, 2007). Chapter 1 offers a survey of African-American views of revelation and the Scripture from the mid-1700s until the present.

10. Downloaded on February 5, 2012 from the website of the African Methodist Episcopal Church, http://www.ame-church.com/about-us/beliefs.php.

11. James H. Cone, *A Black Theology of Liberation: Twentieth Anniversary Edition* (New York, NY: Orbis Books, 1986), 45–46.

12. James H. Cone, *God of the Oppressed* (Maryknoll, NY: Orbis Books, 1997), xi.

13. Howard Thurman, *Jesus and the Disinherited* (Nashville, TN: Abingdon, 1949), 30–31.

14. Michael Joseph Brown, *Blackening the Bible: The Aims of African American Biblical Scholarship* (Harrisburg, PA: Trinity Press International, 2004), 154, 161.

15. Ibid., 23.

16. Ronald N. Liburd, "'Like . . . a House upon the Sand': African American Biblical Hermeneutics in Perspective," *Journal of the Interdenominational Theological Center* 22 (1994): 77, 81. Cited in Brown, *Blackening the Bible*, 52.

17. Femi Adeleye, *Preachers of a Different Gospel: A Pilgrim's Reflection on Contemporary Trends in Christianity* (Grand Rapids, MI: Zondervan, 2011), 87–88.

18. Jonathan Leeman, *Reverberation: How God's Word Brings Light, Freedom, and Action to His People* (Chicago, IL: Moody Publishers, 2011), 47.

Chapter 2

1. Katie G. Cannon, *Teaching Preaching: Isaac Rufus Clark and Black Sacred Rhetoric* (New York, NY: Continuum, 2003), 42.

2. Ibid., 49.

3. Cleophus J. LaRue, *The Heart of Black Preaching* (Louisville, KY: Westminster John Knox, 2000), 6.

4. Marvin A. McMickle, *Shaping the Claim* (Minneapolis: Fortress Press, 2008), 6.

5. Marvin A. McMickle, "What Shall They Preach?" in Timothy George, James Earl Massey, and Robert Smith Jr. (eds.), *Our Sufficiency Is of God: Essays on Preaching in Honor of Gardner C. Taylor* (Macon, GA: Mercer University Press, 2010), 122.

6. Cannon, *Teaching Preaching*, 49. Emphasis added.

7. E. K. Bailey, *Ten Reasons for Expository Preaching* (Dallas, TX: E. K. Bailey Ministries, 2003), 2:1; cited in Robert Smith Jr., *Doctrine That Dances: Bringing Doctrinal Preaching and Teaching to Life* (Nashville, TN: B&H Academic, 2008), 19–20. Emphasis added.

8. John Stott, *Between Two Worlds: The Challenge of Preaching Today* (Grand Rapids, MI: Eerdmans, 1982), 126.

9. Henry H. Mitchell, *Black Preaching: The Recovery of a Powerful Art* (Nashville, TN: Abingdon Press, 1990), 121.

10. Cannon, *Teaching Preaching*, 55.

11. LaRue, *The Heart of Black Preaching*, 19. Emphasis added.

12. Ibid., 13. Italics added.

13. Ibid., 21.

14. Ibid., 20.

15. Mitchell, *Black Preaching*, 105.

16. Ibid., 4. LaRue refers to five nineteenth-century ministers: John Jasper, Alexander Crummell, Francis Grimké, Daniel Payne, and Elias Morris. These five men were roughly contemporaries born during slavery.

17. See, for example, James H. Cone, *A Black Theology of Liberation,* Twentieth Anniversary Edition (New York, NY: Orbis, 2003). I use the terms "Black Theologian" and "Black Theology" to refer to a specific school of black liberation theology founded by James H. Cone. Whenever speaking of the theology of African-Americans in general I use the term "African-American theology."

18. James H. Evans Jr., *We Have Been Believers: An African-American Systematic Theology* (Minneapolis, MN: Fortress, 1992), 10.

19. See, for example, Deborah J. Dickerson, *The End of Blackness: Returning the Souls of Black Folk to the Rightful Owners* (New York, NY: Anchor Books, 2004); Ytasha L. Womack, *Post-Black: How a Generation Is Redefining African American Identity* (Chicago, IL: Lawrence Hill Books, 2010); and Touré, *Who's Afraid of Post-Blackness: What It Means to Be Black Now* (New York: Free Press, 2011).

20. For a brief treatment of the hermeneutics of health and wealth gospel preachers, see Gordon D. Fee, *The Disease of the Health and Wealth Gospels* (Vancouver, BC: Regent College Publishing, 1985), 7–17; David S. Jones and Russell S. Woodbridge, *Health, Wealth and Happiness: Has the Prosperity Gospel Overshadowed the Gospel of Christ?* (Grand Rapids, MI: Kregel Publications, 2010); Adeleye, *Preachers of a Different Gospel.*

21. H. B. Charles Jr., "Explaining What the Text Means," in Cleophus J. LaRue, *Power in the Pulpit: How America's Most Effective Black Preachers Prepare Their Sermons* (Louisville, KY: Westminster John Knox, 2002), 42.

22. For more on this concept, see chapter 1 of Thabiti M. Anyabwile, *What Is a Healthy Church Member?* (Wheaton, IL: Crossway, 2008); Christopher Ash, *Listen Up! A Practical Guide to Listening to Sermons* (Surrey, UK: The Good Book Company, 2009). For an excellent practical guide to listening to and evaluating a sermon for biblical faithfulness, see Chris Brauns, *When the Word Leads Your Pastoral Search: Biblical Principles and Practices to Guide Your Search* (Chicago, IL: Moody, 2010). See chapters 7–9 in particular.

23. Stott, *Between Two Worlds,* 113.

Chapter 3

1. A version of this address was first given at the 9Marks @ Southeastern Conference held September 25–26, 2009 at Southeastern Baptist Theological Seminary in Wake Forest, North Carolina. Audio and video of the address are available at http://apps.sebts.edu/multimedia/?p=239.

2. Henry H. Mitchell, *Black Preaching,* 14. Emphasis added.

3. Ibid. Emphasis added.

4. Matthew D. Kim, "Asian American Preaching," *Preaching Today.com* (August 25, 2005). Emphasis added. Downloaded September 21, 2009 from http://www.preachingtoday.com/skills/2005/august/53--kim.html.

5. Mitchell, *Black Preaching*, 122.

6. Iain H. Murray, *D. Martyn Lloyd-Jones: The First Forty Years, 1899–1939* (Edinburgh, Scotland: Banner of Truth, 1982), 146.

7. Mitchell, *Black Preaching*, 28.

8. Richard Allen, *The Life, Experience, and Gospel Labours of the Rt. Rev. Richard Allen* (Philadelphia, PA: Martin and Boden, 1833), 17.

9. In Richard A. Bailey and Gregory A Wills (eds.), *The Salvation of Souls: Nine Previously Unpublished Sermons on the Call of Ministry and the Gospel by Jonathan Edwards*, 11–12.

10. As preachers, we have the amazing privilege of announcing the good news to our congregations. Each Sunday we get to tell our people what Christ has done for them on the cross and in His resurrection. I don't mean the preacher should give a canned presentation of the gospel or tack it onto the end of a sermon otherwise unrelated. Instead, the preacher should work to present the work of Christ from the text he preaches in a way that's natural to the text. In the case of Nehemiah, one might focus on this weeping and repenting as a place to call the listener to Christ. For an imperfect example, in the original context of this address, I made the following appeal: "If you are here this morning and you have been weeping over your sins as you have listened to God's Word opened and explained, and you have seen that God is holy, I exhort you, I beg you, I plead with you, do not settle for weeping. Repent—yes—but believe that Jesus bore your sin and your curse and satisfied the Father on your behalf and rose from the dead—conquering your death and your hell and your sin and your judgment so that you through faith in Him will live. Trust that promise. Trust that Savior. Place your hope upon Him. He will not disappoint. And you may celebrate eternal life and forgiveness of sin and everlasting righteousness with God. Today is the day of salvation. Repent, believe and live."

11. D. Martyn Lloyd-Jones, *Preaching and Preachers: 40th Anniversary Edition* (Grand Rapids, MI: Zondervan, 2011), 110.

12. Murray, *D. Martin Lloyd-Jones*, 146.

13. Ibid., 146–47.

14. See, for example, Tullian Tchividjian, *Jesus Plus Nothing Equals Everything* (Wheaton, IL: Crossway, 2011); Bobby Ross Jr., "Tullian Tchividjian: Allow Your Critics to Teach You," *Christianity Today* (September 24, 2009), available at http://www.christianitytoday.com/ct/2009/septemberweb-only/138-41.0.html; and Drew Dyck, "War and Peace," *Leadership*

Journal (Fall 2011), available at http://www.christianitytoday.com/le/2011/fall/warpeace.html.

Chapter 4

1. Mitchell, *Black Preaching*, 34.

2. James H. Cone, *Black Theology and Black Power* (Mary Knoll, NY: Orbis Books, 1969), 32.

3. Ibid., 35.

4. Ibid., 35–36.

5. Ibid., 43.

6. Ibid., 38.

7. James H. Cone, *God of the Oppressed* (Mary Knoll, NY: Orbis Books, 1997, new revised edition), 115.

8. James H. Cone, *A Black Theology of Liberation: Twentieth Anniversary Edition* (Mary Knoll, NY: Orbis Books, 1986), 124. Emphasis in the original.

9. Cone, *Black Theology and Black Power*, 40.

10. Cone, *A Black Theology of Liberation*, 128.

11. For examples of Black Theologians extending Cone's thought to other areas of liberation, see Kelly Brown Douglas, *The Black Christ* (Mary Knoll, NY: Orbis Books, 1994); Marcia Y. Riggs, *Plenty Good Room: Women Versus Male Power in the Black Church* (Cleveland, OH: Pilgrim Press, 2003); and Demetrius K. Williams, *An End to This Strife: The Politics of Gender in African American Churches* (Minneapolis, MN: Fortress Press, 2004).

12. Stephanie Y. Mitchem, *Name It and Claim It? Prosperity Preaching in the Black Church* (Cleveland, OH: Pilgrim Press, 2007). For another chapter-length overview of the prosperity gospel, see Ken Jones, "The Prosperity Gospel," in Anthony B. Bradley (ed.), *Keep Your Head Up: America's New Black Christian Leaders, Social Consciousness, and the Cosby Conversation* (Wheaton, IL: Crossway, 2012), 177–96.

13. Creflo A. Dollar Jr., *Not Guilty: Experience God's Gift of Acceptance and Freedom* (Harrison, OK: Tulsa House, 2007), v.

14. Ibid.

15. Ibid., vi.

16. Ibid., 18.

17. Ibid.

18. Ibid., 158.

19. Ibid., 199.

20. Jeremiah A. Wright Jr., "The Continuing Legacy of Samuel DeWitt Proctor," in Iva E. Carruthers, Frederick D. Haynes III, and Jeremiah A. Wright Jr. (eds.), *Blow the Trumpet in Zion: Global Vision and Action for the*

Twenty-First-Century Black Church (Minneapolis, MN: Fortress Press, 2005), 8–9.

21. Gordon D. Fee, *The Disease of the Health and Wealth Gospels* (Vancouver, BC: Regent College Publishing, 2006), 9.

22. Ibid., 17.

23. Mitchem, *Name It and Claim It?*, 21–36.

24. Bruce L. Fields, *Introducing Black Theology: Three Crucial Questions for the Evangelical Church* (Grand Rapids, MI: Baker, 2001), 86.

25. Ibid., 88.

26. Ibid., 91.

27. Anthony Carter, "The Black Church and Orthodoxy," in Bradley (ed.), *Keep Your Head Up*, 160.

28. Cone, *Black Theology and Black Power*, 43–44.

29. Dollar, *Not Guilty*, vi.

30. Ibid., 153.

31. Carter, "The Black Church and Orthodoxy," 161.

32. E-mail correspondence dated February 3, 2012.

Chapter 5

1. Richard Wright, as quoted in Melva Wilson Costen, *African American Christian Worship* (Nashville, TN: Abingdon, 1993), 78–79.

2. Joel C. Gregory, "The Black Church: Alive and Well" (May 5, 2010). Downloaded on January 28, 2012 at http://www.huffingtonpost.com/joel-c-gregory-mdiv-phd/the-black-church-alive-an_b_565411.html.

3. Anthony J. Carter, "Biblical Worship: Experiencing the Presence of God," in Anthony J. Carter (ed.), *Experiencing the Truth: Bringing the Reformation to the African-American Church* (Wheaton, IL: Crossway, 2008), 97.

4. Melva Wilson Costen, *African American Christian Worship* (Nashville, TN: Abingdon, 1993), 127.

5. Carter, *Experiencing the Truth*, 56.

6. Brenda Aghahowa, *Praising in Black and White: Unity and Diversity in Christian Worship* (Cleveland, OH: United Church Press, 1996), 65. Cited in Carter, *Experiencing the Truth*, 100. Emphasis added.

7. Ibid., 134.

8. Carter, "Biblical Worship: Experiencing the Presence of God," 91.

Chapter 6

1. G. A. Smith on the appropriateness of the Bible's shepherd imagery; cited in Timothy Laniak, *Shepherds after My Own Heart: Pastoral Traditions and Leadership in the Bible* (Downers Grove, IL: IVP, 2006), 57.

2. Dale P. Andrews, *Practical Theology for Black Churches: Bridging Black Theology and African American Folk Religion* (Louisville, KY: Westminster John Knox, 2002), 24.

3. Homer U. Ashby Jr., *Our Home Is Over Jordan: A Black Pastoral Theology* (St. Louis, MO: Chalice Press, 2003), 10.

4. Ibid., 36.

5. Samuel D. Proctor and Gardner C. Taylor with Gary V. Simpson, *We Have This Ministry: The Heart of the Pastor's Vocation* (Valley Forge, PA: Judson Press, 1996), 49–50.

6. James H. Cone, "Loving God with Our Heart, Soul, and Mind," in Carruthers, Haynes, and Wright Jr. (eds.), *Blow the Trumpet in Zion*, 60.

7. See, for example, Kathy Lohr, "Senator Probes Megachurches' Finances," National Public Radio (December 4, 2007), downloaded on June 29, 2012 at http://www.npr.org/templates/story/story.php?storyId=16860611.

8. Samuel D. Proctor and Gardner C. Taylor with Gary V. Simpson, *We Have This Ministry: The Heart of the Pastor's Vocation* (Valley Forge, PA: Judson Press, 1996), 53.

9. The following statistics were taken from Richard J. Krejcir, "Statistics on Pastors," downloaded at the Schaeffer Institute on June 30, 2012 and available at http://www.intothyword.org/apps/articles/default.asp?articleid=36562.

10. Ronald M. Enroth, *Churches That Abuse: Help for Those Hurt by Legalism, Authoritarian Leadership, and Spiritual Intimidation* (Grand Rapids, MI: Zondervan, 1992).

11. Timothy Z. Witmer, *The Shepherd Leader: Achieving Effective Shepherding in Your Church* (Phillipsburg, NJ: P&R Publishing, 2010), 9.

12. Contrary to popular usage, the terms "pastor," "elder," "bishop," "shepherd," and "overseer" are synonyms in the New Testament, referring to the same office. Consider, for example, passages like Acts 20:17, 28 and 1 Peter 5:1–2 where these terms are used interchangeably for the same persons and office.

13. I have taken up a lengthier discussion of pastoral qualifications and responsibilities in *Finding Faithful Elders and Deacons* (Wheaton, IL: Crossway, 2012). Readers might also see Benjamin L. Merkle, *40 Questions about Elders and Deacons* (Grand Rapids, MI: Kregel, 2008); Phil A. Newton and Matthew Schmucker, *Elders in the Life of the Church: Rediscovering the Biblical Model for Church Leadership* (Grand Rapids, MI: Kregel, 2014);

and Alexander Strauch, *Biblical Eldership: An Urgent Call to Restore Biblical Church Leadership* (Colorado Springs, CO: Lewis and Roth, 1995).

14. David Dickson, *The Elder and His Work* (Phillipsburg, NJ: P&R Publishing, 2004), 34.

15. Baptist Press, "Most Pastors Unsatisfied with Their Personal Prayer Lives," (June 6, 2005), accessed on July 3, 2012 at http://www.bpnews.net/bpnews.asp?id=20918.

16. William Still, *The Work of the Pastor* (Edinburgh, Scotland: Rutherford House and Christian Focus, 2010), 28.

17. Witmer, *The Shepherd Leader*, 14.

18. Ibid., 43.

19. R. Kent Hughes and Barbara Hughes, *Liberating Ministry from the Success Syndrome* (Wheaton, IL: Crossway, 2008).

Chapter 7

1. For the denomination's description of "Church Mother," see Mattie McGlothen (ed.), *Women's Handbook, Newly Revised Edition of Organization and Procedure* (Memphis, TN: Church of God in Christ Publishing House, 1980), 20–22.

2. Benjamin L. Merkle, *Forty Questions about Elders and Deacons* (Grand Rapids, MI: Kregel, 2008), 161.

3. Ibid.

4. Ibid., 183–87.

5. Witmer, *The Shepherd Leader*, 93.

6. Ibid., 88–93.

7. C. Eric Lincoln and Lawrence H. Mamiya, *The Black Church in the African American Experience* (Durham, NC: Duke University Press, 1990), 276–81.

8. Ibid., 285.

9. The major black Baptist denominations include: the National Baptist Convention founded in 1895, the National Baptist Convention of America founded in 1915, and the Progressive National Baptist Convention founded in 1961.

10. Lincoln and Mamiya, *The Black Church in the African American Experience*, 285–87.

11. Wiggins, *Righteous Content*, 184.

12. Marcia Y. Riggs, *Plenty Good Room: Women Versus Male Power in the Black Church* (Cleveland, OH: Pilgrim Press, 2003), 86.

13. Demetrius K. Williams, *An End to This Strife: The Politics of Gender in African American Churches* (Minneapolis, MN: Fortress Press, 2004), 137.

14. Ibid., 5. Emphasis added.

15. Ibid., 67.

16. Ibid.

17. Ibid., 113.

18. Ibid., 92.

19. Daphne C. Wiggins, *Righteous Content: Black Women's Perspectives of Church and Faith* (New York, NY: New York University Press, 2005), 175.

20. Renita J. Weems, "Womanist Reflections on Biblical Hermeneutics," in James H. Cone and Gayraud S. Wilmore (eds.), *Black Theology: A Documentary Witness, Vol. 2: 1980–1992* (Mary Knoll, NY: Orbis, 1993), 219–20, 222.

21. Ibid., 52–58.

22. Wiggins, *Righteous Content*, 131–33, 139.

23. Anthony C. Thiselton, *1 Corinthians: A Shorter Exegetical and Pastoral Commentary* (Grand Rapids, MI: Eerdmans Publishing, 2006), 170.

Chapter 8

1. "Roman Catholic Sex Abuse Cases," *New York Times* (September 6, 2012), downloaded on September 14, 2012 at http://topics.nytimes.com/top/reference/timestopics/organizations/r/roman_catholic_church_sex_abuse_cases/index.html.

2. Ibid.

3. Jeremiah A. Wright Jr., "The Continuing Legacy of Samuel DeWitt Proctor," in Carruthers, Haynes, and Wright Jr. (eds.), *Blow the Trumpet in Zion*, 5.

4. Rick Bragg, "A Preacher's Faithful Back Both Sinner and Felon," *New York Times* (March 1, 1999).

5. Rick Bragg, "Lyons Steps Down from Black Baptist Group," *New York Times* (March 17, 1999).

6. Sheri Day, "The Rev. Henry Lyons Wants to Lead the National Baptist Convention USA Again," *Tampa Bay Times* (February 5, 2009).

7. See Eryn Sun, "Two Victims Break Silence about Bishop Eddie Long's Sexual Abuse," *The Christian Post* (August 26, 2011); Steve Osunsami, Sarah Netter, and Emily Friedman, "Bishop Eddie Long Denies Sexual Abuse as Plaintiff's Lawyers Promise More Evidence," ABC World News with Dianne Sawyer (September 22, 2010); Audrey Barrick, "Eddie Long Files Response to Abuse Lawsuits," *The Christian Post* (November 2, 2010); and Adelle M. Banks, "Bishop Eddie Long Sexual Misconduct Lawsuit Resolved," Religion News Service (May 27, 2011).

8. Diana R. Garland and Christen Argueta, "How Clergy Misconduct Happens: A Qualitative Study of First-Hand Accounts," *Social Work and Christianity*, 37 (1), 5.

9. For a brief treatment of men's and women's attitudes and responses toward clergy misconduct, see Daphne C. Wiggins, *Righteous Content* (New York, NY: New York Univ. Press, 2005), 54–66.

10. Ibid, 59.

11. See, for example, Eric C. Redmond, *Where Are All the Brothers? Straight Answers to Men's Questions about the Church* (Wheaton, IL: Crossway, 2008).

12. Wiggins, *Righteous Content*, 66.

13. I recognize that a church's or denomination's polity or rules of governance may require differing procedures, from the very defined hierarchical approach of some denominations to the locally-defined processes of independent churches. However, in the discussion that follows, I'm simply attempting to paint some basic biblical responsibilities that ought to be applicable in most church settings.

14. Proctor and Taylor with Gary V. Simpson, *We Have This Ministry*, ix–x.

15. For two excellent, short treatments of pastoral calling, see Edmund P. Clowney, *Called to the Ministry* (Phillipsburg, NJ: P&R Publishing, 1964) and Dave Harvey, *Am I Called? The Summons to Pastoral Ministry* (Wheaton, IL: Crossway, 2012).

16. For a very helpful guide to finding godly, qualified pastors, see Chris Brauns, *When the Word Leads Your Pastor Search*. I've also written a book I hope would be helpful churches in discerning whether a man meets the biblical qualifications for elders and deacons called *Finding Faithful Elders and Deacons*.

17. Wiggins, *Righteous Content*, 66.

18. John MacArthur, *The Master's Plan for the Church* (Chicago, IL: Moody, 2008), 288.

19. The literature and debate regarding restoration of fallen clergy is varied and wide. Representative works on the topic include: John H. Armstrong, *The Stain That Stays: The Church's Response to Sexual Misconduct* (Ross-shire, Scotland: Christian Focus, 2000). Armstrong argues that restoration is not desirable or possible in most cases. See also Don Baker, *Beyond Forgiveness: The Healing Touch of Church Discipline* (Colorado Springs, CO: Multnomah, 1984) and Ray Carroll, *Fallen Pastor: Finding Restoration in a Broken World* (San Jose, CA: Civitas Press, 2011). Baker and Carroll argue that men can be restored following counseling and evidence of repentance.

20. Armstrong, *The Stain That Stays*.

21. Quoted in Eric Reed, "Restoring Fallen Pastors," *Leadership Journal* (Winter 2006). Downloaded on September 17, 2012 at http://www.christianitytoday.com/le/2006/winter/22.21.html.

22. Joe Maxwell, "Devastated by an Affair: How Churches Heal After the Pastor Commits Adultery," *Christianity Today* (January 2007). Downloaded on September 17, 2012 at http://www.christianitytoday.com/ct/2007/january/2.51.html?start=1.

23. Ibid.

24. Proctor and Taylor with Gary V. Simpson, *We Have This Ministry*, 11.

Chapter 9

1. From James H. Cone, "Loving God with Our Heart, Soul, and Mind," in Iva E. Carruthers, Frederick D. Haynes III, and Jeremiah Wright (eds.), *Blow the Trumpet in Zion: Global Vision and Action for the Twenty-First Century Black Church* (Minneapolis, MN: Fortress Press, 2005).

2. For an excellent recent book-length treatment of slave owner resistance to Christian slaves' claim to freedom based on spiritual experience and baptism, see Rebecca Anne Goetz, *The Baptism of Early Virginia: How Christianity Created Race* (Baltimore, MD: Johns Hopkins, 2012).

3. Mark A. Noll, *A History of Christianity in the United States and Canada* (Grand Rapids, MI: Eerdman's, 1992), 201–3. For complete biographies of Richard Allen and studies of the rise of the AME Church, see Carol V. R. George, *Segregated Sabbaths: Richard Allen and the Rise of Independent Black Churches, 1760–1840* (New York, NY: Oxford University Press, 1973) and Richard A. Newman, *Freedom's Prophet: Bishop Richard Allen, the AME Church, and the Black Founding Fathers* (New York, NY: New York University Press, 2008).

4. Mitchell, *Black Preaching*, 25–26.

5. Ibid., 45.

6. For a brief sketch of Haynes's biography, see Thabiti M. Anyabwile, *May We Meet in the Heavenly World: The Piety of Lemuel Haynes* (Grand Rapids, MI: Reformation Heritage Books, 2009), 1–20. See also Timothy Mather Cooley, *Sketches of the Life and Character of the Rev. Lemuel Haynes, A.M., for Many Years Pastor of a Church in Rutland, VT., and Late in Granville, New York* (New York, NY: Harper and Brothers, 1837) and John Saillant, *Black Puritan, Black Republican: The Life and Thought of Lemuel Haynes, 1753–1833* (Oxford and New York, NY: Oxford University Press, 2003).

7. Thabiti M. Anyabwile, *The Decline of African American Theology: From Biblical Faith to Cultural Captivity* (Downers Grove, IL: InterVarsity Press, 2007), 28–29.

8. Daniel Alexander Payne, *Recollections of Seventy Years* (Nashville, TN: AME Sunday School Union, 1888).

9. Mitchell, *Black Preaching*, 44–46.

10. C. Eric Lincoln and Lawrence H. Mamiya, *The Black Church in the African American Experience* (Durham, NC: Duke University Press, 1990), 98. Lawrence and Mamiya refer to studies conducted by Harry V. Richardson, *Dark Glory: A Picture of the Church Among Negroes in the Rural South* (New York: Friendship, 1947) and Ralph Felton, *These My Brethren: A Study of 570 Negro Churches and 542 Negro Homes in the Rural South* (New York, NY: Committee for the Training of the Negro Rural Pastors of the Phelps-Stokes Fund and the Home Missions Council of North America, 1950).

11. Lincoln and Mamiya, *The Black Church in the African American Experience*, 129, citing Benjamin E. Mays and Joseph Nicholson, *The Negro's Church* (New York, NY: Russell and Russell, 1969, reissue).

12. Ibid.

13. Charles Shelby Rooks, *Revolution in Zion: Reshaping African American Ministry, 1960–1974* (New York, NY: Pilgrim Press, 1990), 29.

14. Ibid., 30.

15. Ibid., 4.

16. Ibid., 21–24.

17. Ibid., 59–60.

18. Ibid., 150.

19. Ibid., 155–56.

20. Robert M. Franklin, *Another Day's Journey: Black Churches Confronting the American Crisis* (Minneapolis, MN: Fortress, 1997), 6.

21. Lincoln and Mamiya, *The Black Church in the African American Experience*, 98.

22. Association for Theological Schools, "Diversity in Theological Education" (Association for Theological Schools). Downloaded on October 17, 2012 at http://www.ats.edu/Resources/PublicationsPresentations/Pages/default.aspx.

23. Lincoln and Mamiya, *The Black Church in the African American Experience*, 129.

24. Michael I. N. Dash and Christine D. Chapman, *The Shape of Zion: Leadership and Life in Black Churches* (Cleveland, OH: Pilgrim Press, 2003), 96.

25. Association for Theological Schools, "Diversity in Theological Education." See table "Racial/Ethnic Enrollment by Decade 1969–1999."

26. For a complete listing of program participants in the various scholarship programs, see Rooks, *Revolution in Zion*, 193–216.

27. Ibid., 29, 83.

28. Association for Theological Schools, "Diversity in Theological Education." See table "African American M.Div. Enrollment in ATS Schools 1990–1999."

29. Learn more about the Rebuild Network at http://therebuildnetwork. org.

30. For more information on the African American Leadership Initiative at Reformed Theological Seminary, see http://www.rts.edu/site/rtsnearyou/jackson/aali.aspx.

Chapter 10

1. Collin Hansen, "Why Johnny Can't Read the Bible," *Christianity Today* (May 24, 2010). Downloaded on February 12, 2013 at http://www. christianitytoday.com/ct/2010/may/25.38.html.

2. Michael J. N. Dash and Christine D. Chapman, *The Shape of Zion: Leadership and Life in Black Churches* (Cleveland, OH: Pilgrim Press, 2003), 33–34, and Stephen C. Rasor and Michael J. N. Dash, *The Mark of Zion: Congregational Life in Black Churches* (Cleveland, OH: Pilgrim Press, 2003), 29.

3. Rasor and Dash, *The Mark of Zion*, 57.

4. Roland G. Hardy Jr., "Christian Education: Making the Process Work," in Lee N. June and Matthew Parker (eds.), *Evangelism and Discipleship in African-American Churches* (Grand Rapids, MI: Zondervan, 1999), 91.

5. William C. Turner Jr., *Discipleship for African American Christians: A Journey through the Church Covenant* (Valley Forge, PA: Judson Press, 2002), 37.

6. Lloyd C. Blue, "The Pastor's Role," in June and Parker (eds.), *Evangelism and Discipleship in African-American Churches*, 68.

7. Colin Marshall and Tony Payne, *The Trellis and the Vine: The Ministry Mind-Shift that Changes Everything* (Kingsford, Australia: Matthias Media, 2009), 14. Emphasis added.

Chapter 11

1. Joseph Washington, "How Black Is Black Religion?" in James J. Gardiner and J. Deotis Roberts (eds.), *Quest for a Black Theology* (Maryknoll,

NY: Orbis Books, 1993), 5. Cited in Homer U. Ashby Jr., *Our Home Is Over Jordan: A Black Pastoral Theology* (St. Louis, MO: Chalice Press, 2003), 76.

2. This pressure to join the church or face social sanction is why some researchers refer to the Black Church as a "semi-involuntary institution." Wiggins, *Righteous Content*, 164–65, provides a brief overview of this thesis.

3. I am aware that faithful Christians have differed over the proper subjects of baptism for nearly four hundred years now. Though I take the view commonly called "believer's baptism," which identifies those who repent and make a public profession of faith as the appropriate subjects of baptism, I happily recognize as fellow Christians the many believers who believe the children of believing parents may also receive the sign of the new covenant. If interested in a brief, friendly discussion from Baptist and Presbyterian views, see Thabiti Anyabwile and J. Ligon Duncan, III, *Baptism and the Lord's Supper* (Wheaton, IL: Crossway, 2011).

4. An excellent exploration of the way love and authority are meant to be exercised in church membership and discipline is Jonathan Leeman's, *The Church and the Surprising Offense of God's Love* (Wheaton, IL: Crossway, 2010).

5. Gregory A. Wills, *Democratic Religion: Freedom, Authority, and Church Discipline in the Baptist South, 1785–1900* (New York, NY: Oxford University Press, 1997), 68.

6. Ralph Basui Watkins, *Hip-Hop Redemption: Finding God in the Rhythm and the Rhyme* (Grand Rapids, MI: Baker, 2011), 50–51. Emphasis added.

Chapter 12

1. Charles V. Willie and Richard J. Reddick, *A New Look at Black Families* (Walnut Creek, CA: Altamira Press, 2003), 135–36.

2. Eric Mason, *Manhood Restored: How the Gospel Makes Men Whole* (Nashville, TN: B&H Publishing Group, 2013), 30, 34.

3. Bruce Waltke, *Genesis: A Commentary* (Grand Rapids, MI: Zondervan, 2001), 88.

4. Mason, *Manhood Restored*, 104.

5. William Julius Wilson, *More than Just Race: Being Black and Poor in the Inner City* (New York, NY: Norton, 2009).

6. Ibid., 10.

7. Ibid., 10, 41.

8. Ibid., 28–39. Of course, there have been other policies that have been developed with explicit attention to race. For an excellent discussion of how policy and public spaces have been used to reinforce racial disparity,

see W. Fitzhugh Brundage, *The Southern Past: A Clash of Race and Memory* (Cambridge, MA: Harvard, 2005).

9. Ibid., 62.

10. Ibid., 45.

11. Ibid., 71–73.

12. Ibid., 80. For a book-length treatment, see Elijah Anderson, *Code of the Street: Decay, Violence, and the Moral Life of the Inner City* (New York, NY: Norton, 1999). Emphasis added.

13. Ibid., 116–17.

14. Howard Brown, "Sexuality in the Black Community," in Anthony B. Bradley (ed.), *Keep Your Head Up: America's New Black Christian Leaders, Social Consciousness, and the Cosby Conversation* (Wheaton, IL: Crossway, 2012), 71.

15. Wilson, *More than Just Race*, 117. Wilson defines "social structure" as "the way social positions, social roles, and networks of social relationships are arranged in our institutions, such as the economy, polity, education, and organization of the family." Such forces can incentivize or punish certain behaviors, whether through markets, policies, or social roles. Wilson defined "culture," on the one hand, as "the sharing of goods and modes of behavior among individuals who face similar place-based circumstances (such as poor segregated neighborhoods) or have the same social networks as when members of particular racial or ethnic groups share a particular way of understanding social life and cultural scripts that guide their behavior." Wilson argues that social acts (i.e., stereotyping, stigmatizing, and discrimination) and social processes (i.e., laws, policies, institutional practices) work to determine group outcomes. Some groups are more vulnerable to social forces than others. This remains true for African-Americans, especially in large cities.

16. Ibid., 100–101.

17. Ibid., 102–3.

18. M. Belinda Tucker and Claudia Mitchell-Kernan (eds.), *The Decline in Marriage Among African Americans* (New York, NY: Russell Sage, 1995), 351.

19. Neha Sahgal and Greg Smith, "A Religious Portrait of African Americans" (Washington, DC: The Pew Forum on Religion and Public Life, 2009). Downloaded at http://www.pewforum.org/A-Religious-Portrait-of-African-Americans.aspx on July 16, 2013.

20. Franklin, *Another Day's Journey*, 89.

21. Ibid.

22. Ibid., 90–91.

23. Kaila Heard, "Why Aren't More Black Men Attending Church?" *The Miami Herald* (March 24, 2012). Accessed July 16, 2013

at http://miamitimesonline.com/why-aren%E2%80%99t-more-black-men-attending-church%C2%A0.

24. Karla F. C. Holloway, *Codes of Conduct: Race, Ethics, and the Color of Our Character* (New Brunswick, NJ: Rutgers University Press, 1995), 139.

25. Ibid, 140–41. Emphasis added.

26. Touré, "How to Talk to Young Black Boys about Trayvon Martin: Eight Talking Points about the Potentially Fatal Condition of Being Black," Time.com (March 21, 2012). Downloaded at http://ideas.time.com/2012/03/21/how-to-talk-to-young-black-boys-about-trayvon-martin on July 17, 2013.

27. Holloway, *Codes of Conduct*, 141. Emphasis added.

28. Ibid., 142.

29. Wesley Stephenson, "Are There More U.S. Black Men in Prison or College?" *BBC News Magazine* (March 17, 2013). Downloaded on October 7, 2013 at http://www.bbc.co.uk/news/magazine-21791038.

Chapter 13

1. Raphael G. Warnock, *The Divided Mind of the Black Church*, 1.

2. Ibid., 2.

3. Henry Mitchell, *Black Church Beginnings: The Long-Hidden Realities of the First Years* (Grand Rapids, MI: Eerdmans Publishing, 2004), 130.

4. Albert J. Raboteau, *Canaan Land: A Religious History of African Americans* (New York, NY: Oxford University Press, 1999), 22.

5. Ibid., 25. See pages 21–25 for Raboteau's summary of the founding of key individual black churches and denominations. For a more complete list of the founding of independent black churches, see appendix III in Mitchell, *Black Church Beginnings: The Long-Hidden Realities of the First Years*.

6. Ibid., 68–69. Emphasis added. For a chapter-length examination of black Baptist withdrawal from white denominations, see Leroy Fitts, *A History of Black Baptists* (Nashville, TN: Broadman Press, 1985), chapter 2.

7. Sylvia R. Frey and Betty Wood, *Come Shouting to Zion: African American Protestantism in the American South and British Caribbean to 1830* (Chapel Hill, NC: The University of North Carolina Press, 1998), 150.

8. Ibid., 66. Emphasis added.

9. Fitts, *A History of Black Baptists*, 109.

10. Absalom Jones, "A Thanksgiving Sermon," cited in Ibid., 33.

11. Fitts, *A History of Black Baptists*, 77.

12. Raboteau, *Canaan Land*, 72–73.

13. Ibid., 33–34.

14. See John Marrant, *Narrative of the Lord's Wonderful Dealings with John Marrant, a Black,* in Henry Louis Gates Jr. and William L. Andrews, *Pioneers of the Black Atlantic: Five Slave Narratives from the Enlightenment, 1772–1815* (Washington, DC: Counterpoint, 1998), 61–82.

15. Fitts, *A History of Black Baptists,* 109–10. See also Sylvia R. Frey and Betty Wood, *Come Shouting to Zion: African American Protestantism in the American South and British Caribbean to 1830* (Chapel Hill, NC: The University of North Carolina Press, 1998), 131.

16. Grant Gordon, *From Slavery to Freedom: The Life of David George, Pioneer Black Baptist Minister* (Hantsport, NS: Lancelot Press Limited, 1992), 163.

17. For the organizational history of Baptist missionary efforts, see Fitts, *A History of Black Baptists,* 64–98.

18. Sylvia M. Jacobs, "African Missions and the African American Churches," in Vaughn Walston and Robert J. Stevens (eds.), *African-American Experience in World Mission: A Call beyond Community* (Pasadena, CA: William Carey Library, 2002), 31.

19. Ibid., 97.

20. See, for example, Mitchell, *Black Church Beginnings,* 130–40; Warnock, *The Divided Mind of the Black Church*; Peter J. Paris, *The Social Teaching of the Black Churches* (Philadelphia, PA: Fortress Press, 1985); Gayraud Wilmore, *Black Religion and Black Radicalism: An Interpretation of the Religious History of African Americans* (Maryknoll, NY: Orbis, 1988).

21. Albert J. Raboteau, *Canaan Land,* 25.

22. Ibid., 63.

23. Ibid., 65.

24. Fitts, *A History of Black Baptists,* 68–69.

25. Lillian Kwon, "Black Christians Largely Absent from U.S. Missionary Force," *The Christian Post* (October 6, 2010), downloaded on January 24, 2014 at http://www.christianpost.com/news/black-christians-largely-absent-from-us-missionary-force-47088.

26. Ibid.

27. Andy Butcher, "Cross-Cultural Missions the 'Great Omission' of the Black Church, Study Says," *Missions Frontiers* (March 1, 2000). Downloaded on January 24, 2014 at http://www.missionfrontiers.org/issue/article/cross-cultural-missions-the-great-omission-of-the-black-church-study-says. The phrase is attributed to Jim Sutherland, a missiologist who has served in African-American communities for more than twenty years. His eighteen-month study examined the experiences of African-American missionaries, denominations, and missionary-sending agencies.

28. Sarah Eekhoff Zylstra, "Black Churches Missing Missionaries: Black Churches Are Booming. Why They Are Not Sending," *Christianity Today* (April 2, 2013). Downloaded on January 24, 2014 at http://www.ctlibrary.com/ct/2013/april/missing-missionaries.html.

29. Ibid.

30. Ibid.

31. Michael Johnson, "Am I My Brother's Keeper? The Search for African American Presence in Missions," in Walston and Stevens, *African-American Experience in World Mission*, 17.

32. Robert D. Woodberry (2012), "The Missionary Roots of Liberal Democracy," *American Political Science Review*, 105 (2), 244–74. Retrieved February 4, 2014 from http://www.academia.edu/2128659/The_Missionary_Roots_of_Liberal_Democracy.

33. See, for example, The International Mission Board's Global Research website at http://public.imb.org/globalresearch/Pages/default.aspx; The Joshua Project's website at http://joshuaproject.net/; and People Groups at http://www.peoplegroups.org. These websites feature information on people groups around the world, current efforts to reach groups, and useful information for distributing to churches.

34. Tess Rivers, "SBC President: We Need African Americans on International Mission Field," *Baptist Press* (Feb. 13, 2013). Retrieved on February 4, 2014 from http://www.bpnews.net/bpnews.asp?id=39697.

35. Rebecca Walston, "Missions in the Local Church: Four Pastors' Perspectives," in Walston and Stevens, *African-American Experience in World Mission*, 8.

36. Ibid., 9.